DISUNITED
STATES

DISUNITED STATES

JOHN D. DONAHUE

BasicBooks
A Division of HarperCollins*Publishers*

Designed by Elliott Beard

Library of Congress Cataloging-in-Publication Data

Donahue, John D.
    Disunited states / John D. Donahue.
        p. cm.
    Includes bibliographical references and index.
    ISBN 0-465-01661-8
        1. Federal government—United States.   2. United States—
Politics and government—1993–   .   I. Title.
JK325.D66 1997
320.8'0973—dc21   97-3921
                                                                  CIP

97 98 99 00 01   10 9 8 7 6 5 4 3 2 1

For Kate

CONTENTS

PREFACE AND ACKNOWLEDGMENTS

This book seeks to show why the ascendancy of America's separate state governments may be a worse idea than current sentiment and practice suggest. Like most books published under the Basic imprint, it is meant to engage expert opinion while inviting any interested citizen into the conversation. Certain risks are inherent in such an enterprise. One is tilting too much toward the expert audience and leaving general readers drumming their fingers with impatience at all the caveats, conditions, and invocations of scholarly authority. The other risk is leaving the specialists—in this case including economists, political scientists, economic development practitioners, lawyers, and historians—gasping in horror at the reckless pace with which I traverse hazardous terrain. Two tactics are deployed to reduce these risks. For the more specialized audience I avoid, so far as I am able, letting stylistic informality degenerate into imprecision, and I include extensive notes (as well as an appendix) containing references, supplemental information, and refinements that are a step less central to the argument than the material in the main text. For general readers I try to keep the writing clear while banishing most technicalities to the notes and highlighting the central themes in the first and last chapters.

One special stylistic observation: Some writers capitalize "Federal" but not "state;" some capitalize "State" but not "federal"—in each case,

I find, usually sending a signal with the details of the spelling. Since I'd rather not count on typeface to carry my message, and since capitalizing both gives the text too much of a German or Old English look, neither "federal" nor "state" is capitalized.

This started out a long time ago as a different kind of book, and I have incurred many debts on the way to the current version. In 1990 I began to explore the themes of Chapter Five and Chapter Six—state-level economic activism against a backdrop of federal laissez-faire, and the net effects of state competition for business investment. That project was suspended as I spent much of 1991 observing the post-Communist transformation in Eastern Europe, an opportunity made possible by Project Liberty and its director, Shirley Williams, and by the Institut für Angewandte Wirtshsaftsforschung in Tübingen. While nominally a detour, that experience altered this project. Witnessing the fresh wreckage of cultures gone wrong in Poland, eastern Germany, and what was then Czechoslovakia raised my ambitions, and I returned to undertake broader historical and theoretical research on America's federal-state balance than I had originally intended. Then came another interruption, this time for nearly three years, while I served in the Clinton Administration. Meanwhile, the topic moved several notches up the scale of practical urgency, and I left government in 1995 in large part to complete this work. As the project's shape shifted and finally settled I benefited, as always, from the counsel of Alan Altshuler, Robert B. Reich, and Richard J. Zeckhauser.

Throughout I have relied upon the logistical and financial support of the Center for Business and Government at Harvard's John F. Kennedy School of Government under the directorship of John Dunlop, Richard Cavanagh, John White, and now Roger Porter, and upon the admirable assistance of its administrative director, Beverly Raimondo. Paula Holmes-Carr and Patience Terry have provided diligent administrative support. The Taubman Center for State and Local Government has also contributed to this project at several crucial junctures. Participation in the Harvard project on Visions of Governance in the Twenty-first Century has helped me set this enterprise in a broader context, and gave me the opportunity to tap a little of Paul Peterson's deep expertise on federalism.

Gregory Feldberg, Farron Levy, Megan Matey, John B. Ostrick, and Nikhil Srinivasan have served as research assistants at different points throughout the project, and each contributed his or her own brand of care and resourcefulness. Data and interpretive advice were also provided by William Hulcher of the Governments Division at the Commerce Department's Census Bureau; Doug Norwood of the Budget Analysis Branch at the Office of Management and Budget; Michael R. Mazerov of the Multistate Tax Commission; William Schweke of the Corporation for Enterprise Development; and David Sullivan at the Department of Commerce, Bureau of Economic Analysis.

Alan Altshuler, Timothy J. Bartik, Paul Dimond, Mickey Edwards, Claudia Goldin, Naomi Goldstein, Thomas Kane, Zackary Karabell, Lawrence Katz, Alan Krueger, Robert Lawrence, Richard Neustadt, David Osborne, Robert Putnam, Robert B. Reich, Jeremy Rosner, Frederick Schauer, F. M. Scherer, Raymond Vernon, and Ralph W. Whitehead, Jr., generously read earlier drafts and offered valuable suggestions. Paul Golob of Basic Books carried out his editorial duties with energy, good judgment, and no mercy at all.

I owe a special debt of thanks to the Andrew W. Mellon Foundation and its president, William G. Bowen, for a major grant that covered travel and research expenses and allowed me to devote much of 1996 to the completion of this book.

None of the people or institutions mentioned here, of course, bear any responsibility for errors of fact, interpretation, or judgment, which remain wholly my own.

My wife, Maggie Pax; my daughter, Kate, to whom this book is dedicated; and my son, Ben, whose birth in 1995 marked the resumption of this project, remind me daily why it matters to get the policies right.

DISUNITED
STATES

CHAPTER ONE

The Ascendancy of the States

What shall be the answer of our generation, pressed upon by gigantic economic problems the solution of which may involve not only the prosperity
but also the very integrity of the nation, to the old question of the distribution of powers between Congress and the States?

Woodrow Wilson, 1908
Constitutional Government in the United States[1]

Within America's troubled public sector, the states are gathering
strength. The ascendancy of the states figured in the 1996 presidential
election chiefly as one of those conventional pieties (like family values
or fiscal rectitude) that each candidate strained to claim as his own.
Senator Robert Dole regularly brandished a copy of the Tenth Amendment—affirming the principle of state primacy—and President Bill
Clinton likewise endorsed the "inexorable move to push more basic
jobs of the public sector back to the state level." So uncontroversial was
the trend that the 1996 Democratic platform featured the taunt "Republicans talked about shifting power back to states and communities—Democrats are doing it."[2]

The wisdom of shifting the public sector's center of gravity away
from Washington and toward the separate states enjoys something as

3

close to consensus as American politics often sees. Proponents promise greater efficiency, lower costs, stepped-up innovation, and even a softening of antigovernment sentiments as power moves closer to the people. Nor, to be sure, are such virtues implausible. The ills of bureaucracy generally worsen with size, and for that reason alone state agencies may not match the federal government's worst in terms of sheer organizational sclerosis. The benefits of experimentation and innovation by states are undeniable, and the vigor and inventiveness that many state governments display contrast starkly with the federal government's frequent bouts of sour paralysis. In a diverse national economy operating on a continental scale, uniformity in laws and regulations can be spectacularly wrongheaded, and fine-tuning policy to fit local conditions has an obvious appeal.

Yet the tilt toward state-based government promises perhaps more fundamental and far-reaching consequences than the noisier debate over the federal deficit. And the decentralization of public power—an ingenious remedy against ancient political ills—can carry risks of the gravest sort when taken in the wrong dosage or in the wrong conditions.

Enthusiasm for devolution is not restricted to the United States, nor is shifting authority downward from national to subnational governments the only transfer of power presently under way. Public authority around the globe is being diminished, transformed, augmented, and rearranged as conditions and expectations evolve.[3] Sovereignty is flowing *upward* from the nation-state to multinational institutions like the World Trade Organization and the European Union, while flowing *downward* to subnational units like Catalonia, Scotland, Quebec, the former Soviet republics, and (potentially) Italy's Lombard League.[4] Yet the theme plays out in America with a special historical resonance, and a disproportionate focus on the binary choice between state and nation. For federal-state tension is etched into our country's design.

After a failed first attempt at nationhood under the Articles of Confederation, the United States has stuck to the same organizational blueprint since 1789. Our Constitution is an astonishingly successful governmental innovation, and among its many virtues is a radical ambiguity about the relative power of national and state governments. In part, this ambiguity reflects eighteenth-century political realities: Mindful of the muddle with which the weak Articles of Confederation had afflicted the country, the Framers were bent on strengthening the central government. Some of the more ardent nationalists expected (and intended) a virtual withering away of the states. Yet other leaders, aghast at the prospect of surrendering hard-won sovereignty to a central government, sought only minor changes to the Articles. State legislatures, of course, picked the delegates to the Constitutional Convention and approved the final product, and no document emerging from such a process could fail to preserve substantial state powers.

In greater part, however, the tension between levels of government was a product of conscious strategy. The Framers sought to shatter political theory's age-old tradeoff between order and liberty by crafting a government strong enough to get things done but equipped with built-in bulwarks against excessive or unaccountable power. Three distinct branches of government would check and balance one another at the federal level. The coexistence of state and national governments, with neither able to dominate the other, would offer a separate structural safeguard against tyranny.

A consequence of this ambiguous division of authority is that the balance between levels of government can, and does, shift widely from era to era. Advocates of flatly contrary federalist visions—from Southern leaders asserting the right to opt out of the nation in the 1860s to Lincoln denying them that right; from FDR's vast expansion of federal ambition in the New Deal to today's chorus calling for a shrunken national government and more powerful states—can find support for their views in the Constitution and the compendium of pro-Constitution political advertisements collected as the Federalist Papers. This is not to suggest that the Constitution is feebly permissive or vague about values. Its principles are defined with breathtaking clarity. But the Framers left ample room for those principles to take effect in different ways to meet different conditions. And they inaugurated a permanent American argument over what version of federalism—at each particular time, in each particular set of circumstances—would be truest to the nation's bedrock values.

One hesitates to suggest that today's economy would have been unimaginable to the likes of Madison, Jefferson, and Hamilton, who proved capable of imagining a lot. Nor, for that matter, are the specific challenges of our time so different from those they confronted. (One of the Framers' goals was to curb the excesses of economic rivalry among state governments, after all, and another was maintaining a common front in the face of international economic pressures.[5]) But the stresses

America must master today are surely different, at least in detail and degree, than those of two hundred years ago.

A defining challenge for contemporary America is to maintain our middle-class culture in a world grown inhospitable to that heritage. Our heirs will judge the present generation by whether we succeed or fail at this task—unless our failure is so complete that the future finds small meaning in the middle-class values we cherish today. The reshaping of the industrial landscape, the maturation of mid-century transportation and communications revolutions, and the emergence as economic rivals of huge populations long dismissed as backward, are transforming the planet into an ever-more-integrated market.[6] Economic globalization, to be sure, is less novel than we sometimes think; Benjamin Franklin was long employed as the European agent of several American colonies, and Thomas Edison's launch of the electric lighting industry triggered a rapid collapse of London gas stocks across the Atlantic.[7] But there is certainly something new about the pace with which cheaper, better transportation and communications are lubricating the interconnection of markets across the planet and intensifying the impact of technological change.[8]

Like a previous era of industrial upheaval in the late 1800s, today's economic transformation is widening consumers' options, expanding opportunities for those who are able to seize them, conferring staggering wealth on a select few—and stranding those unable to adapt. Observers with the luxury of taking the long view, or those with no special stake in any single country, may find this moment in history to be richly promising. But it is by no means assured that America's magnificent achievement of broadly shared prosperity will survive. (The emphasis here on America's middle class doesn't imply indifference to the far grimmer condition of the underclass. But only by acting to secure middle-class prosperity can government ever again hope to win popular permission to confront the problems of poverty.)

Some lament that the forces sculpting America's economy are simply too powerful to deflect. Others dismiss the mid-century surge in mass living standards as an unnatural interlude that must fade away. But grant, provisionally, that the withering of the middle class would be calamitous for this country. Grant, too, that we are not yet powerless to affect the future. The metric for judging governmental strategies then becomes whether they promise to shore up, or to further erode, the economic foundations of our culture.

Three generic approaches await assessment by this metric, three different blueprints—not mutually exclusive, but competing nonetheless for first claim on our hopes and energies—by which to align America's public sector to its contemporary challenges. The most obvious strategy is austerity. As wage stagnation stiffens resistance to taxation, few politicians have failed to at least invoke the rhetoric of smaller government. Beyond the rhetoric, moreover, there has been real downward pressure on many (though by no means all) categories of public spending, including the Reagan Administration's domestic cutbacks, the shrinkage of the federal workforce and discretionary programs in the first Clinton Administration, and an apparent resolve to continue down the path toward a balanced federal budget.

The second generic strategy is national reform. An explosion of efforts to "reinvent" the federal government has overtaken Washington. While there is an undeniable quotient of faddism and sloganeering involved, necessity has incubated some honest invention. Among the most promising elements of this broad strategy are efforts to delegate the delivery of public services to private firms and other organizations more specialized in operational efficiency than federal bureaus can be, or to shift resources from conventional programs to voucher systems crafted to amplify individual discretion.

The third general strategy is devolution, emphasizing the rearrangement (rather than reform or diminution) of public authority. Devolution is often cast as a superior substitute for federal reform. In fact, as will be seen, it is not so much a separate strategy as it is the overture to automatic austerity. Yet while budget reductions and reinvention loom largest in the explicit debates over government's future, as a country we have been quietly weighting our bets toward devolution. By the measures that best gauge governmental power—authority, resources, and legitimacy—the tide is flowing away from Washington.

AUTHORITY

Welfare reform is the most vivid example of authority cascading to lower levels of government. National legislation passed and signed in 1996 repudiates a sixty-year tradition of federal responsibility for antipoverty policies. An intricate and little loved federal-state system that previously assured at least some minimal level of assistance to poor families with children has been replaced by freestanding state programs whose nature will emerge only over time. The national role is restricted to providing the states with block grants at whatever scale Congress deems appropriate, with no ongoing link to either need or effort. (For the first few years, the size of the federal transfers is based on early-1990s welfare spending.) The grants come with few strings attached, beyond an imperative of austerity that includes strict time limits on the collection of benefits and incentives to reduce caseloads—by getting recipients employed, if possible; by other means, if necessary.

Other examples, if individually less dramatic, suggest the breadth of the trend. With few exceptions the federal government has renounced the goal of guiding or accelerating industrial change. In part this reflects a considered bipartisan conviction that markets should trump politics in resource allocation; in part it reflects straitened budgets that bar even ardent activists from doing very much. But under the elastic banner of "economic development," state officials engage in ambitious efforts to mold their economies. Overseas offices, marketing trips by governors and their staffs, industrial technology institutes, targeted training programs, special tax breaks, and direct subsidies all serve as tools by which states seek to alter the pace and direction of their economies' evolution.

The 1991 Intermodal Surface Transportation Efficiency Act expanded state authority over transportation policy. Separate transport financing programs, each traditionally dominated by congressional barons, were swept together into a single pool of money to serve whatever priorities the states perceive as most urgent. The act authorized up to $152 billion—mostly funded from federal gas tax revenues—to be spent on highway and mass transit programs, with the states paying one-fifth of the cost while wielding most of the authority.[9]

Legislation championed in 1995 by both the Republican Congress and the Clinton Administration sheltered states from "unfunded mandates," through which Congress claims credit for advancing popular goals while leaving to other governments the obligation to deliver on the promises. The law requires Congress henceforth to identify and estimate the size of any obligation imposed on states and cities by new legislation, and then either to come up with a way to pay for the burden or to explain explicitly why it should not.[10] Barriers to the imposition of unfunded mandates, while a welcome step toward more accountability in government, act to amplify the states' voices in any conflict of priorities.

A package of 1996 amendments to the Safe Drinking Water Act of 1974—cosponsored by both Senate Majority Leader Bob Dole and Minority Leader Thomas Daschle, and supported by the Clinton Administration—expanded states' authority over drinking water standards. The legislation diluted the power of the Environmental Protection Agency to set requirements, restricted the federal role to one of providing information and money, and enlarged state discretion over how (and how aggressively) to ensure that the water flowing from citizens' taps is fit to drink.[11]

The Supreme Court—which to the dismay of strict constructionists has long deferred to congressional judgments of where the federal-state division really lies—is on the cusp of a historical tilt toward state authority. The Court's 1995 decision in *United States v. Lopez* constricted the scope for invoking the Constitution's commerce clause to justify federal action; its 1996 decision in *Seminole Tribes v. Florida* limited citizens' ability to sue states that violate federal laws. Most court-watchers expect the next few sessions to unleash a series of decisions augmenting state power.

RESOURCES

The common notion that state and local governments are dwarfed by the federal behemoth is somewhere between oversimplified and preposterous. The simplest metric involves money. Figure 1 traces the trajectory of public spending since 1960, using multi-year averages to dampen the transitory effects of economic cycles. The most striking trend is the shrinkage of national defense and foreign affairs spending as the Cold War wound down, and the parallel growth of transfer payments and interest on the debt. Defense and international programs dropped from nearly 10 percent of the economy in the first half of the 1960s to well under 4 percent in the mid-1990s, as the total of tranfers and interest payments more than doubled, from a little over 6 percent to nearly 15 percent. The other major trend, however, is the rising importance of state and local government *within* the domestic sphere. Within what most Americans think of as "the government," states and cities occupy a large and growing share of the terrain. State and local spending supported by state and local resources now exceeds 10 percent of America's gross domestic product. Even before taking into account the many programs run by cities and states but paid for with federal

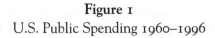

Figure 1
U.S. Public Spending 1960–1996

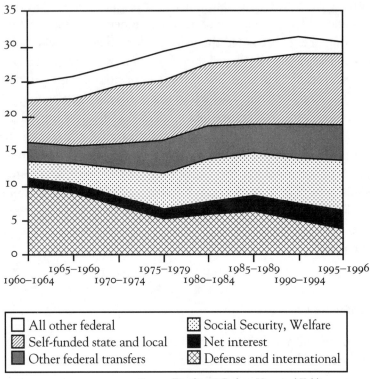

Source: Fiscal 1998 Budget, Historical Table 15.5

grants (which shortshrifts the states' involvement in both "all other federal" and "other federal transfers"), lower-level government dwarfs federal domestic spending aside from transfer payments. The federal government now spends less on all domestic activities other than transfers than it spends to service its massive debt.[12]

The financial data compiled by the federal Office of Management and Budget on which Figure 1 is based commingle state and local spending and hence can't confirm, on their own, the states' ascendancy. But a different data series collected by the Census Bureau tracks state and local finances separately. Between 1960 and 1964 state spending averaged only a little over one-third of the state and local total. Over 1990–93—the most recent period for which data are available— it exceeded one-half. It is chiefly the states, and not the cities, that are waxing as Washington wanes.[13] Nor do the OMB data disaggregate nonfederal spending to isolate the growing role of transfer payments. Figure 1 thus overstates somewhat the relative importance of state and local *operations*, since transfers are not netted out as they are for the federal figures. The National Income and Product Accounts (while less useful for some other purposes, and while not directly comparable to the OMB figures) *do* track transfers separately. They show that AFDC, Medicaid, and other transfer programs have indeed risen as a share of state spending, from under 20 percent in the early 1960s to around 30 percent in the early 1990s. Yet the NIPA data underscore the prominence of lower-level governments in running things, as distinct from writing checks. In 1995 (the most recent year covered) transfers claimed less than half as large a share of state and local budgets as they did of federal budgets.[14]

Some declare it misleading to count *any* public spending as under state or local control, since federal officials (the argument goes) dictate the disposition not merely of intergovernmental grants, but even of the funds states and localities raise themselves. Such assertions, however, characteristically dissolve upon inspection. As John J. DiIulio, Jr., and Donald F. Kettl observe in an assessment of devolution proposals in the 104th Congress, despite "many gripping anecdotes" of federal micromanagement, "an entire generation of empirical research on intergovernmental affairs reveals that the rule is more nearly the reverse: Washington has had, and continues to have, tremendous difficulty in executing even relatively straightforward policies precisely because state and local governments enjoy such wide latitude in deciding how best to translate federal policies into action, or whether, in fact, to follow federal policies at all."[15]

The same tide away from Washington can be discerned in the flow of *human* resources—arguably the more meaningful gauge of comparative importance. The net growth in federal civilian employment between 1962 and 1995 was 15 percent. State and local employment grew by 150 percent over the same period.[16] (Such huge discrepancies in growth rates commonly turn out to result from a much smaller starting point for the faster-growing category. But state and local employment was nearly three times as large as federal employment at the *start* of the period.) The tide appears to be quickening: Between January 1993 and March 1996, federal employment fell by 11 percent while state and local employment grew by 5 percent.[17] (Much of the fall in federal employment reflects defense downsizing, but by no means all.)

The rising quality of state government intensifies the quantitative

shift. There has been a quiet, decades-long migration of talent toward
state capitals. Twenty or thirty years ago state politics was decidedly
minor-league; today the caliber of state officials frequently exceeds the
federal standard. This rise in professionalism was driven, for a time, by
the need to administer the surge of Great Society–era federal grants.
But the more enduring reasons are political, and quite different for the
two parties. Many Republicans feel a genuine ideological affinity for
state government and a corresponding distaste for Washington. Many
Democrats, facing grim career prospects in the federal executive branch
for all but a few years between 1969 and 1993, dedicated themselves to
state-level versions of the activism then out of fashion nationally. As
the capacity and profile of state government has risen, governors and
former governors—Clinton of Arkansas, Reagan and Wilson of California, Carter of Georgia, Cuomo and Pataki of New York, Engler of
Michigan, Whitman of New Jersey, Dukakis and Weld of Massachusetts, Kerrey and Nelson of Nebraska, Thompson of Wisconsin, Bayh of
Indiana, Alexander of Tennessee, and many others—have been among
the most prominent political leaders of both major parties.

LEGITIMACY

Ultimately the most important asset that government can command—
at least in anything resembling a democracy—is not legal authority, or
fiscal resources, or even talented personnel, but *legitimacy*. Nothing can
compensate for the loss of popular confidence, or the withdrawal of citizens' cooperation. State governments have been spared the worst of
Americans' disenchantment with the public sector, and claim a growing advantage in most measures of governmental legitimacy.

To some extent this reflects a return to the American norm after
an uncharacteristic dalliance with centralized power. In our country's
early years the states enjoyed far more legitimacy than the distant national government. Washington's rise (and fall) in public esteem has
been a twentieth-century phenomenon. The Depression, the New
Deal, World War II, and the civil rights movement all tended to de-
tach popular loyalties from the states and move them toward Washington. A 1936 Gallup Poll found that 56 percent of Americans
favored concentrating power in the federal government, while 44 percent favored state authority. Forty-one percent of respondents on a
1939 Roper Poll felt the federal government was "most honest and ef-

ficient in performing its own special duties." The states came in last in this New Deal-era survey at 12 percent, with 17 percent awarding their confidence to local government.[18]

Contemporary opinion surveys, by contrast, show dwindling faith in the federal government and (at least in relative terms) rising state legitimacy. In regular polls commissioned by the Advisory Commission on Intergovernmental Relations, the fraction of respondents identifying the federal government as "the level from which you feel you get the *least* for your money" rose by 10 points (to 46 percent) between 1989 and 1994 alone.[19] Mid-1990s polls conducted by the Gallup Organization, the *Wall Street Journal* and NBC News, *Business Week* and the Harris Group, Hart and Teeter, and Princeton Survey Research Associates found, with a striking consistency, support for enlarging the role of the states. Majorities of respondents—often lopsided majorities— favored state rather than federal leadership in education, crime control, welfare, job-training, low-income housing, highway construction, and farm policies.[20] Late 1994 polling on trust in government among Missourians and Kansans found about a six-to-one advantage for the states.[21] A bellwether poll conducted by Princeton Survey Research Associates in 1995 for the *Washington Post*, the Kaiser Family Foundation, and Harvard University found that by a margin of 61 to 24 percent, respondents trusted their state governments over the federal government to "do a better job of running things." Except for Jewish voters (who favored the federal government by a 44 to 36 margin) and black voters (tied, at 43 percent) every subgroup gave the edge to the states, including self-defined liberals (who favored the states by a margin of 49 to 36 percent), Democrats (48 percent to 35 percent), and voters under age thirty (72 to 21 percent).[22]

Not just instinct and tradition, but some powerful logic as well, supports the ascendancy of the states. Supreme Court Justice Louis D. Brandeis framed a resonant metaphor when he wrote that "a single courageous state may, if its citizens choose, serve as a laboratory, and try social and economic experiments without risk to the rest of the country."[23] Richly varied state strategies continually test and winnow policy alternatives, providing the nation with information about what works and what doesn't. Beyond the "laboratories of democracy" scenario, in which diversity invites the discovery and diffusion of best practice, there can be value in diversity itself. Since both citizens and corporations differ in their priorities, the country may be better off if within its borders constituents can find a range of alternative packages of services, regulatory regimes, and tax burdens among which individuals and institutions may choose.

A related line of reasoning stresses the virtues of competition. One engine of private-sector efficiency is the pressure enterprises face to match the pace set by ambitious rivals. Should not the same logic extend to units of government? States that must compete for citizens and investment with other states might be expected to be more creative, less complacent, more diligent in carrying out the tasks of governance, than an unchallenged leviathan in Washington.

A quite different argument for devolution as a core strategy for public-sector reform—an argument tinged with both poignancy and cynicism—is commonest among those with direct experience in or around the federal government. It varies in its details, depending on the adherent's specific exposure to the crippling debt and toxic politics that have come to dominate Washington. But in its essence, it boils down to a kind of grim gratitude—since we have wrecked one level of government—that the Founding Fathers had the foresight to provide a spare.

One can mount a contrary conceptual case that the shift toward the states is precisely the wrong way for America to engage a maturing global market system. Impeded by ideology in the development of any real sense of national commonwealth, and long spared by its peculiar history from the natural consequences of such an impediment, the ever-less-united United States now squanders its leverage in the world economy. Paralysis in Washington and wholesale devolution invites the balkanization (in that metaphor's updated, more ominous sense) of America.

At this pitch of abstraction, of course, both the case for and the case against stepped-up decentralization amount to proverbs rather than policy assessments. This book aims to deepen the debate, while establishing the predicate for an ultimate conclusion at odds with the prevailing consensus on devolution's virtues: The ascendency of the states cannot relieve us of the imperative to confront our problems as a *nation*, and devolution will prove to be (at best) a detour on America's path to renewal.

Chapter Two traces the ingenious blueprint of the Framers' architecture for American government and reviews the two-century argument over precisely how to strike the balance between national and state authority. Next, Chapter Three identifies some of the gauges that help calibrate the fit between our values and our evolving institutions.

We cherish autonomy; we cherish community. We cannot evade choices where the two values are (at least partially) in conflict, so the clearer the markers on the path we must tread, the lower the risk of going needlessly astray. Engaging these issues is a prerequisite to any effort at judging whether our present trajectory—a fading central government and resurgent states—should be reckoned as the restoration, or the erosion, of the American ideal.

The stage is then set for Chapter Four's contention that the intricate network of economic and cultural connections veining the modern United States in fact tends to intensify the hazards of fragmented public authority. The stronger and more numerous are such links, the more powerfully do the consequences of one state government's actions affect citizens of other states who are disenfranchised, in effect, through undue decentralization. The scope for compartmentalized decision-making is becoming narrower, not broader, in an era of integrating markets and explosive advances in communications. Chapter Five explores America's characteristic aversion to economic activism by the federal government, coupled with unruffled acceptance of economic strategizing on the state level. The focus changes in Chapter Six to a long-standing practice with some ominous new twists—interstate rivalry for business investment. As capital becomes more mobile (both within and among nations), the time-honored tactics that states deploy to lure investment may be rendered at once more consequential and less benign in their ultimate effects.

Chapter Seven broadens the frame to pose some more fundamental questions and to make some more pointed predictions about how competition among increasingly autonomous states will affect the scope, the ambition, and the agenda of the country's public sector. Taking up an issue with special implications for America's future as a middle-class culture, Chapter Eight examines education and training policies and explores how the configuration of governmental authority can shape the pattern of investment in citizens' productive skills. Chapter Nine, finally, distills some lessons for the next stage of America's endless argument over the elusive equilibrium between nation and state.

CHAPTER TWO

America's Endless Argument

One of the most elegant definitions of the term "federalism" comes from the Czech-born scholar Ivo Duchacek, who described it as "two governmental layers superimposed on the same territory, neither being at the mercy of the other."[1] (The word is never defined in America's Constitution; indeed, it is never even used.) Federal systems are still rare, despite Europe's cautious construction of a continental level of government and moves toward decentralization in Mexico, Italy, Spain, and elsewhere. As the demise of Communism let peoples sever unwilled ties, federations in Yugoslavia, Czechoslovakia, and the USSR have shattered, while democratic federations like Canada and India struggle against centrifugal pressures.

Even within the small club of federal systems, America is special. For many federations—Nigeria, Switzerland, even Germany—provincial autonomy is the residue of separate histories or a surrender to deep differences among regions. American federalism, by contrast, is less an accommodation to territorial diversity than one part of an ingenious answer to a fundamental political question: How to bridle anarchy while preserving liberty?

"In sovereignty," wrote Samuel Johnson in 1775, "there are no gradations."[2] Around a decade later a collection of patriots, intellectuals, and visionaries gathered in Philadelphia to prove Johnson wrong. The strategy they crafted sought to render power less hazardous to liberty by scattering it throughout an elaborately divided government. Authority thus subdivided was meant to be able to govern, but unable to tyrannize. The Framers at Philadelphia launched not only a nation, but an appropriately endless argument over the proper balance between federal and state authority—an argument whose intensity ebbs and flows and whose content evolves, but which is never really settled.

THE FRAMERS' WORK

America's first try at being a nation did not go very well. The crucible of the Revolutionary War had forged a degree of unity among colonies that, while jointly declaring their independence from Britain, had in that declaration referred to themselves, in the plural, as "free and independent States."[3] Two historians recount how General George Washington very consciously constructed his immediate staff of young officers from every colony, thus "personalizing his own commitment to what was still for most people rather an abstraction, the 'United States.'"[4] John Adams, anxious to reinforce his beleaguered Massachusetts as the war intensified, advocated a strong form of union melding the states "like separate parcels of metal, into one common mass."[5]

The pace of nation-building, though, slackened markedly in peacetime. The Articles of Confederation adopted in 1781 provided for only a feeble form of union, specifying at the start that "[e]ach state retains its sovereignty."[6] The central government's economic authority was tightly constrained—it could not collect taxes, regulate trade, or levy tariffs on imports—and was largely mediated through the constituent states. There were several reasons behind this weakness. Officials in the separate states were jealous of their authority and resisted any hint of subordination. The English and Scottish political traditions in which most American intellectuals were steeped celebrated the radical new idea of limited government. Beyond the prevailing philosophical climate in the English-speaking world, the fine-pored filter of transatlantic migration ensured that the American character was disproportionately defined by those especially averse to undue authority. And the just-won struggle for freedom from the British empire had elevated independence to the highest ranks of political virtues. Small wonder, then, that the Articles bound the former colonies together with only the loosest of ties. The very vocabulary of American government memorializes this heritage. In political discourse elsewhere, the word "state" normally refers to the nation as a whole. The term used for our national assembly, "congress"—instead of "parliament" or its equivalent—recalls the Confederation Congress, a gathering of delegates from sovereign states, as distinct from the popular assembly of a single nation.

But as the glow of wartime triumph faded, the drawbacks of disunity grew increasingly apparent. The most obvious involved money. America's monetary system in the 1780s presented a patchwork of foreign coins and paper currencies that varied from state to state. Even the definition of the pound differed, from 1,547 grains of silver in Georgia to 966 grains in North Carolina. Inflation plagued the new nation, but unevenly; some states let their currencies plummet in value, while other were more cautious. Separate currency systems, and the absence of any overarching national authority, made both public and private finance chaotic and treacherous. Some states refused to recognize other states' paper money at all. Others passed laws declaring their own questionable currency to be legal tender for all purposes, allowing the states' citizens and governments to pay off out-of-state creditors at a deep discount while foreclosing court challenges. "Nothing did more to bring about the adoption of the Constitution," according to historian Allan Nevins, "than the recognition by business interests that they needed a safeguard against this invasion of justice."[7]

The struggle over repayment of the Revolutionary War debt likewise underscored the fragility of the Articles of Confederation. In 1781 Congress approved a 5 percent import tax, primarily to service the national government's share of the war debt and to shore up its precarious reputation for creditworthiness. But under the Articles, the tax could not be imposed without the unanimous consent of the states. Despite a pro-tax propaganda blitz from the pen of Thomas Paine—who had been hired for the task by George Washington, among others—Rhode Island refused its approval, and the financing plan died.[8] Congress was forced to negotiate for the funds, and the negotiations brought great complications and small success. New York and Rhode Island bluntly refused to help pay off the debt; other states sought to attach onerous conditions to their contributions. The allocation and financing of the war debt remained a source of confusion and antagonism throughout the whole period of the Articles.[9]

Conflicting economic development policies, in an era when the mercantilist spirit was still strong, also strained relations among the states and stifled the sense of nationhood. Once war and the uncomfortable peace that followed had diminished America's reliance on manufactured imports from Britain, competing commercial interests in the separate states scrambled to fill the gap. States levied taxes on shipping that worked to promote their own shipowners by increasing the cost to merchants of moving goods on vessels registered elsewhere.[10] Tariffs on manufactures, the major source of government revenue, metamorphosed into mercantilist weapons. Massachusetts used trade protection as an industrial development tool to promote its glass, woolen, and sugar industries, and all four New England states as well as New York and Pennsylvania had erected protective tariffs by 1786. Connecticut even passed legislation giving foreign manufactures advantages over goods produced in adjoining states.[11] These maneuvers not only afflicted consumers and warped industrial development— economists' classic critiques of mercantilism—but they also built economic barriers against the new nation's political integration.

Perhaps the deepest and most consequential economic divisions among the postrevolutionary American states concerned international trade. The unbridled assertion of particular state interests caused two kinds of trade problems. First, "gateway" states with the best harbors and rivers—including Maryland, Pennsylvania, New York, and Massachusetts—laid heavy taxes on imported goods destined for inland states, thus financing their governmental operations on the backs of that least vocal constituency, out-of-state consumers. Tariffs paid by Connecticut citizens, for example, at one time covered about a third of New York's budget.[12] This "taxation without representation," not surprisingly, sparked resentment. New Jersey sought to enlist Congress as an ally against New York by withholding its 1785 contribution to the Treasury until Congress pressed New York to lighten its tariffs, and Connecticut merchants attempted a boycott of New York ports.[13]

The central government's weakness, and the struggle for advantage among the separate states, squandered what limited political and economic leverage the new country commanded in its dealings with foreign powers. After the war, Britain barred American ships from trading with its remaining New World colonies, both as a punitive measure against the breakaway nation and as a precaution against the emergence of a regional economic rival. The national government declared a campaign of retaliation, aimed at lifting this formidable impediment to America's economic growth, and New Hampshire, Massachusetts, and Rhode Island flatly banned British ships from their ports. But other states, including Connecticut, South Carolina, and Delaware, broke the boycott and welcomed British shipping. This had the effect of promoting the development of *their* ports, while rendering pointless the sacrifices of other states and draining all force from the national effort at retaliation. The central government had no power to enforce its policy, and a 1783 statement by the Pennsylvania legislature warned that the "exercise within the States of the power of regulating and controlling trade can result only in discordant systems productive of internal jealousies and competitions, and illy calculated to oppose or counteract foreign measures."[14] By the mid-1780s Britain sought to bypass the national government altogether and conduct its trade negotiations exclusively with the individual states. Thomas Jefferson, inspired in part by frustration over America's failure to face Britain with a common front, wrote in 1785 that "the interests of the States ought to be made joint in every possible instance, in order to cultivate the idea of our being one nation."[15]

One scholar has written that "the 'United States' in 1787 was not much more than the 'United Nations' was in 1987: a mutual treaty conveniently dishonored on all sides."[16] The economic liability of interstate division was not the only or even the most important issue alarming patriots in the 1780s—many were more troubled by the small-minded fractiousness of the period's state politics and the dimming of the republican vision that had been so bright a beacon during wartime[17]—but it was one major cause for the mid-decade movement to rethink the terms of American commonwealth so as to "form a more perfect Union." Forging unity among a people who loved liberty above all else posed a considerable challenge. But on the job in 1787 were the best minds of an extraordinary generation—in particular the intense young Virginian, James Madison.

Their task was to improvise, under pressure, a practical synthesis of a century's philosophical musings on the possibilities, and the limits, of democratic government. Thomas Hobbes had warned that only if the people ceded sovereignty to an unchallenged governmental Leviathan could brutal anarchy be kept at bay. The Framers—informed by familiarity with French, English, and Scottish political thought, and equipped with a spirit of pragmatic eclecticism—aimed to build a living rebuttal to Hobbes's argument. Greatly on display at the Constitutional Convention was the political gamesmanship that is an eternal component of such assemblies. Less predictably, perhaps, the convention spawned intellectual work of breathtaking originality and power.[18]

The core dilemma the Framers faced was that weak government tends to degenerate into muddle or mob rule, while strong government tends to harden into tyranny. The key to their solution was to craft a government that would be, in total, quite strong, but to *divide* that strength along two dimensions.

The first dimension of division was *within* the national government. Powers were separated among distinct legislative, judicial, and executive branches. The second dimension involved sharing sovereignty between the central government and the constituent states. Such a scheme offered hope for merging the virtues of small and large polities, while avoiding the worst evils of each.

Precisely *how* to subdivide sovereignty between state and national levels was hotly controversial. Some favored a continued "confederation" of states joined only at the top, where the national role would be restricted to foreign affairs, defense against external enemies and, perhaps, against internal coups. This group aimed for an edited version of the Articles of Confederation, establishing a more durable kind of association among state *governments*, while retaining the Articles' limited scope for direct dealings between citizens and the national government. But Alexander Hamilton, staking out the bluntest version of a growingly shared concern, argued that both other nations' histories and the recent travails of the United States displayed confederal arrangements of this sort as the "cause of incurable disorder and imbecility."[19] Others envisioned a diminishing role for the states as American nationhood matured. If Hamilton was the most avid of the "nationalists," Pennsylvania's Gouverneur Morris was perhaps the most candid. "We must have it in view," Morris argued, "eventually to lessen and destroy the state limits and authorities."[20]

The outcome fell somewhere in between the goals of those who wanted to strengthen the ties among essentially separate entities, and those who sought a new nation to supersede the states as the locus of commonwealth—though precisely *where* it fell remains disputed to this day. The national government was authorized to regulate foreign and interstate trade, coin money, award and enforce patents, make war and negotiate peace, and intervene if any state strayed egregiously from the practice of democracy.[21] But the Constitution makes great use of that timeless political expedient, ambiguity. Article VI declares federal supremacy in ringing terms: "This Constitution, and the Laws of the United States which shall be made in Pursuance thereof . . . shall be the supreme Law of the Land . . . any Thing in the Constitution or Laws of any State to the Contrary notwithstanding." The last of the ten original amendments seems equally clear: "The powers not delegated to the United States by the Constitution, nor prohibited by it to the States, are reserved to the States respectively, or to the people."

No one with the slightest exposure to the sophistication of the Framers' thinking can interpret this seeming inconsistency as a simple blunder. For one thing, there is no inconsistency, strictly speaking—taken together, the two clauses say that national authority is supreme wherever valid national laws exist, and not otherwise. The apparent conflict (at least in rhetoric and tone) springs from the political delicacies of getting the Constitution approved, first by the convention itself and then by the states. The supremacy clause affirms the priorities of the slim majority of nationalists; the Tenth Amendment (with the rest of the Bill of Rights) was meant to reassure some of the Constitution's more reluctant supporters among the Framers, and to aid in the effort to win ratification by defensive state legislatures. Madison, in particular, saw adding the Bill of Rights as a tactical concession to the Constitution's opponents, according to historians Stanley Elkins and Eric McKitrick, providing "the most convenient possible forum whereby they might change their minds."[22] Madison's own view was that the Bill of Rights was redundant with the body of the Constitution. What counted was not so much codifying the right rules—in a list that would inevitably be incomplete and out of date—but to structure a sound process for producing, over time, the rules a healthy republic required.

The Framers believed that the allocation of responsibility across levels of government would need to change with the times, and the Constitution sets broad parameters around the allowable division of powers between state and national governments.[23] Within those limits, the Framers left it to the wisdom of their successors to find the right balance to fit the circumstances of the world to come and the priorities of future generations of Americans. From that point onward, Americans have debated the precise width of those limits, the proper exercise of the freedom the Framers bequeathed, and the riddle of reconciling the supremacy clause and the Tenth Amendment.

DIVISION, WAR, AND RECONSTRUCTION

The early decades of America's second attempt at nationhood—insofar as a tumultuous half-century can be said to have any central theme—saw national union haltingly consolidated, though the argument over the division of federal-state authority barely slackened. The Jefferson Administration, in spite of the President's principled distaste for central authority, deployed federal resources to speed westward expansion by subsidizing infrastructure and education.[24] John Marshall, who led the Supreme Court through its formative early decades, played an enormous role in defining the judiciary as a steward of national unity. His experience as a combat commander in the Revolutionary War—including the hardships the underfunded army endured at Valley Forge—informed Justice Marshall's conviction that "state particularism and national weakness were as deadly as British musket fire."[25] Ambiguities were settled in favor of national unity by the Marshall Court's key decisions in *McCulloch v. Maryland* (1816) and *Gibbons v. Ogden* (1824).[26]

The doctrine of "nullification," asserting the right of states to reject federal laws they felt transgressed the boundaries of national power, originated with opposition to the notorious Alien and Sedition Acts of John Adams's government, but came to a head with an economic issue. New tariffs put in place under Andrew Jackson outraged import-dependent states and led the South Carolina legislature to enact an "Ordinance of Nullification" in 1832, declaring self-determination in economic matters. But while Southern sentiment in favor of the nullification principle remained strong, in practical terms, as Woodrow Wilson wrote, the "federal government was conceded the power to determine the economic opportunities of the States."[27]

As the nineteenth century reached its midpoint, however, the eternal argument became heated and American federalism neared its most searing test. Pressures accumulated along the fault line of slavery. A growing fraction of Americans judged the institution repugnant. Their willingness to tolerate its practice elsewhere in the name of state discretion eroded. The slave states, meanwhile, held that whatever the institution's moral qualities might be, the principles enshrined in the Tenth Amendment left decisions about slavery to the states alone. As absolutes collided, the sentiment of union crumbled. The South asserted what it declared to be the defining right of sovereign states—the right to opt out of the union. State authority, Lincoln countered, did not go so far. The matter was settled by the most traumatic passage in American history.

The Civil War and Reconstruction saw a marked shift of authority away from the states and toward the federal government.[28] Prosecuting the war had itself accelerated the growth of Washington's power, and preserving the union by force of arms made vividly concrete the notion of American nationhood. The virtual occupation of the defeated South, and protracted federal monitoring of the former slave states' governments, symbolized the preeminence of national authority. And three new amendments, the legacy of the triumphant Republican Party, etched this postwar spirit into the Constitution. The Thirteenth Amendment, barring slavery, may not in itself impose a strikingly greater restriction on state discretion than, say, the Constitution's prior prohibition of retroactive laws or aristocratic titles. But the accompanying amendments went deeper. The Fourteenth Amendment mandates an ambitious standard of respect for human rights as the obligation of every state, and the Fifteenth extends this guarantee to all citizens, including former slaves. The federal government, crucially, was declared the enforcer of the newly codified rights.

For some scholars and politicians, the Reconstruction era marks the renunciation of the vision of limited national government that had inspired the Constitution. Those who interpret American federalism as requiring state supremacy (or at worst an equal balance) lament that "the Fourteenth Amendment was . . . bootlegged into the Bill of Rights" during a chaotic interval of our history.[29] Others see the Reconstruction amendments as the germination of seeds sown at Philadelphia. By this view, the postwar surge of federal power marked the affirmation of a nationalist project that had been present in the Framers' work, but buried by the political imperative of soothing antifederalist sentiments.[30] In either event, it is clear that midway through American history the balance of sovereignty shifted away from the state capitals and toward the District of Columbia.[31]

The Argument's Twentieth-Century Evolution

Herbert Croly's book *The Promise of American Life*, widely credited as the conceptual catalyst of the Progressive movement, was published at the beginning of the century in a period (not unlike our own) when stepped-up economic change was intensifying the debate over American fundamentals. "The Promise of American life must depend less than it did upon the virgin wilderness and the Atlantic Ocean," Croly wrote, "for the virgin wilderness has disappeared, and the Atlantic Ocean has become merely a big channel."[32] Croly's grand design hinged on a sharp consolidation of national economic authority. "The regulation of commerce, the control of corporations, and the still more radical questions connected with the distribution of wealth and the prevention of poverty—questions of this kind should be left exclusively to the central government," Croly argued, and states' economic activities should be undertaken essentially "as the agents of the central government."[33] Yet Progressivism, paradoxically, had its greatest impact at the *state* level. Justice Louis Brandeis celebrated the states as "laboratories of democracy," the wellsprings of progressive initiatives that could be adopted more widely if they worked, and otherwise discarded. Felix Frankfurter echoed the theme in a 1930 speech at Yale: "The states need the amplest scope for energy and individuality in dealing with the myriad problems created by our complex industrial civilization."[34] As Frankfurter spoke, however, America was on the cusp of the next surge in central authority.

The era of the Great Depression witnessed furious debate on the federal-state balance (as on much of the rest of the American system.) Virtually each initiative in the policy salvo Franklin Delano Roosevelt launched shifted the balance of power a bit more toward Washington. The Supreme Court initially resisted on constitutional grounds, then yielded, and loosed the flood of FDR's ambitions. Legislation barring interstate trade in goods produced by child labor, for example, was at first struck down. The Court had argued that "if Congress can thus regulate matters entrusted to local authority by prohibition of the movement of commodities in interstate commerce, all freedom of commerce will be at an end, and the power of the States over local matters may be eliminated."[35] That bulwark of state sovereignty (and many others) was dislodged by New Deal–era Supreme Courts, making way for legislation solidifying the federal government's role. An unprecedented degree of governmental activism on the economy, orchestrated from the center, meant an unprecedented concentration of authority.[36]

Even so, Roosevelt's government was careful to pay obeisance to the principle of balance. As a system of state-run but nationally mandated unemployment insurance was taking shape, Roosevelt's powerful Committee on Economic Security (which spearheaded the effort) was careful to specify that "all matters in which uniformity is not absolutely essential should be left to the states."[37] Yet the range in which uniformity, or at least an unaccustomed degree of national integration, was considered "absolutely essential" greatly expanded during the New Deal. Roosevelt not only articulated, but also acted upon, what in earlier eras would have seemed a startling proposition: that it is the responsibility of the national government to diminish differences in living standards across states. In response to a 1938 National Emergency Council report on grim conditions in the southern states Roosevelt declared that "the South presents right now the nation's No. 1 economic problem—the nation's problem, not merely the South's."[38] That same year Harold Laski, in a famous New Republic article, argued that the imperative of a centralized governmental response to centralized modern capitalism meant that "the epoch of federalism is over."[39] Even if many disagreed with so sweeping a conclusion there was little appetite in the late 1930s for rolling back the New Deal in the name of states' rights.

The massive national mobilization of the Second World War (and the Cold War that followed) was a further force for centralization. And the prosperity of the first postwar decades softened once hard-edged questions about the locus of economic responsibility. Macroeconomic fine-tuning, orchestrated (according to scientific principles) from the very peak of the federal policy-making system seemed to make lower-level interventions superfluous. The argument did not die down completely, to be sure, and there were some postwar pressures to reverse course: A group of governors petitioned the Truman Administration to loosen strings attached to federal aid; in 1949 a presidential commission led by Herbert Hoover proposed a more rational sorting-out of functions and revenue sources across levels of government; Eisenhower initiated new commissions in 1955 and again in 1957 to revisit the balance. But the tide toward Washington was not to be turned.[40] An early postwar Supreme Court decision, H.P. Hood and Sons v. Du Mond, declared explicitly that "our economic unit is the Nation."[41] The Interstate Highway Act of 1956 marked a major expansion of the federal government into transportation policy.[42] In 1960 a business-group official lamented that state-level economic policy had become "a swampy backwater in the United States."[43]

Events beyond the economic realm, meanwhile, reinforced the shift toward Washington. As the struggle for civil rights escalated, both the oratory, and the policy initiatives it inspired, echoed Reconstruction. "States' rights" became an unsavory code phrase, and recalcitrant southern states faced vigorous assertions of federal authority.

By the 1970s, the federal government had gained some sort of role in virtually every public function, in virtually every state. Washington both influenced the ends of a wide range of policies and delivered much of the means for pursuing them.[44] An apt metaphor was provided by Morton Grodzins.[45] In earlier conceptions of federalism, American government could be described as a layer cake, with the national and state levels connected to each other but distinct, and with state government retaining a discernibly independent identity. In the new reality, Grodzins wrote, federalism was like a marble cake. State and national authority were indissolubly intermingled. Just as there were no sharp boundaries on the effects of a policy, so there should be no rigid delineation of which level of government held authority over which set of activities. The "marble cake" theory is a sunnily optimistic view of federalism, and indeed of government itself. It envisions national, state, and local officials—who are rooted in the same professional culture and who share a devotion to good government—working together to advance well-defined public goals.

The architects of Lyndon Johnson's Great Society gave life to the "marble cake" metaphor through the surge of targeted intergovernmental transfers that powered most of Johnson's new social initiatives. The Great Society is commonly, but erroneously, seen as an expansion of direct federal activism. Instead, it was an expansion of state and local activism catalyzed by Washington. In 1965 alone, 109 new categorical grant programs were created, and a total of 240 between 1964 and 1966.[46] Funding for such programs grew from $7.7 billion in 1962 to $41.7 billion in 1973.[47] (Significantly, the Great Society intergovernmental programs treated cities and states similarly, despite the special constitutional status that set states apart.)

This benign "marble cake" interpretation of the blurring lines between levels of government quickly inspired a reaction. The counterattack is represented most famously by a book coauthored by Jeffrey Pressman and Berkeley political scientist Aaron Wildavsky, bearing the bland title, *Implementation* and the telling subtitle, *How Great Expectations in Washington Are Dashed in Oakland.*[48] *Implementation* is a scholarly tragicomedy. It explains, in painful detail, how a nobly-intended federal program to boost economic development in blighted locales, carried out with arrogant disregard for local goals and conditions, collapsed into rubble and dust. Against the Great Society ideal of harmonious partnership among federal, state, and local professionals, Pressman and Wildavsky deploy an object lesson of unmitigated muddle, where dreamers, incompetents, and knaves conspire to unleash chaos. *Implementation* generalizes the story to suggest that nearly all grand ambitions emanating from Washington, but *especially* those requiring cooperation from other governments, are fated to founder on the perverse complexity of the world outside the Beltway. The book was as influential as it was pessimistic, and presaged the intellectual fashions to come: a presumption in favor of lower-level governments, overlaid with cynicism about government in general and an expectation that most policies will fail.

"New Federalism," Old and New

The durable term "new federalism" surfaced in American political rhetoric at least a century ago, and figured in the title of a much-noted book published in the 1930s.[49] Two modern Republican presidents, Nixon and Reagan, each launched major restructurings flying the "New Federalism" banner, although they used the same words to mean quite different things. (Interestingly, the counterpart phrase the "New Nationalism" was the slogan not of the New Deal, but of Theodore Roosevelt's administration.[50]) Congressional Republicans of the mid-1990s, meanwhile, employed the term for their own distinctive purposes.

Nixon's initiative, in the main, was the realization of a proposal first laid out by Walter Heller, chief economist for the Kennedy Administration. The basic idea was to shift from the Great Society's "categorical" grants, which cast state and local governments as Washington's agents or subcontractors, to spending *funded* by the federal government but *controlled* at lower levels.[51] This was in essence a step toward the fiscal model prevailing in other modern federations—including Australia, Canada, and Germany—where a substantial fraction of the revenue raised centrally flows on to the states to spend as they see fit. General revenue sharing surged from less than $500 million in 1970 to over $8.6 billion in 1980.[52]

Ronald Reagan's New Federalism, paradoxically, was both more narrowly pragmatic than Nixon's, and a far more aggressive repudiation of the turn that American history had taken. It was pragmatic in its concern for shielding the federal treasury. Instead of providing resources while ceding control, Reagan sought to renounce the federal government's responsibilities over large areas of policy. It was profound, indeed radical, in its theme of undoing several stages of national consolidation. The Reagan plan aimed to redress the shift toward coordinated social policy that had occurred under Johnson's Great Society, and sought as well to reverse much of the New Deal's centralization of power.

The 1981 Omnibus Budget Reconciliation Act that set the tone for the Reagan era consolidated roughly one-tenth of the 534 existing categorical programs into nine block grants.[53] The good news, for the states, was that there were fewer restrictions on how they could use the money Washington sent; the bad news was that there was a good deal less money.[54] Reagan's 1982 State of the Union address featured yet bolder (if ultimately little-heeded) calls to turn back responsibilities to the states while rearranging the financial burdens of social welfare programs. General revenue sharing, the hallmark of Nixon's New Federalism, dwindled steadily under Reagan until it disappeared in 1986. Overall transfers from Washington to states and cities, which had surged from about 1.5 percent of the overall economy in the mid-1960s to about 3.5 percent in the mid-1970s, retreated to around 2.5 percent of GDP.

The New Federalism in its Reagan-Bush variant, in short, left the states to go their own ways in many areas of economic and social policy that previous national administrations had centralized. Thomas Swartz and John Peck exaggerate, but only slightly, when they say that the underlying precept of 1980s intergovernmental relations was "if you cannot pay for a service at the level where it is provided, then do without it."[55] Veteran federalism scholar John Shannon coined the evocative term, "fend-for-yourself-federalism."[56] It would be another decade, though, before the movement toward competitive state autonomy would mature, and before its broader implications would become manifest.

The decentralization efforts that Nixon (and later, Ford) had pursued under the New Federalism label were directed to a substantial degree at bolstering *local* governments, which have no definite constitutional status and (for the most part) a secondary role in the American argument over governmental balance. Nixon's initiatives, in delegating delivery to cities and states alike, had at least as much to do with administrative efficiencies as they did with the locus of sovereignty.[57] The Reagan restructuring, conversely, stressed the *states*, and cut closer to the core of the basic argument. Categorical programs that used to fund city governments and community organizations were replaced by block grants whose allocation was controlled or greatly influenced by governors. The Job Training Partnership Act, for example, replaced a profusion of intergovernmental (and heavily local) training programs with consolidated state-based funds, granted with only the flimsiest of federal strings attached.[58]

Meanwhile, the brutal arithmetic of entitlement spending meant that a few remaining federal programs claimed an increasing share of the funds. Intergovernmental grants earmarked for health care (chiefly Medicaid) and income security (chiefly AFDC) rose from less than two-fifths of the total in 1970 to two-thirds in 1995, as Figure 2 shows.

THE SUPREME COURT AS INCONSTANT ARBITER

The Supreme Court has served as umpire in America's endless argument over federal-state balance. But its judgments have been shifting and inconsistent (although doubtless no more so than should be expected for an institution made up of men and women, and two centuries' worth of different men and women charged with settling society's hard cases). The changing composition of the court, the evolving economic and political context, and the ambiguity of the Constitution itself have made for a tortuous history of Court decisions and a convoluted tangle of precedents.[59]

Earlier sections have noted the Court's role in the national consolidation of the early nineteenth century and its eventual acquies-

Figure 2
The Allocation of Intergovernmental Grants, 1970–1995

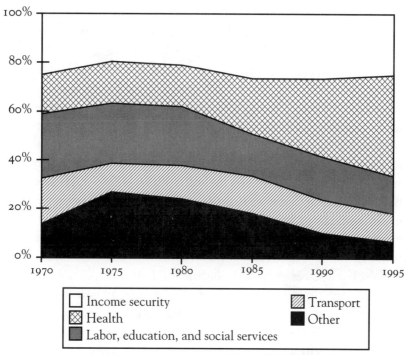

Source: OMB, FY97 Budget, Historical

cence in Roosevelt's New Deal. But the past two decades have been particularly turbulent. In a 1976 case, *National League of Cities v. Usery*, the Court sought to shore up the sovereignty of the states by declaring that Washington had no authority to extend to state governments the wage and hour regulations it enforced on private employers.[60] Nine years later, the Court explicitly repudiated this precedent in *Garcia v. San Antonio Metro Area Transit Authority*, with a divided ruling that "the Constitution does not carve out express elements of state sovereignty that Congress may not employ its delegated powers to displace."[61] *Garcia* enraged adherents of shared sovereignty with its suggestion that the states should advance their claims on the federal government through political action, like any other interest group.[62] And in 1988, after South Carolina and the National Governors' Association challenged new restrictions on state debt's traditional exemption from federal taxation, the Court rejected their claim in *South Carolina v. Baker*.[63] This case, like most other Court decisions on federalism, had tilted toward the nationalist side of the argument by the narrowest of margins. But the close decisions were soon to start splitting the other way.[64]

The next turn in the Court's arbitration of the debate over balance was signaled in 1992 by *New York v. United States*, which struck down a federal law requiring the states to take responsibility for the disposal of nuclear waste.[65] As the Rehnquist Court reached its stride in the mid-1990s, *United States v. Lopez* took on the time-honored practice of using the commerce clause as a sort of wild card to legitimate federal activism. Congress had invoked the commerce clause to justify the Gun-Free School Zones Act that required states to ban weaponry from the vicinity of schools—an argument that the Court found farfetched.[66] Shortly thereafter a dry and initially obscure case, *Seminole Tribes v. Florida*, turned out to frame with brutal clarity the question of when citizens can turn to the federal government with complaints against the actions of states. The Court found for Florida in a decision that essentially declared states immune to lawsuits to force compliance with federal environmental, regulatory, and health and safety laws. Justice John Paul Stevens, in a dissent from the 5-to-4 decision, described *Seminole Tribes* as "a case about power," the importance of which "cannot be overstated."[67] Within a few weeks after *Seminole Tribes*, the Supreme Court vacated an appeals court decision allowing an Ohio agency to be sued in federal bankruptcy court; scheduled a case that could extend the principle by immunizing state officials (not just state institutions) from suit under federal law; and in a symbolically important move, had agreed to hear state complaints against the Brady Bill, which required states and localities to police handgun purchases.[68] "What we're seeing from the judicial branch," observed Paul D. Gewirtz of Yale, "is an across-the-board restriction on national government power on every front, and a bolstering of state sovereignty."[69]

ON THE CUSP OF A NEW PHASE

The early years of the first Clinton Administration were marked by ambivalence on the federal-state balance. The economist Alice Rivlin, a respected arbiter of mainstream Democratic opinion, published a plea for expanded state autonomy in 1992, shortly before taking a senior

Clinton policy post.[70] Yet other voices within the new administration called for federal activism and, in any case, most of the initiatives that would have decisively engaged the issue failed to survive the passage to legislation. The administration's agenda for federalism, in the event, became considerably less determinative with the 1994 congressional elections. John J. DiIulio, Jr., and Donald Kettl have noted that the Contract with America, the collective campaign manifesto of House Republicans, marked the "birth of the third 'new federalism' in a quarter century."[71] On devolution, if not on the rest of their agenda, the new majority found a receptive public. Texas Senator Kay Bailey Hutchinson seemed to speak for many when she declared that the "states can be more efficient and more responsible if Washington just gets out of the way."[72]

At the same time, the composition of the cast of characters ensured that Washington itself would have considerable sympathy with the view from the states. Bill Clinton, of course, had made his reputation and honed his instincts as a creative small-state governor. The 104th Congress included seventeen former governors and thirty-eight former state legislators among the one hundred senators, and nearly half of the members of the House had previously served as state legislators.[73] In a feature of the 1994 elections that was less noted than the turnover in Congress, but perhaps not less significant, the number of Republican governors leaped from nineteen to thirty-one. There was now a critical mass of fresh conservative leaders at the state level—thirsty for authority, unified in how they would deploy it, and in synch with their congressional counterparts.

Seizing the momentum of their surge to the forefront of American government, some state leaders laid plans for a new Constitutional Convention—the first since 1787. Their hopes for having the century's final word in the argument over federalism's proper balance were undercut, however, by bipartisan nervousness about the consequences of unleashing on the Constitution the passions of the mid-1990s. Erstwhile advocates of a Constitutional Convention settled instead for a "Federalism Summit" that united nine governors and scores of other state officials in a 1995 convocation on "restoring the balance" in the American system.

Michael O. Leavitt, the articulate governor of Utah, led the effort to convene the summit, and in a passionate speech at its commencement invoked the ghosts of Thomas Jefferson, James Madison, and

Alexander Hamilton in support of his call to strengthen the role of the states. "As stewards of their creation, the Constitution of the United States," Leavitt said, "I believe they would tell us we have an obligation to restore the balance."[74] The options the summit promoted to recalibrate American federalism prominently featured what Leavitt termed a "people's legislative recall"—a constitutional provision that would allow a majority of states to veto any federal law or regulation. (James Madison, whose spirit Leavitt summoned, had actually favored a *federal* veto on *state* laws. And Madison, Hamilton, and Jefferson hardly comprise a harmonious chorus on the proper federal-state balance.[75] But however debatable Leavitt's history, he had a good eye for the contemporary trajectory of America's endless argument.)

As advocates of state primacy found their voice, the nationalist side of the argument was strangely muted. Washington acquiesced in the ascendancy of the states, and not only because of Republican dominance of both Congress and the statehouses. President Clinton, from what precise mix of conviction and stratagem it is difficult to say, proved broadly agreeable to letting Washington cede leadership to the states. Throughout the debate over the devolution of welfare policy, for example, Clinton and the Republicans differed chiefly in degree and tactics, not principle. Even before approving legislation that gave the states formal control over antipoverty policy, the administration had granted waivers from federal regulations to forty states. The notion of national welfare, in other words, had effectively dissolved well before the legislation was signed. "What separates the President and Senator Dole on this issue," ABC's Brit Hume reported during the height of the rhetorical wars over welfare, "is not so much the issue itself. They both want to give the states more control, but they both want to be seen as the leader on it."[76] Beyond welfare reform, Clinton seemed quite comfortable with the broad devolutionary theme. The administration proudly noted, in a report on labor-market trends, that federal government employment had fallen by over one-tenth on its watch (from January 1993 to March 1996) while state and local government employment had grown.[77]

But the Clinton Administration's acquiescence in the shift toward the states is most dramatically on display in its budget proposals. Figure 3 arrays the major categories of public spending shares of America's overall economy, based on averages from 1990 through 1996. The public sector, in total, claimed slightly under one-third of the coun-

Figure 3
Share of U.S. Gross Domestic Product, 1990–1996 Average

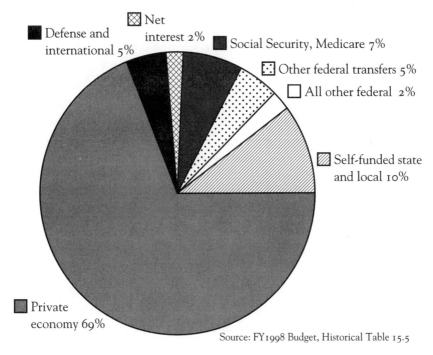

Source: FY1998 Budget, Historical Table 15.5

try's gross domestic product. (In the other industrialized countries of the Organization for Economic Cooperation and Development [OECD], total government spending averaged 49 percent of GDP in the mid-1990s.[78]) Federal transfer payments totaled about 12 percent of GDP, and along with interest payments on the federal debt and federal spending on defense and international affairs account for about three-fifths of the overall public sector. Domestic public spending *other than* federal transfers and interest totaled just under 12.5 percent of the economy over this period, with most of this (10.2 percent) representing self-funded state and local spending. Federal domestic spending (aside from transfers and interest) fell from around 3 percent of the economy at the start of the 1990s to less than 2 percent in 1996. And under the administration's budget plans, federal domestic spending will continue its decline.[79]

Consider, against this backdrop of shrinking real federal domestic discretionary spending, some alternative scenarios for the future of sub-national government.[80] One possibility is that "the era of big government is over" at lower levels of government as well as in Washington. Suppose state and local spending grows at the same restrained pace as federal domestic programs, as projected by the Office of Management and Budget. As government budgets at all levels lag behind the economy's growth, by this scenario, America's public sector would shrink to something under 30 percent of the gross domestic product by 2002. Another possibility is that Washington cuts back, according to schedule, over the last years of this century and the first years of the next. But state and local spending continues to grow at the same average pace as it did over the 1980–95 period—an annual rate of about 7.8 percent. Under this scenario the overall public sector shrinks very slightly from the share of the economy it represented in the first half of the 1990s, while its composition shifts: Self-funded state and local spending would edge out federal entitlements and debt service as the largest category of public spending.

A third possibility is that as the federal government retreats, states and localities will advance to occupy the abandoned terrain so that the public sector, taken as a whole, stays at the same share of the economy as during the 1990–96 period. Under this scenario, self-funded state and local spending would sharply outstrip federal interest and entitlements as the largest category of American government. Still more striking is the shift this scenario implies in the composition of domestic government: Spending controlled by states and localities in 2002—the sum of self-funded state and local spending and federal grants to cities and states—would reach about fifteen times the level of federal domestic spending (other than interest and entitlements). Even more than it does today, American government would wear a state and local face.

These scenarios, to be sure, do not exhaust the alternatives. Washington might slacken its pace toward budget balance, forestalling the trend toward state and local dominance. It is also quite likely that states will turn out to embrace austerity with *more* fervor than Washington does—due to recession; to the structural bias in state tax codes that tends to keep revenue growing more slowly than the economy; to competitive pressures to shrink spending; or to ideological conviction—so that overall public spending in an era of devolution will fall faster than even the first scenario suggests.

Yet however rooted in conjecture, the scenarios do illustrate some fundamental implications of federal budget plans. Aside from sending checks to health-care providers, Social Security claimants, and debt holders, the federal government will be a shrinking presence in most Americans' lives well into the early years of the twenty-first century. So the United States' public sector—already small by comparison to those of other industrialized countries—will shrink further. Or the relative importance of the cities and states will soar. Or both.

CHAPTER THREE

Unity and Autonomy: The Weights on the Scale

The tension between autonomy and commonwealth ranks high among political philosophy's primal themes. The human spirit is instinctively drawn to the advantages of community but (no less instinctively) bridles at the concomitant imperative of compromise. Common sense affirms the virtue of balance; contemporary political rhetoric often ignores it. Proponents of some particular increment of unity, or of some particular increment of autonomy, can anticipate being battered by lurid depictions of an extreme version of the principle they seek to advance. But either principle, of course, is pathological in excess. Floods can be fatal. So can droughts. Societies can starve from too little community, or smother from forced conformity. Recent history affords ample evidence of cultures made miserable by too much unity, and by too little—sometimes, as in the case of the former Yugoslavia, the same culture separated by a few years.

America's federal system is structured to improve the odds, issue by issue, of reaching the right equilibrium between unity and autonomy. "The general lines of definition which were to run between the powers granted to Congress and the powers reserved to the States," wrote Woodrow Wilson in his happier, prepresidential days as a professor, "the makers of the Constitution were able to draw with their characteristic foresight and lucidity; but the subject-matter of that definition is constantly changing, for it is the life of the nation itself."[1] This chapter introduces some of the principles that animate debates over how the federal-state division should be drawn for particular issues that matter for the life of the nation in our times; later chapters put the principles to work.

While the reasoning on any specific policy choice quickly becomes complex and technical, the generic task is to find the point, on the broad continuum of allowable possibilities, where national unity and state autonomy are best in balance. Before we set out to calibrate some of the weights on the scale, however, we must face up to an intimidating obstacle—the claim that the debate over balance is not ours to engage, but a debate that raged and was settled, once and for all, in 1787. An ancient and honorable faction holds that the division of responsibilities between state and national governments was determined by the Framers—not merely in general terms, as Wilson suggests, but in great detail, or at least all the detail we need. By this view the Constitution presents no broad continuum of possible divisions anchored by a few absolutes, but, to the contrary, provides specific instructions for running the government. Thus it would be at best presumptuous, in general imprudent, and perhaps even unpatriotic to discuss which responsibilities ought to lodge at which level.

Yet assigning contemporary judgment a role in adjusting the federal-state balance is an equally ancient, equally honorable intellectual tradition. Alexander Hamilton, of course, had no qualms about defining the national government's functions elastically. In Federalist 34 he wrote: "Nothing . . . can be more fallacious than to infer the extent of any power proper to be lodged in the national government from an estimate of its immediate necessities."[2] James Madison as well (at least until his later alarm over Hamilton's application of their shared principle shifted him several degrees toward strict constructionism) saw the balance between federal and state power in similarly pragmatic terms.[3] The two levels of government, Madison wrote, are "but different agents and trustees of the people, constituted with different powers and designed for different purposes."[4]

This basic proposition that no *government* has any rights at all, but can only claim instrumental rights as the agent of popular power, carried the debate in the Framers' day, and should carry it in our own. Antifederalists attacked the proposed Constitution as an affront to the sovereign rights of the separate states. The core of the Federalists' rejoinder, as summarized by Elkins and McKitrick, was that

> state sovereignty was not being invaded because sovereignty had never resided there. Sovereignty resides ... in the whole body of the people.... And such is the supreme authority of the people that although the people may not, indeed cannot, part with any portion of that sovereignty—which is to say that sovereignty is in some final sense indivisible after all—they may still distribute its functions in as many ways as they choose, and yet again revoke them should prudence so advise it.[5]

America is a pragmatic country, and practical arguments about what national economic role would serve the people best have usually prevailed over abstract absolutes that claim to supersede and render superfluous the analysis of alternatives.[6] For example, the Constitution does not give the federal government the power to issue paper currency. But the disadvantages of state currencies, the preferability of a single national standard, and the inconvenience of gold and silver coins have proven so obvious that hardly anyone objects to the dollar on constitutional grounds anymore.[7] Yet even if few strict constructionists are quite *that* strict, I am aware (as should be the reader) that some scholars and political figures will view the reasoning of this chapter in much the same way as Christian or Islamic fundamentalists perceive secular moral philosophy—as impious claptrap.[8]

For those willing to continue with the debate, its terms include *state diversity*, the advantages and disadvantages that come with *governmental scale*, the role of autonomous states as *policy laboratories*, and the alignment of choice and consequence to minimize policy *externalities*. (The overarching issue of competition among state governments merits a later chapter all its own.)

DIVERSITY

Citizens differ in preferences and circumstances. Sometimes those differences are related in some systematic way to geography; citizens of one region tend to be like each other, and less like citizens of other locales. To the extent America's states constitute collections of like-minded people, a degree of state autonomy in economic affairs would make sense even if there were no other arguments in its favor. Citizens may differ state by state in the values they cherish, in the problems that confront them, in the options at hand for addressing those problems, and so on. What matters is not so much the dimensions of state diversity, but how homogenous states are internally, and how reliably different from other states.[9]

John C. Calhoun, a leader of the Southern sectarian view that eventually inspired secession, argued early in our history that "the very idea of an *American People*, as constituting a single community, is a mere chimera. Such a community never for a single moment existed."[10] Few contemporary observers would go quite so far, but neither would many contend that the states are all the same. Rhode Island's thickly clustered population is as characteristic as Montana's wide open spaces. Nearly every state considers its own culture unique, and even outsiders concede the distinctiveness of many (including California, Texas, Alaska, and Louisiana.) The personal reserve that defines good manners in Minnesota or Indiana can strike New Yorkers as borderline autism. North Carolina is characteristically genteel and traditional; Massachusetts is sharp-elbowed and progressive. And so on. Even though regions are becoming more ideologically similar over time, state populations still differ measurably on the liberal-to-conservative spectrum. Empirical work by political scientists has found state-by-state differences in prevailing political sentiment to be correlated, appropriately, with variations in policy.[11]

Economic theorists have long probed the perils of collective choice. The more diverse the group, the lower the odds that a collective decision will gratify the typical member, suggesting that the inherent problems of public spending will be mitigated, to a degree, by pushing decisions down to smaller and more homogenous communities.[12] Contemporary scholars have affirmed and elaborated on the advantages of leaving states free to tailor policies to their particular conditions and values.[13] President Reagan issued an executive order—to limited effect—calling on federal agencies to defer whenever possible to state discretion since "in most areas of governmental concern, the States uniquely posses the constitutional authority, the resources, and the competence to discern the sentiments of the people and to govern accordingly."[14]

Even when states vary, of course, there are arguments for uniformity. Institutions and individuals who live or do business in several states face the expense, bother, and confusion of coping with different (and sometimes conflicting) rules. Inconsistencies among state laws and regulations can lead to disputes of great complexity, and to resolutions of limited appeal. (After taking its case all the way to the Supreme Court, for example, a cruise ship operator won the right to be sued only in Florida by aggrieved passengers who had been on a trip between Washington State and Mexico.[15]) Woodrow Wilson—proving his own argument that the proper federal balance can alter over time—had dismissed proposals for a federal child labor law as involving "obviously absurd extravagancies of interpretation" of the commerce clause.[16] Such a law was passed about a generation later. It is difficult to believe that Wilson, were he living today, would call for its repeal. Indeed, not even today's most avid decentralizers propose abandoning national child labor statutes and inviting Wisconsin, say, to compete for business by advertising to factory owners its ample workforce of nimble and compliant twelve-year-olds if its internal politics endorsed such a strategy.

Among the most fervent advocates of regulatory uniformity are corporations (such as the major automakers) who sell nationwide, since they would be robbed of scale economies if they had to produce a different product to meet each state's regulatory code.[17] An engineering study has blamed the predominance of local regulations—and the resulting patchwork of inconsistent building codes—for the "technological backwardness of the American construction industry."[18] Since new techniques could only be replicated awkwardly, or not at all, across different regulatory regimes, construction companies had limited incentive to innovate. Similarly, as financial markets become more integrated the downside of decentralized regulations has become apparent. The National Securities Markets Improvement Act, which became law late in 1996, preempted state regulation of many categories of financial securities on the grounds that a single set of national rules will be far more efficient.[19]

On almost any issue there are plausible arguments for state auton-omy and plausible arguments for standardization. Sometimes the bal-ance is worked out quietly under the auspices of a quasi-official coordinating group called the National Conference of Commissioners on Uniform State Laws; sometimes the issue is settled in a more visible political forum.[20] Consider highway safety. For several decades policies on speed limits and other aspects of safety have tended toward national convergence. Assertions of a national interest in limiting oil imports helped justify a uniform fifty-five-mile-per-hour maximum speed; the partial pooling of national medical costs through Medicaid was invoked to warrant requiring every state to have a minimum drinking age and motorcycle helmet laws as a condition for getting federal highway fund-ing. But as the oil crisis passed, safety alone couldn't sustain the case for uniform national speed limits. Highway speeds that would be homicidal on the crowded, twisting roads of the Northeast may be entirely pru-dent on the Great Plains.

Opponents of mandated state helmet laws based their arguments not on diversity of conditions—motorcyclists are no more skillful in one state than another, and skulls are no sturdier—but rather on diver-sity of values. Citizens of some states find the whiff of paternalism in-volved in mandatory helmet laws worth enduring in the name of limiting the worst consequences of road mishaps; citizens of other states find it intolerable. After many years of effort, national requirements for helmet laws and maximum speed limits were repealed in late 1995. Within a few months motorcyclists could let their hair blow free in sev-eral states, most Western states had set seventy-five mph limits, and Montana had no daylight speed limit at all.[21]

EXPERIMENTATION

The notion of states as the "laboratories of democracy" is one of the commonest and most intuitively appealing arguments for weakening Washington's hand and giving the states more room to maneuver. Pub-lic problems are sufficiently complex, and policy-makers' judgment is sufficiently fallible, that rarely is the one right answer obvious—even in the rare case where a single solution (once discovered) turns out to fit every state. As states innovate, their experience informs not just their own policy choices, but those of the other states as well. The freer states are to experiment independently, the deeper will be the common well of expertise about what works and what doesn't.

The payoff from policy innovation offers one of the strongest generic arguments for maintaining an ample range of state autonomy.[22] In the mid-1990s Ohio conducted a massive experiment, with useful if somewhat sobering lessons for other states, on the impact of crafting welfare rules to encourage teenage parents to stay in school.[23] The states opened a new front in the war against smoking when attorneys general began suing tobacco companies to recover some of the huge sums states have spent on smoking-related illnesses. Georgia under Governor Jimmy Carter found business to be more concerned with transparent environmental rules and rapid processing of permit applications than with the rules' stringency or laxness, and Georgia's innovation of "streamlined permitting" was rapidly adopted by most other states.[24] As health maintenance organizations came to dominate health care in many parts of the country, a number of scandals erupted over HMO rules forbidding doctors to discuss certain costly treatment options with their patients, or to reveal their own financial interest in limiting the cost of care. In 1996 alone, sixteen states adopted laws barring such physician "gag rules."[25] While a similar law had been proposed in Congress, state legislators were able to deliver results with more speed and flexibility (at least in those sixteen states), and states' experience will surely improve any eventual federal legislation. Competency tests for teachers, public financing for election campaigns, and sunset laws to trigger automatic review of legislation were all products of state-level experimentation.[26]

The greater the uncertainty about what works and what doesn't, and the greater the ability and willingness of states to share information, the more valuable are state-level policy innovations and the more costly is any requirement of national uniformity. There is a certain method, when viewed through this lens, in the distinction drawn between AFDC and Medicaid in the 1996 restructuring of antipoverty policy. Congress at first pushed to shift both to the states; the administration resisted; and the eventual solution left Washington with substantial authority over Medicaid while devolving most decisions about welfare. This would make sense under the (not implausible) hypothesis that true welfare reform is stymied by ignorance of what works and the paucity of alternative models, while the options for Medicaid essentially involve greater or lesser degrees of austerity within a relatively well-understood undertaking.

The real measure of an experiment's value, of course, is the wide-spread application of its lessons. And here the "laboratory" metaphor can be stretched too far. States don't innovate in order to augment the pool of common knowledge. They innovate to solve their own problems. Generalizable evidence is a serendipitous by-product. States may have limited interest in making the lessons they've learned available to other states, or limited ability to spread the word. (In part to compensate for these shortfalls, the Ford Foundation has mounted a major project to identify governmental innovations and accelerate their diffusion.[27]) Indeed, states can be frankly hostile to the diffusion of an innovation, if the knowledge held close would confer a proprietary advantage in interstate competition. In other words, the states may be laboratories for national policy in much the same way as a rain forest, say, is a laboratory for the biological sciences. There is a lot going on. Much if it has great potential relevance for improving the state of the art. But the rain forest's drama of predator and prey, its roiling interplay of survival strategies, are not set in motion to test hypotheses or to speed the progress of theory. A great deal of this ferment of activity, moreover, goes unobserved, doing little or nothing to advance best practice.

SCALE

"Close to the People"

The advantages and disadvantages of governmental scale enter into calculations on the federal-state balance at several levels. Among the most fundamental arguments is the claim that the emotional bonds of commonwealth simply can't stretch very far, and that only small polities can command popular fealty. In a letter to Madison during the Constitutional Convention, Connecticut's Roger Sherman put it bluntly: "The people are more happy in small than in large States."[28] Massachusetts Governor William Weld expressed the same sentiments in the political idiom of 1996: "We're closer and more directly answerable to our citizens than the cloud-dwellers in Washington are."[29] The primal psychological argument that only small republics are workable was the core of Montesquieu's politics, which Madison so ingeniously sought to amend through the intellectual architecture of our Constitution. George Washington's one intervention in the Constitution's drafting was to insist that congressional districts be small enough to permit a personal style of politics.[30] Nor is this an outdated concern; a contemporary communitarian school celebrates the virtues of the compact community: In an era of economic globalism, political philosopher Michael Sandel has written, "the politics of neighborhood matters more, not less. [31]

Even Rhode Island, however, is far larger than the intimate republics that Montesquieu envisioned. (For that matter, even in the Framers' day the smallest state exceeded the size of such a republic, as Hamilton pointed out.[32]) States, even in principle, fall short of the ideal of grassroots democracy. Modern information technologies have somewhat eroded the advantages of small-scale government, at the same time, since citizens no longer must rely on direct observation or word of mouth to keep abreast of public affairs. Indeed, relentless coverage by the news media can mean that Washington is *better* understood by the average citizen than state and local governments that are less thoroughly scrutinized by the press. As continued technological progress— the profusion of cable channels, specialized Web sites—makes it easier to keep up with state and local issues, this factor could fade. Similarly, the shift of resources and authority to the states could alter the allocation of press attention.[33] On the other hand, if the real constraint is the time citizens can allocate to public affairs, the fragmentation of authority could worsen confusion and alienation.

Administrative Efficiencies

Slightly subtler than the claim that humans are simply designed for compact commonwealths are arguments about the relative *administrative* efficiency of large-scale and small-scale government. The conceptual case can go either way. On the one hand, some functions of government (like some industries) can display significant economies of scale. The cost of a car falls substantially as the scale of production rises. The same is not true of haircuts. Where the administrative economics of government looks more like car-making than like barbering, centralization can increase efficiency. Air-traffic control, the maintenance of standard weights and measures, and international diplomacy are areas where economies of scale are plausible, even if not inevitable. If a particular culture generates relatively little top talent in public administration—as is arguably the case in America—centralization may

economize on such scarce personnel, while the profusion of adept bureaucrats in Germany, for example, loosens personnel constraints on
government decentralization.[34]

On the other hand, there are reasons to anticipate that administrative efficiency will erode, not improve, as government grows in scale:
Complexity rises, communication becomes garbled, coordination becomes more difficult, and the opportunities for waste and confusion
multiply as any organization expands its size and the scope of its responsibilities. Public organizations, chronically more plagued by administrative muddle than their private counterparts, can become even more
fumble-prone as they grow. While there are exceptions, the worst administrative inefficiency is often to be found in large multinational organizations; somewhat less in national governments; less still in
smaller-scale governments; and even less in individual families.[35]

Decentralized government, on balance, does seem to offer the more
compelling *conceptual* case for administrative efficiency. Thomas Jefferson, in his 1821 autobiography, emphasized the administrative advantages of decentralization: "Were not this country divided in to States,
that division must be made that each might do for itself . . . what it can
so much better do than a distant authority."[36] Philip Burgess contends
that beyond the bias toward decentralization that prevailed even in Jefferson's day, in our own era modern technology systematically favors
small-scale organizations, so that the federal government has been rendered obsolete, a "mainframe government in a PC world."[37] Burgess and
many other proponents of stepped-up devolution base their case as
much on the states' presumed efficiency advantages as on constitutional claims of state sovereignty. Ohio Governor George Voinovich,
for example, presents as a "simple fact" the proposition that "states often excel when the federal government falters."[38]

There is only limited evidence, unfortunately, by which to assess
this proposition. Seldom do state and federal governments do the same
thing, or close enough to the same thing, to simply measure costs and
compare. Even were many such side-by-side enterprises on record,
state accounting conventions differ, making it difficult to tally administrative costs on a comparable basis. Where there *are* decent data,
they usually find at best a modest efficiency edge for lower-level governments. The Urban Institute studied the results of the Reagan-era
transformation of several federal programs into block grants, representing a large-scale shift from national to state administration. Gains in

administrative efficiency had been one of the rationales behind block grants, and there *were* some administrative savings. But they were much smaller than had been advertised in advance, typically in the range of 3 to 5 percent.[39] Michigan's ambitious mid-1990s welfare reforms cut annual administrative costs by about $100 million out of a total budget of $7 billion, for savings of less than 1.5 percent.[40]

For an enterprise that is essentially a matter of writing checks, it is not surprising, perhaps, that even the most energetic reformers can't find huge administrative savings—administration simply isn't where the money is. The significance of this straightforward point, however, is easy to miss. The federal government, at least on the domestic side of the budget, is now mostly in the business of moving money—from current workers to Social Security recipients, from those who buy Treasury debt to those who are due repayment, from taxpayers to welfare recipients and health-care providers, and so on. There is almost always *some* room for improvement in how financial transfers are administered, but in general the way to reduce the cost of check-writing operations is to write smaller checks. This limits rather severely the potential for administrative efficiencies.

The Quality of Politics

If the quality of political processes is better at one level of government than at another, the resulting efficiency improvements may swamp any plausible differences in administrative efficiency. There are some good reasons to predict that smaller-scale governments will do better, on average, at making public choices that accord with the public's true values and interests. Homogeneity within a community eases consensus. Political issues tend to be simpler and political procedures more transparent in smaller polities, facilitating the public comprehension that permits effective participation. But there are other aspects that complicate this optimistic generalization.[41]

One issue concerns the relative capacity of legislators to represent their constituents' interests. The federal Congress is held in such low esteem that one might reflexively assume the state versions are superior. Indeed, state legislatures generally come somewhat closer to the ideal of the citizen-lawmaker. Short sessions, low pay, and term limits in many states tilt the balance away from career politicians and toward part-timers and short-termers, which may improve lawmakers' identification with the typical citizen. Yet legislative professionalism is not without its advantages, and amateurism is not an unalloyed virtue. The limited expertise of many state legislatures may degrade the quality of deliberation on some issues, and increase the leverage of professional staffers, interest groups, and the executive branch.

Small-scale politics may mean superior accountability at the ballot box, if a manageable set of issues and more transparent processes allow voters to reward and punish officials more easily than when they must sort through a larger number of issues, and untangle complex skeins of cause and effect, in order to fix responsibility and vote accordingly. But here, too, the evidence is scanty, and mixed.[42]

The role of lobbyists merits special mention. Popular disaffection with Capitol Hill has much to do with the perception that special interests, fronted by sophisticated lobbyists, shout down the voice of the people. If state politics turned out to be freer of special-interest maneuvering, one would expect better decisions, on average, to take shape in state capitals than in Washington. Yet there is little reason to believe that this is the case. As power has migrated from Washington to the states, so, too, have the resources devoted to lobbying. Electoral politics may be simpler and less professionalized at the state level. But lobbying increasingly operates with a scale and sophistication comparable to the norm in Washington.

As the states have grown in importance, virtually every state has seen a sharp growth in lobbying; the number of registered state-level lobbyists increased by one-fifth between 1986 and 1990 alone. Total lobbying expenses in Connecticut swelled nearly fivefold between 1985 and 1995.[43] Business lobbying has grown with special intensity—the proportion of trade associations monitoring state-level politics doubled between 1982 and 1987—and lobbyists for business groups almost surely exercise greater relative influence at the state than at the federal level.[44] The federal government's restrictions on the role of money in politics have become notoriously porous, but in most states there is not even a gesture toward limiting campaign contributions by lobbyists.[45] While the *relative* power of different interest groups vary, in sum, it is hard to support any general claim that narrow interests wield less clout in the statehouses than on Capitol Hill.

Externalities

Efficiency requires that an action's full effects be felt by its authors. If there are external consequences (either positive or negative), then the true tally of costs and benefits will be different from what decision-makers take into account. Misalignment between choice and consequence leads to bad decisions—actions taken that should not be, because some costs are ignored; options passed up that should be seized, because some of the benefits are reaped by others.

The notion of "externalities" is fundamental to economic theory, but holds an equally central place—though often under different terms—in American political traditions. The Framers justified a strong central government by reference to issues where the consequences of a policy choice could not be contained within state borders, and where the Articles of Confederation were too weak to defend the broader national interest. When James Wilson set out to persuade his fellow Pennsylvanians to approve the Constitution, he invoked its principle of assigning responsibilities to federal or state governments in accord with the scope of the function's impact:

> Whatever object of government extends, in its operation, beyond the bounds of a particular state, should be considered as belonging to the government of the United States. Whatever object of government is confined in its operation and effect, within the bounds of a particular state, should be considered as belonging to the government of that State.[46]

Daniel Webster, defending the imperiled principle of national union a half-century later, summoned the example of harbor improvements undertaken by the federal government in Delaware Bay, a waterway serving several states. "Would Pennsylvania ever have constructed it? Certainly never . . . because it is not for her sole benefit. . . . It could not be done, therefore, but by the general government."[47] Just as the federal budget can be cast, at least from an idealized perspective, as a device for coordinating national benefits, so can the federal judiciary be seen as a bulwark against efforts to foist burdens onto the citizens of other states. The political impotence of out-of-state voters is a time-honored rationale for federal judicial review of state laws.[48]

There is no shortage of thoughtful modern discussions of external costs and benefits and the complexities they impose on any system of multiple governments. Fritz Scharpf has noted the tendency, within a federal system, "for positive or negative externalities to be neglected. Through a decentralized decision-making structure—by the standard of the collective optimum—either too much or too little of a particular sort of activity is undertaken."[49] Mancur Olson finds "systematic forces which work against allocative efficiency in any situation where the boundaries of a government and a collective good do not coincide."[50]

External costs and benefits form much of the justification—at least much of the *economic* justification—for the very existence of government; if our acts had no consequences for others, "publicness" would be an empty term. But except for the simplest kinds of unitary government, externalities also complicate public policy. Ohio bans the use of most fireworks on safety grounds—but Ohio merchants are free to sell fireworks for use out of state.[51] All states now have "lemon laws" requiring dealers or manufacturers to repair or repurchase faulty cars, and restricting the resale in-state of cars declared "lemons." But few states extend any protection to out-of-state purchasers of defective cars, and there have been growing complaints of "lemon laundering" as vehicles repurchased from unhappy customers are resold, without disclosure, in other states.[52]

The misalignment of costs and benefits presents opportunities for destructive political gamesmanship as politicians burnish their images with voters by claiming credit for benefits while maneuvering costs onto other jurisdictions.[53] Product-liability law, for example, is largely a state responsibility. Some scholars and politicians have argued that externality problems have led to liability laws tilted toward aggrieved consumers and against manufacturers, since the benefits of broad-minded rules for proving damage and claiming compensation accrue mostly within the state, while the burden falls disproportionately on out-of-state manufacturers.[54] Conversely, state-level economic policies affect the nation's macroeconomic trajectory in ways that state officials have little incentive to consider when framing their own choices.[55]

The failure of choice and consequence to correspond underlies some fundamental problems of intergovernmental relations. One broad category, noted earlier, bears the label "unfunded mandates," where a higher level of government "solves" a problem simply by requiring lower levels of government to solve the problem—without providing the resources required. Legislatures with the power to assign unfunded mandates have limited incentives to ensure that the costs and the benefits of a policy, broadly measured, are in balance. They will tend to make mistakes, sometimes subtle mistakes, of the sort that a more precise alignment of choice and consequence would prevent.

The 1964 Civil Rights Act and the 1970 Clean Air Act Amendments, while clearly imposing mandates on the states, were relatively cheap, and served goals that most state officials (albeit certainly not all) shared as well. But the subsequent proliferation of federal mandates—whether flat legislative requirements, or conditions for participating in federal grant programs—included some goals that states saw as trivial or unwise, and some costs they saw as burdensome. Noteworthy examples include the Americans with Disabilities Act of 1990, the Clean Air Act Amendments of 1990, transportation regulations requiring truck drivers to be tested for alcohol use, and the "Brady Bill" requiring states and localities to do background checks of prospective handgun owners.[56] Even if state and local officials wholeheartedly share the goals of such federal action, they can legitimately resent federal officials who declare that goals must be accomplished but refuse to come up with the funds to pay for their accomplishment.

The fundamental problem with unfunded mandates is not that one group of politicians is shabbily treated by another group of politicians, however much that theme has flavored the public debate. It is rather that decisions about the commitment of public resources are likely to be made with far less care when the pursuit of benefits is uncoupled from any calculation of costs. (Legislation curbing unfunded mandates became law in 1995, though the barriers are neither complete nor insurmountable.)

There is a precisely symmetrical misalignment problem with intergovernmental grants. Over one-fifth of state and local spending consists of funds raised as federal taxes and transferred to the cities and states.[57] There are excellent reasons for collecting funds at the broadest possible level of government. But there is also an undeniable invitation to inefficiency: Just as unfunded mandates allow federal officials to be reckless about requiring activities that other governments must fund, so intergovernmental grants lift from state and local officials the burden of raising taxes to pay for grant-funded activities. In theory, one might expect grant-funded programs to be managed less carefully than tax-funded programs, and state officials to try to substitute federal money for their own resources. In practice, of course, this is often just what one does observe.[58]

There are devices for lessening the incentive problems of intergovernmental grants—matching requirements, grant conditions, eligibility rules, performance rewards and penalties—but no simple fix. The tighter the federal accountability rules, in general, the less local conditions and priorities can guide spending, and the more the intergovernmental grant programs look like simple central-government action, with all its normal defects and some others as well.[59] The weaker the accountability rules, the higher the quotient of inefficiency to be anticipated when one government spends money that another government raises.[60]

The surest solution to misaligned authority, of course, is to arrange that communities are of precisely the right scale to capture all the benefits and bear all the costs of communal decisions.[61] Yet the boundaries of cost for some particular undertaking will often differ from the boundaries of benefit; the borders relevant to one activity won't necessarily correspond to the borders relevant to all others (or indeed *any* others); and the perimeters of cost and benefit will seldom correspond to the jurisdictional boundaries that a capricious history has inscribed upon the landscape. The imperatives of operational efficiency, on their own, would dictate arrangements very different from the coarse configuration of federal, state, and local authority we see today.

The gap between the theoretical ideal and actual practice, in the United States and elsewhere, has inspired feverish creativity on the part of theorists. Gordon Tullock, in a conceptually rich 1969 essay, suggests that efficiency requires a world in which "the individual citizen would be a member of a vast collection of governmental units, each of these governmental units being to some respect of a different geographical coverage than the others, and each one dealing with a separate activity."[62] Conceding the possible inconveniences such an arrangement might entail, Tullock suggests that costs and benefits of unity and autonomy might be best in balance if each individual belonged to "somewhere between five and eight" governments, differing in their policy portfolios and geographical coverage, bearing no necessary resemblance to the world in which we happen to live.[63] The related theoretical approach known as "club theory" views government in general as an ill-advised solution to the problem of collective action, and envisages instead an intricate arrangement of private clubs by which individuals pursue those interests that are difficult to advance in isolation.[64] (Some may be relieved, and others disappointed, to learn that a team of economic theorists has recently found that geographically defined governments may turn out to be a good idea after all.[65])

One might be tempted to dismiss all this as arid abstraction. But in fact real-world politics has been generating just the sort of jurisdictional proliferation and fragmentation such theories suggest. Beyond the townships, counties, municipalities, and other jurisdictions bundled together as "local government" are thousands of school districts, port authorities, and special districts for transportation, waste management, and other functions. There are also new kinds of jurisdictions that (much as some of the more exotic conceptual schemes prescribe) blur the distinction between public and private organizations and invite individuals to buy into the commonwealths that best fit their preferences. "Gated communities" essentially replace local government with private alternatives; "business improvement districts" levy private "taxes" on companies within specified urban areas to supplement the police, sanitation, and other services traditionally, but inadequately, supplied by city government. (In late 1995 there were thirty-four such districts in New York City, covering some 550 urban blocks.[66])

Special-purpose commonwealths doubtless have the potential to simplify collective decision-making—but at a cost. Consider, for example, the creation of autonomous transit authorities, as an alternative to transportation divisions of urban government. This makes it easier to address transport needs that spill beyond a single jurisdiction, and allows the kind of managerial focus that can improve efficiency. But it also shields the authority's officers from the scrutiny that municipal officials normally confront. And it walls off resources from the claims of education, law enforcement, and other competing uses outside the transportation area. More generally, at some point the proliferation of governments starts to strain the capacity of self-government. There are limits to people's ability to pay attention, and limits to the resources, such as the media, that facilitate the exercise of citizenship.

A degree of disjuncture between choice and consequence is more the norm than the exception, which summons a general cautionary note. Unless we are willing to follow some of the more exuberant theorists into scrapping nation, state, and city in order to start afresh on the puzzle of human community, then a large measure of imprecision is inevitable. If authority must be lodged with a general-purpose government, rather than one custom-tailored to fit the task, then choice and consequence will only with great rarity be in perfect alignment. Distressing as this may be to some tidy minds, the choice between flawed federal and state alternatives is still worth worrying about. Getting it a bit closer to right can make a great deal of difference in how faithfully, and how effectively, government works to serve citizens' interests.

CHAPTER FOUR

The National Commons

The Framers sought to ensure that the national government would posses what powers it required—no more, and no less—to deal with issues beyond the compass of the separate states. In their day, the need for such powers was modest, and more pronounced in the political than in the economic realm. While it may have been workable in the 1780s for states to pursue most of their interests in isolation—with only subordinate concern for the national consequences of state decisions—the scope for such isolated decision-making has narrowed.

From a vantage point three-fifths of the way between James Madison's day and our own, Woodrow Wilson wrote that the "common interests of a nation bought together in thought and interest and action by the telegraph and the telephone, as well as by the rushing mails which every express train carries, have a scope and variety, an infinite multiplication and intricate interlacing, of which a simpler day can have had no conception."[1] The interconnection of American interests cannot, on its own, settle the question of federal-state balance. The Framers' basic blueprint retains its vitality even in an age of air freight, interlinked computers, nonstop currency trading, and site-shopping global corporations. Yet while the change is a matter of degree, it is an *important* matter of degree. Issues in which other states' citizens have no stakes, and hence no valid claim to a voice, are becoming rarer.

An illuminating metaphor—the concept of "the commons"—helps to cast in a clearer light the perils of fragmented decision-making on issues of national consequence. In what has been termed "perhaps the most influential article ever written in the environmental field,"[2] biologist Garrett Hardin (borrowing from an obscure 1833 mathematical pamphlet) invoked the parable of a herdsman pondering how many cattle to graze on the village commons. Self-interest will lead him to increase the size of his herd even if the commons is already overburdened, since he alone benefits from raising an extra animal, but shares with his fellows the consequent damage to the common pasture. As each farmer follows the same logic, overgrazing wrecks the commons. In "The Tragedy of the Commons," Hardin extended his grim scenario of collective catastrophe flowing from rational individual action to air and water pollution, overfishing on the high seas, and (his main target) population growth in underdeveloped countries.[3]

The metaphor is historically questionable—colonial New Englanders, for example, governed common land with more good sense and far better results than the Hardin scenario suggests—but has been used to gain insight into situations ranging from water policy in the arid West and petroleum extraction in the Middle East to corruption among police officials and the behavior of airlines following deregulation.[4]

Examples arise in unexpected places. Nearly all of the blood bought by hospitals in the United States is contributed by volunteers, who endure the minor unpleasantness of blood donation to make concrete their humanitarian convictions. The groups that run blood drives—most prominent among them the Red Cross—are not-for-profit, but nonetheless are driven (if only in part) by financial imperatives. Even if they have no investors who demand maximum profits, their revenues still must cover expenses, and the sale of blood to hospitals has become a major source of funds. Dependence upon blood-sale revenues has bred tensions among collection organizations, including incidents of high-pressure tactics to induce volunteers to roll up their sleeves for one organization instead of another. Some worry that the scramble for blood donors is polluting the atmosphere of selflessness and goodwill on which voluntary donation depends. The commons problem is clear: Each organization finds it rational to push a little harder for donors, even impugning rival organizations.

But such tactics endanger the spirit of voluntarism on which they all depend.[5]

Even outer space can be seen as a commons at risk of abuse. By the late 1980s there were some seven thousand pieces of junk in orbit around the planet—spent booster rockets, defunct satellites, tools fumbled by astronauts, and so on—posing a threat to space operations. The accumulation of space trash is unfortunate for all current and potential space-faring nations. But none has sufficiently strong incentives to clean it up on its own, or even to incur major costs to avoid worsening the problem, since the dropped wrench, left to drift, may collide with a European or Russian spacecraft instead of an American one. A State Department official told the United Nations in 1988 that it "makes little sense for the United States to try to solve the problem of orbital debris by itself."[6] Nor does it for any other nation; if the problem is ever addressed, it will be through international action.

Back on earth, and back to the topic of this book, the commons is an exceptionally useful concept for clarifying the consequences of fragmented state authority in a nation richly veined with economic and cultural connections. Where the nation as a whole defines a commons—whether as an economic reality, as a political ideal, or as a cultural imperative—and states take action that ignores or narrowly exploits that fact, the frequent result is the kind of "tragedy" that Hardin's metaphor predicts: Collective value is squandered in the name of a constricted definition of gain. States win advantages that only seem worthwhile because other states bear much of the cost.

America's earliest history affords some examples of this syndrome in the area of public finance. In the late 1700s, states reluctant to raise taxes instead paid public debt with paper money that had progressively little gold or silver behind it. Even states like Georgia, Delaware, and New Jersey that exercised some restraint in issuing paper money saw merchants lose confidence in their currencies, as the flood of bad bills debased the reputation of American money in general.[7] In the mid-1800s, defaults and debt repudiations by Pennsylvania, Arkansas, Florida, Illinois, and a few other states—which for the states concerned were unfortunate, but apparently preferable to the alternative of paying what they owed—polluted the common American resource of creditworthiness, and for a time froze even solvent states and the federal government out of international credit markets.[8]

Presidential primaries are run state by state. Primaries have grown in importance in recent decades, and states have attended more closely to their roles in the process. Early votes signal legitimacy and feed momentum, and states that vote sooner not only have more leverage over the eventual nominees—which inspires candidates to pledge fealty to the favored states' particular priorities—but also gain commercial benefit from the incursion of candidates and media and (not least important) the psychological gratification of a quadrennial day in the national spotlight. Yet while each state prefers to vote early, most analysts agree on the superiority of a protracted primary season. If the nomination process is stretched out over several months, voters have more opportunity to learn about the nuances of each candidate's character and agenda. What seemed bold in early February might appear simply shrill by May; the candidate of plain common sense might by and by be seen as simplistic; and a candidate who starts off seeming complex or dull may grow on voters over the course of six months.

In recent presidential election seasons—and especially the 1996 Republican primaries—states have wrecked the common resource of an extended primary process in a rational (but nonetheless tragic) pursuit of parochial advantage.[9] New Hampshire cherishes its first-in-the-nation status, and defends it with a state law requiring its primary to be held at least seven days before the *next* earliest state's primary. Over time, other states moved their voting dates up on the calendar. California's primary in June 1992 had come too late to matter. Anxious to avoid another episode of irrelevance four years later, it staked out March 26 for its vote. But several other states, whose *own* votes would be rendered superfluous once California's crowd of delegates was selected, rescheduled their primaries in response. A spiral of competitive rescheduling led to ugly squabbles as Delaware and Louisiana crowded New Hampshire's traditional franchise; a mass of state primaries ended up bunched right behind New Hampshire, and a grotesquely compressed primary season ensued. The outcome was clear by the first days of March, and California's primary—although held two months earlier than it had been in 1992—was just as irrelevant.[10] Most voters perceived the 1996 primary season as a brief spasm of televised name calling. Even supporters of the eventual nominee felt that Senator Dole, and the voters, had been ill-served. Officials were soon at work on a new system that would give states incentives to delay their primaries to promote the common interest in a more deliberate process.[11]

Term limits for representatives and senators present a similar commons problem. Despite a flurry of term-limits legislation at the state level, anyone convinced that the United States should have a less professionalized Congress should not count on state term-limit laws to accomplish the goal. If less entrenched legislators make for better law— a plausible although not invulnerable proposition—then a citizen-legislature is a common benefit for the nation as a whole. Yet an individual state is usually better off when represented by politicians with a deep reserve of past favors on which to trade and wisdom in the ways of Washington. Even if a majority of a state's citizens would like to see a Congress of fresh faces, they would rationally prefer to see *other* states restrict representatives and senators to a few years' service, while keeping their own old lions on the job.[12]

The Constitution's "full faith and credit" clause, a court case in Hawaii, and the quadrennial uptick in political tawdriness brought an unusual sort of commons problem to center stage in 1996. The issue was whether the definition of "marriage" should be broadened to include same-sex unions. Some years earlier a handful of Hawaiian same-sex couples had asserted the right to have their relationships reckoned under state law as no different from heterosexual marriages.[13] The case quietly ground its way through Hawaii's courts—despite tepid support from civil liberties and mainstream gay rights organizations—eased by unusual provisions in the state constitution that bar sex discrimination in almost any form, arguably requiring men and women to be allowed the same choices about the gender of their spouses. When a wholesale shift in the composition of Hawaii's supreme court made a seemingly lost cause suddenly viable, it dawned on advocates and opponents alike that if Hawaii recognized same-sex marriage, those unions would have to be recognized nationwide under Article IV's requirement that "Full Faith and Credit shall be given in each State to the public Acts, Records, and judicial Proceedings of every other State." If any homosexual couples—at least those able to afford two tickets to Hawaii— could bypass more restrictive laws in their home states, the rapid result could be a national redefinition of what marriage means, without anyone outside Hawaii having any voice in the outcome.

While the Hawaiian case was still pending, opponents of gay marriage staged a preemptive strike as Senator Don Nickles of Oklahoma and Representative Bob Barr of Georgia introduced the Defense of Marriage Act. The legislation required the federal government to counter heterodoxy in Hawaii or anywhere else by proclaiming a *na-*

tional definition of marriage—one man, one woman, and that's that. Beyond excluding same-sex spouses from any federal program (such as survivors' benefits under Social Security) the act gave states the right to refuse recognition to other states' marriages.[14] The issue's public profile was so high that in the summer of 1996—while not a single same-sex union had ever been recognized by any state—56 percent of voters said a candidate's position on gay marriage would be important in their choice between congressional contenders.[15] The Defense of Marriage Act raced through Congress with a velocity (and a rhetorical volume) at odds with its negligible immediate importance. President Clinton, while opposed to the notion of same-sex marriage, denounced the bill as unnecessary and politically motivated. But he signed it nonetheless—without ceremony, and (literally) in the middle of the night.[16]

The bill's authors were undeniably driven in part by the partisan spirit of the election year. But whatever their motivations—and however one feels about same-sex marriage—they had a point: The definition of marriage in the United States should be settled by national deliberation, not by accidents of politics, timing, and constitutional structure in a single state. There is an interesting historical irony here, however. Not so long ago, divorce was only a little more common, and only a little less out of the mainstream, than homosexual unions seem today. While the causes for its increase are many and complex, the pace was set by states' calculations of parochial advantage. Around the turn of the century legislators in several Western states—notably Nevada—passed liberal divorce legislation in part to encourage economic development. Unhappy couples facing onerous divorce laws in their home states could head West for a few weeks or months. There they could dissolve their union, while solidifying the local economy, in some striving desert town.[17] Other states might have resisted the trend to more lenient divorce laws. But any couples—at least any able to afford two tickets to Reno—could bypass their home-state restrictions. If a legislature held the line it would only be subjecting its citizens to extra expense while sending money out of state.

The wholesale liberalization of American divorce laws is often seen as a mistake—if not from the perspective of men who can cast off unwanted obligations with minimal bother, at least from the perspective of women and, especially, young children who all too often are left economically stranded.[18] Which summons an interesting question: If states should be free to refuse recognition to marriages made elsewhere, on the grounds that another state's definition of marriage offends local morals, should they also be able to refuse to recognize out-of-state divorces? Suppose further that Vermont, say, passed legislation toughening divorce laws, and declaring Vermont marriages immune to dissolution by any other state's laws. If the legislation survived constitutional challenge (which is rather doubtful, as it is for the Defense of Marriage Act's comparable provisions) there would be some definite advantages: More traditional states could fend off unwelcome national trends; a potential spouse could signal the depth of his or her commitment by proposing a Vermont wedding. On the other hand, the United States would become a little bit less of a nation.

In one of the less glorious episodes in American history, this country attempted to define human slavery as an issue each state could settle on its own, according to its own economic and ethical lights. Northern states, however, eventually proved unwilling to accept the proposition that the moral commons could be so neatly subdivided. The Fugitive Slave Act, solidified by the Supreme Court's notorious Dred Scott decision, required antislavery states to make room in their moral world for slaveholders to transport their "property" for use anywhere in the nation. The repercussions ultimately led both to attempted secession and to the national abolition of slavery. The definition of marriage may be another moral issue so basic that it must be dealt with through a national deliberation, protracted and painful as that will doubtless turn out to be.

The gay marriage issue also demonstrates that a consciousness of the national commons is not restricted to any particular ideology, even if conservatives are somewhat more inclined to invoke common interests on cultural than on economic grounds. For example, conservative senators called for federal action to counter the effects of 1996 ballot initiatives liberalizing state marijuana laws in Arizona and California.[19] And at about the same time as the Defense of Marriage Act was passed and signed, so was legislation to require every state to notify local officials upon the arrival of any once-convicted sex offender. (The legislation was triggered by a searing New Jersey crime.) Unless one suspects that the child-rapist lobby somehow commands a disproportionate influence on state legislatures that only Congress can counter, it is hard to justify making this a federal issue *except* as the assertion of a moral commonwealth.[20]

The rest of this chapter explores some economic issues where concepts introduced in Chapter 3 play out against a backdrop of a national commons. Consider first a policy area close to Hardin's original metaphor: environmental protection.

ENVIRONMENTAL REGULATION

While some kinds of pollution affect only a fixed location, and while a few states are shielded by their size or isolation from most environmental problems originating in other states, antipollution law is perhaps the most obvious application of the commons metaphor to economic federalism. If a state maintains a lax regime of environmental laws it spares its own citizens, businesses, and government agencies from costly burdens. The "benefits" of environmental recklessness, in other words, are collected in-state. Part of the pollution consequently dumped into the air or water, however, drifts away to do its damage elsewhere in the nation. If states held all authority over environmental rule making, the predictable result would be feeble regulations against any kinds of pollution where the in-state costs and benefits of control are out of balance. Even in states whose citizens valued the environment—even if the citizens of *all* states were willing to pay heavily for cleaner air and water—they would calculate that their sacrifice could not on its own stem the tide and reluctantly settle for weaker rules than they truly prefer.

A second factor threatens to intensify the incentive of separate states to shortchange the environment. If a clean environment forms a commons shared among the states, so, too (in a somewhat different sense), does business investment. Much of the cost of pollution abatement falls, at least in the first instance, on industry. Many companies, including polluting businesses, are able to move from one state to another if cost differentials are sufficiently large. A state contemplating tough antipollution rules might calculate that not only will its citizens pay the full costs for environmental improvements that will be enjoyed, in part, by others, even worse, by imposing higher costs on business than do other states, it risks repelling investment, and thus losing jobs and tax revenues to states with weak environmental laws. A House Committee Report on the 1970 Clean Air Act explicitly invoked the specter of a "race for the bottom"—competitive loosening of environmental laws in order to lure business—to justify federal standards that would "preclude efforts on the part of states to compete with each other in trying to attract new plants."[21] The race-to-the-bottom rationale employed by Congress was even starker for the 1977 amendments to the Clean Air Act, which further limited state discretion over air pollution standards:

> Without national guidelines for the prevention of significant deterioration, a State deciding to protect its clean air resources will face a double threat. The prospect is very real that such a State would lose existing industrial plants to more permissive States. But additionally the State will likely become the target of "economic-environmental blackmail" from new industrial plants that will play one State off against another with threats to locate in whichever State adopts the most permissive pollution controls.[22]

The logic of the commons, and even some of the terminology, characterized the wave of national environmental legislation of the 1970s.[23] Major choices about how aggressively to act against pollution were moved from the separate states to the federal government. While the details of many rules as well as enforcement remained largely state responsibilities—introducing another level of complications[24]—the trade-off between environmental and economic values moved much closer to a single national standard. Once America decided it was rich enough to make the environment a priority, large parts of the enterprise had to be national. Subsequent proposals to return authority over environmental laws to the states have been resisted, for the most part.[25] (A 1980 decision to devolve responsibility for nuclear waste turned out badly.[26])

But there *are* some complexities to note, even in this seemingly straightforward case. First, national regulation in a diverse economy has an undeniable downside. States differ in their environmental problems, in their relative prosperity, and in the priorities of their citizens. Requiring all states to accept the same balance between economic and environmental values imposes some real human costs and generates real political friction. Pollution control, moreover, is a relatively new, relatively technical enterprise, and independent state action, even at a depressed level, would doubtless have generated some useful innovations and evidence that we sacrifice by choosing a national approach.

Even if the tilt toward national authority we adopted in the 1970s is on balance the correct approach to environmental regulation, there is reason to doubt we got all the details right. For example, logic suggests that the federal role should be stronger for forms of pollution that readily cross state borders, and weaker for pollution that stays put. But federal authority is actually weaker under the Clean Air Act and the Clean Water Act than under the Comprehensive Environmental Response, Compensation, and Liability Act of 1980. Toxic waste sites, which the law's "Superfund" provisions are meant to address, can certainly pose major environmental threats. But most waste sites are situated within a single state, and stay there.[27]

Moreover, anxieties that states would be forced to weaken environmental standards to lure or preserve business—a prospect which figured so prominently in congressional thinking in the 1970s, and which is certainly plausible in principle—turns out to be somewhat overblown. The reason is simple: The costs of complying with environmental laws, on average, are quite modest. Few firms find it in their interest to change their location, or even determine the location of a new investment, in the name of weak antipollution rules. An empirical study by Timothy Bartik, an expert in the economics of industry location, found that the costs of compliance with environmental regulations were so small, relative to other business costs, that "even sizable increases in the stringency of state environmental regulation are unlikely to have a large effect on the location decisions of the average industry."[28] A team of economists including Adam Jaffee and Robert Stavins reviewed five separate empirical studies, all of which found either small or statistically undetectable effects of state environmental regulations on manufacturing plant locations.[29] Even among nations, where environmental rules differ dramatically, it is difficult to find any impact on business location from tighter or looser antipollution rules.[30] Most researchers believe there must be *some* effect. But the lure of weak environmental rules, or the repulsion of stringent ones, is simply swamped, in most cases, by other factors. (As will be seen, we cannot simply extend from environmental regulation to other areas the conclusion that policy doesn't matter much for business location decisions.) In the absence of national antipollution rules, states might well have other motives to shortchange the shared environment—even if firms had *no* ability to move in response to regulatory costs. The evidence suggests that competition for mobile investment, however, would not in itself undercut a state's commitment to environmental protection.

Corporate Chartering

Few questions about the division of economic authority across our federal system have received the enormous investment of intellectual energy as has state chartering of corporations. The issue is a classic commons scenario. Since corporations can operate nationally, whatever their state of incorporation, state decisions on chartering have national implications. Until the Securities Act of 1933, there was no federal law at all on corporate governance. While federal rules constrain tender offers and disclosure practices, states still govern most important aspects of corporate law.

If states reap advantages when firms choose to incorporate under their laws—and there is ample evidence that they do—then shouldn't the tragedy of the commons lead them to contort their legal codes to attract firms? The state that tilts furthest in favor of managers wins taxes, fees, and job opportunities for corporate attorneys, while the costs of unbalanced corporate law are spread widely, wherever the state has operations, sales, creditors, or investors. The commons scenario would predict a progressive weakening of the conditions of incorporation.

In part because the issue harbors some fascinating intellectual puzzles, in part because the stakes are high, and in part because the interested parties include people who argue for a living, much ink has been spilled on the chartering controversy. The background facts are fairly clear. In the eighteenth and most of the nineteenth centuries, corporate charters were granted under far more stringent conditions than they are today, usually on the understanding that demonstrable public good would result from the corporation's activities. As corporations came to be seen less as agents of the public interest; as states came to presume, instead of demanding proof of, public benefits from business enterprise; and as some firms became sufficiently national to have meaningful choices about which state to call home, the specific terms of state chartering came to matter more.

In 1896 New Jersey adopted aggressively liberal chartering rules and soon became the legal home of choice for major corporations. New Jersey shifted to a somewhat tougher chartering law in 1913, however, and rapidly lost its hegemony to Delaware, which had altered its own incorporation provisions to mirror New Jersey's previous law. Delaware has tenaciously defended its dominant place in corporate chartering ever since. While its population is smaller than that of San Jose, it is the legal home of over half of the Fortune 500 manufacturers and over two-fifths of all companies listed on the New York Stock Exchange, and claims over 80 percent of all firms *changing* their incorporation from one state to another.[31] (Many "Delaware" companies, it is important to note, have vanishingly few assets or employees located within the state.)

Herbert Croly, the Progressive intellectual, considered state chartering a silly anachronism by 1909, arguing that "a state has in the great majority of cases no meaning at all as a center of economic organization and direction."[32] Many business enterprises— especially the small service operations that formed the largest number of businesses in Croly's day as in our own—affected only local economies, and could be left to municipal regulations. Larger firms with national impact, however, should be chartered by the federal government, not by the states. Croly's call for national chartering was made "not because there is any peculiar virtue in the action of the central government, but because there is a peculiar vice in asking the state governments to regulate matters beyond their effective jurisdiction."[33]

The catchphrase "race to the bottom" was introduced in 1933 by Supreme Court Justice Louis Brandeis—who also, recall, popularized the term "laboratories of democracy"—in connection with corporate chartering. Multistate companies, Brandeis said, sought charters "in states where the cost was lowest and the laws least restrictive. The states joined in advertising their wares. The race was one not of diligence but of laxity."[34] The modern debate over the prudence of state chartering got under way in the early 1970s with an article by William L. Cary in the *Yale Law Journal* on the pernicious effects of interstate competition for corporate charters.[35] Cary (and other critics) argued that any state attempting to impose even the mildest conditions on the maintenance of corporate charters—in the name of shareholders, employers, or other interests—could anticipate losing corporations to a less demanding state. (That state, by all odds, would be Delaware.[36]) Competition for charters among states hungry for such revenue, critics warned, would make it impossible to hold corporations accountable. By

1976 the Senate Commerce Committee was conducting hearings on "Corporate Rights and Responsibilities," in which eighty law professors from sixty-two law schools endorsed the principle of federal action to brake the "race to the bottom" among states.[37]

The counterarguments were not long in coming. Some defenders of rivalrous state chartering argued that Delaware's advantage lay not in weak conditions of incorporation, but rather in its efficient procedures for chartering—streamlined administrative rule making, courts dedicated to corporate law, a specialized private bar, and a tradition of depoliticizing corporate law made sustainable by the paucity of actual corporate *operations* within the state.[38]

But the more interesting rebuttal to the "race for the bottom" critics came from a group of scholars who emphasized the importance of market rationality in the crafting of corporate law. Ralph Winter, in an influential 1977 article, started by acknowledging that states compete to maximize their share of the nation's corporate charters, and that they do so primarily through loosening the conditions of chartering. (Indeed, both sides of the debate take as axiomatic that states compete for the revenues that charters bring, and that mobile corporations shop for favorable chartering rules.[39]) But the race was to the *top*, not the bottom, Winter and like-minded analysts argued, because the goal toward which states raced, and the pace of their scramble, turned out to be set *not* by corporate managers but by investors.

The story goes like this: Corporations must attract capital. People who hold investable assets will be more likely to commit them to firms whose charters require managers to do right by investors. Corporate governance is a tricky business, and state-by-state experimentation, driven by competition, will generate valuable innovations in the science of structuring the rules of the corporate game. The least likely outcome, by this reasoning, are rules that let managers have their way at the expense of shareholders, since a "state which 'rigs' its code to benefit management will drive debt and equity capital away."[40] To the contrary, Winter argued, we should "expect competitive state legal systems to tend toward economically optimal rules governing the corporation-shareholder relationship." By the same token, an "expanded federal role in corporate governance would almost surely be counterproductive"[41] because the monolithic federal government, free from competitive pressures, would have no incentive to undertake the analytically and politically difficult task of crafting rules that give managers the right incentives to create value on the product market, and to dutifully pass the proceeds on to investors.

"If incorporation in Delaware were really harmful to shareholders," Daniel R. Fischel argued, continuing Winter's logic, "shares of firms located there would trade for less, managers would reduce the value of their services, and the firm might be an attractive takeover candidate with the probable result that existing managers would be displaced. Since managers have no incentive to injure themselves in this fashion, a far more likely explanation is that Delaware has achieved its prominent position because its permissive corporation law maximizes, rather than minimizes, shareholders' welfare."[42] Frank Easterbrook established empirically that firms saw their stock price *increase*, not drop, when they announced plans to reincorporate in Delaware, and concluded that the "impression that the race—surely real—was for the 'bottom' was uninformed."[43] For those who are convinced that all interesting dimensions of value are embodied in stock prices, this is a persuasive line of reasoning.

Roberta Romano contributed an exceedingly clever additional explanation of Delaware's role as a corporate homeland, drawing on new thinking in game theory and organizational behavior. Unlike other states, Delaware is deeply dependent on the corporate chartering business. A significant fraction of state revenue comes from chartering fees. The structure of state government, including the judicial system, is geared to the efficient handling of corporate affairs. Many of the state's most influential citizens and private organizations are exclusively devoted to delivering business services. It would be flatly disastrous for Delaware to lose its franchise as corporate America's favorite state. Companies and investors, anxious to avoid surprises, can be confident that Delaware politics will produce no unwelcome changes in its corporate law, since the long-term damage to Delaware from frightening away corporations would overwhelm any conceivable short-term advantage from changing the rules. Much of Delaware's economy, in other words, is a hostage to corporate America's continued favor. No other state can make that claim, or so convincingly promise that its hospitable climate will not change. So for perfectly legitimate reasons, Delaware's dominance in corporate chartering is self-reinforcing.[44]

A wave of state antitakeover laws in the 1980s ran counter to the predictions of the efficient-competition theorists. Lucian Bebchuck observed that while maximizing share prices offered one way for managers to deter a takeover and keep their jobs, they might prefer a more direct approach and deploy their influence with legislators accordingly. He also argued that even if states must maintain regimes of corporate law that, on balance, are shareholder-friendly, they still have the opportunity and incentive to craft rules that gratify managers at little cost to shareholders.[45]

All sides in the debate accept that corporations shop for favorable regimes of state law, and that interstate competition helps to explain the light hand with which America constrains corporate discretion. Scholars differ over whether efficient capital markets force managers to do their state-by-state shopping as faithful agents of shareholders, or whether managers can put their own interests first. While some of its more elaborate manifestations strain credulity, the efficient-competition school probably has the better argument. The market seems close enough to efficient to bridle managers' natural hunger for regulatory regimes that leave investors vulnerable. Managers are empowered by their ability to choose the state of incorporation. But shareholders have far more than fifty choices about where to invest their funds, and can redeploy their resources with greater ease than a firm can reincorporate.

The United States is an extraordinarily friendly country for investors. The benefits of this climate flow not just to managers and investors (including, with increasing importance, pension investors), but throughout the rest of the economy. Competitive state chartering contributes to this benign environment. The wealth of verifiable financial information at investors' fingertips, the confidence with which one can assess the worth and risk of unseen assets, the ease of buying and selling securities, all form a common national advantage that is on balance augmented, not eroded, by independent state action. But this is not quite the end of the conversation. Interstate competition promotes laws that favor investors not because legislators are directly solicitous of shareholders, but because investors have leverage over managers, and managers have leverage over state policy-makers. By this same logic, interests with a weaker claim on managers' devotion have no reason to expect that interstate competition will generate favorable rules.

One such group, for example, consists of the creditors of firms that have not quite entered bankruptcy, but are skating on such thin ice that it would be prudent to conserve resources. These creditors might prefer limits on dividend payments by distressed firms, to boost the odds of collecting their debts. Stockholders, however, would prefer looser rules. The resolution, as summarized by one legal scholar, is that state laws limiting dividend payouts by cash-short firms "are generally so weak and ineffectual as to have no practical significance."[46] Similarly, the dynamics of state competition for corporate chartering are unlikely to generate a national pattern of laws that strengthen the hand of employees within the firm.[47] The opposite result, indeed, is both more plausible in principle, and more commonly witnessed in practice.

LEGALIZED GAMBLING

There has never been a time in America when a person determined to gamble could not find some kind of action. Nor is *legal* gambling, for that matter, anything new. The Continental Congress fed and armed Washington's army, in part, with revenues from a lottery, and state-sanctioned games of chance financed the early growth of Harvard and other colleges.[48] In the modern era, however, gambling has often operated in the economic shadows. Except for the exotic enclave of Nevada, government's stance toward gambling ranged, until recently, from vigilant hostility—as late as the 1970s an Iowa priest was tossed into jail for running a parish bingo game[49]—to narrowly circumscribed tolerance.

This has changed with an astonishing speed and completeness. In 1988 Nevada and New Jersey were alone in allowing casino gambling. Eight years later there were around five hundred casinos operating in twenty-seven states, and some form of gambling was legal in all but two states. The total annual amount wagered legally was about $500 billion.[50] (For a sense of scale, consider that America's entire economic output is in the range of $7000 billion a year.) A casino executive predicted in 1994 that by the end of the century, 95 percent of Americans would live in a state with legal casino gambling, and trends since have been consistent with such a trajectory.[51]

Gambling brings some obvious benefits to the state that runs the lottery or hosts the casinos. It can generate relatively high-paying jobs even for workers without advanced training. It yields welcome revenues for the state treasury. States took in $27 billion from lotteries in 1994, and had $9.8 billion in revenues left over after paying off winners and covering administrative costs.[52] Beyond the swelling lottery take, 1994

taxes paid by casinos alone yielded $1.4 billion for states and locali-
ties.[53] Legalized gambling can also produce political benefits, most directly the rich lodes of campaign contributions available from a highly
profitable industry that is so intensely dependent on political favor.
The gambling industry has quickly vaulted into the top ranks of con-
tributors, spreading campaign cash across levels of government and to
candidates of both major parties.[54] Politicians also cherish the indirect
political benefit of gambling-fueled job growth. (Political analysts attributed the reelection of Mississippi governor Kirk Fordice in 1995 in
part to good times powered by the expanding gambling industry.[55])

Yet there are costs as well. Some people will gamble whether it is legal or not, but many more do so when the law allows. Access to legal
opportunities for gambling has been found to increase the number of
people who develop a gambling problem. The consequences range from
mild economic inconvenience to bankruptcy, embezzlement, divorce,
and suicide. In 1995—ten years after their state launched a lottery, and
four years after the first legal riverboat casino opened—nine out of ten
Iowans indulged in gambling. One in twenty reported having a gambling problem, and Iowa social service agencies were coping with a
surge of collateral family and financial damage.[56] Some commentators
complain more broadly of moral decay as gambling becomes a commonplace part of the culture and as dreams of sudden wealth undermine the work ethic.

Grant that there are both plusses and minuses—the same can be
said of any economic issue. Why should we doubt that the surge in liberalized gambling laws, on balance, is a good thing? Shouldn't we leave
it to officials in each state (unless we suspect them to be too heavily influenced by campaign money) to tally up the expected costs and benefits and make the right decision for their own state? And shouldn't we
expect these state-by-state decisions to sum to the right pattern of policies for America as a whole?

The logic of the commons makes this less than likely. If a state
loosens its own restrictions on gambling, it gains the benefits in jobs,
tax revenues, and political favor. It also suffers costs—but not *all* the
costs. When citizens of *other* states buy the lottery tickets and visit the
casinos, they leave their money behind when they return home, but
take their gambling-related problems back with them. Consider the
perspective of a state that would *prefer* to restrict gambling, but finds
that citizens thwarted by local laws find it easy to travel to more open-

minded states in search of some action. These states suffer much of the damage from the national trend toward legalized gambling, but without sharing in the benefits. They might conclude that there's no real point to holding the line, and liberalize their laws in turn. (The rapid expansion of gambling on Indian reservations, which the states were powerless to constrain, surely helped to fuel the transformation.) Once Nevada was no longer the isolated exception to the rule—as transportation costs fell, as budget pressures made states less fastidious, and as New Jersey and the Indian casinos triggered the rush to lift the rules—the tragedy of the commons was set in motion.

Iowa, in fact, had maintained stringent antigambling laws until the mid-1980s. But as a growing number of Iowans played lotteries in neighboring states it became harder to resist proposals to revitalize a battered economy through riverboat casinos aimed at attracting out-of-state gamblers, especially from the prosperous, casino-less Chicago area. At first, Chicagoans did come, by the busload. But Illinois legislators, seeing gambling dollars heading down the interstate to Iowa, opted to allow riverboat gambling in their state, too.[57] Iowa's initial liberalization law had tried to lower the risk of problem gambling by limiting the size of any one bet and (more importantly) the amount any person could gamble away in a single day. But when Illinois, Mississippi, and Louisiana introduced riverboats *without* any limits, Iowa lifted its own restrictions.[58] In a similar way, after Montana allowed slot machines in taverns in 1985, neighboring South Dakota called and raised, allowing slot machines in bars *and* convenience stores.

As public opposition to gambling's further expansion began to harden in the 1990s, industry lobbyists deployed the logic of the commons as a political tool. The lobbying firm promoting casino gambling in Florida found that 56 percent of citizens opposed legalization, even if the state's share of the take was strictly earmarked for programs to aid the elderly. But if the survey question was framed to emphasize that gambling was already widespread in the regions, and that voting down legalization would only make Florida "miss out on the revenue and economic development casinos generate," opposition fell to 43 percent.[59]

New York Governor George Pataki, calling in mid-1996 for liberalized gambling laws to prop up the state's tourism industry, emphasized that "the most important thing is to be able to stop losing billions of dollars to surrounding states."[60] At the same time as New York was responding to New Jersey and Connecticut's growing gambling industries, the prospect of losing racetrack revenue as neighboring Delaware allowed slot machines in its racetracks led to intense pressure on Maryland's Governor Parris Glendening to rescind his earlier opposition to casino-style gambling.[61]

By 1996 the only two states with no legal gambling at all were Utah, whose Mormon culture was uniquely resistant to the national trend, and Hawaii, where it is a good deal harder than average for citizens to do their gambling in a neighboring state. The federal government's absolute deference to the separate states began to bend that same year with legislation establishing a commission to examine the broader national impacts of gambling. A Nevada congresswoman denounced the bill as "the nose under the tent of Federal interference with the right of states to regulate gambling."[62] She was entirely correct. But it is questionable whether exclusive state control over an issue with such sweeping implications for our culture ever made much sense. There are common interests at stake in the regulation of gambling, and a common process of deliberation is called for.

Not every issue, to be sure, can be cast as a commons problem. And even in cases where states are tempted to gain an edge at others' expense, it is not automatically true that the shared loss exceeds the advantages of state autonomy, or that an acceptable way can be found of safeguarding common interests without straining the framework of our federal system. But the examples cited here do suggest the importance, and the complexity, of thinking through the implications of scattered authority over matters with common consequences.

There are two basic strategies for overcoming the confusion of incentives that trigger the tragedy of the commons. One is to fragment the commons into private holdings where property rights are unambiguous. The other is to develop an architecture of rules to curb narrow claims and give force to common interests. Either approach is often workable, though they embody different values. The broad debate over the future of America's federal-state balance can be seen, in a sense, as pivoting on this strategic choice. Devolution, in its purer manifestations, seeks to simplify incentives by subdividing the commons into separate plots. Federal reform requires accepting the challenge of balancing multiple interests within the national commonwealth.

CHAPTER FIVE

The Industrial Policy Paradox

Imagine an aspiring entrepreneur—one who is not above seeking a little help from the government—cruising the Internet in search of open-minded public agencies that might offer some support to a business venture. He lands at random on the Indiana Department of Commerce home page, and clicks on the icon labeled "Assistance and Business Incentives." There he finds over twenty different kinds of financial assistance on offer—from the Capital Access Program and the Hoosier Development Fund to the Indiana Community Business Credit Corporation—along with four export-assistance programs, technical help from the Indiana Micro-Electronics Center and the Indiana Business Modernization and Technology Corporation and seven other programs, and several sorts of workforce assistance.[1] (There is nothing unusual about this; he will find a similar array of government assistance proffered by nearly every other state.) As he checks out the details on how to apply for assistance, he reflects with gratitude on his country's principled aversion to government meddling in the marketplace, and with even more gratitude on the uneven application of that admirable precept.

The profusion of state aids to business and other programs to shape or accelerate economic development is nothing new and, with few exceptions, is boringly uncontroversial. Seldom is the ambivalence of American ideology so starkly on display as it is with the comparative legitimacy at the federal level, and in the states, of economic intervention. An activist stance that remains ideologically suspect in Washington—including, for the most part, under the Clinton Administration—is the unremarkable norm in the states.

THE DEBATE OVER FEDERAL INDUSTRIAL POLICY

Periodically throughout America's economic history, an interventionist impulse inserts a counterpoint to the dominant national theme of laissez-faire. Alexander Hamilton's fervor for forcing the pace of his new country's development was the first such phase; the loose alliance of agendas briefly united under the industrial policy banner is among the most recent. Its long run of postwar prosperity tripped up by the economic upheavals of the Nixon, Ford, and Carter years, America struggled for conceptual footing. In certain precincts of academia and government, this puzzlement evolved into a deep reexamination of the doctrinal fundaments of American economic policy. The enterprise came to carry the label "industrial policy." It may seem hard to imagine a blander or more rhetorically inert term for policies having to do with industry, and the phrase is commonplace in political discourse in other countries. But in the United States, industrial policy was to become a political and intellectual circus, featuring elements of the sophisticated, the cynical, and the simply silly.

In the waning days of the Carter Administration, the cabinet-level Economic Policy Group launched an inquiry into the potential for targeted microeconomic policies. In August 1980 Carter used the term "industrial policy" to describe the strategic economic agenda then taking shape within the White House. As a supplement to the macroeconomic regime being pursued under the direction of Federal Reserve chair Paul Volker, Carter promised a (still ill-defined) campaign of sector-specific intervention to cushion the fall of declining industries and steer resources into more promising fields of endeavor. The initiative had little practical effect—Carter's bid for reelection was defeated three months later—and the President's final economic report ended up repudiating "attempts to pick winners or reinvigorate declining industries."[2]

Industrial policy was utterly at odds with Ronald Reagan's economic vision. "The most important cause of our economic problems," Reagan's first economic agenda declared, "has been the government itself."[3] Any mention of strategic meddling was banished from the corridors of power, and industrial policy advocates scattered to universities and think tanks. The diaspora, however, only intensified their obsession with the country's industrial troubles, as the economic grimness of the early Reagan years offered additional motive. Joblessness and the trade deficit continued to rise in 1981 and 1982, and the economy remained stagnant as major industrial sectors still bled. A proliferation of work on the potential for strategic governmental intervention provided an intellectual counter to Reaganomics in the early 1980s. Academics diagnosed industrial sclerosis and dysfunctional relationships among business, labor, and government and called (with varying proportions of caution and urgency) for explicit adjustment policies.[4] Legislators (mostly Democratic) held hearings, commissioned studies, and drafted proposed legislation.[5]

The high-water mark for the industrial policy debate came in 1983. Investment banker Felix Rohatyn, who had overseen the bailout of New York City in the mid-1970s, called for elevating the rescue's key principles into national policy. A national development bank, controlled by business, labor, and government leaders, would orchestrate ongoing negotiations among the economy's major stakeholders, using the promise of fresh resources to cement consensus on adjustment measures.[6] *Business Week*'s July 4 issue pointed to a "decade of recessions, bouts of roaring inflation, near-depression levels of unemployment, the deteriorating competitiveness of basic industries, sliding productivity, the painful adjustment to dependence on high-priced foreign oil, and a stagnating standard of living" as ample cause for reconsidering laissez-faire orthodoxy; an editorial explicitly (albeit cautiously) endorsed a more strategic industrial policy.[7] Robert B. Reich published *The Next American Frontier*, a sweeping assessment of the social causes and consequences of the country's economic ills.[8] Ronald Reagan appointed a Presidential Commission on Industrial Competitiveness, headed by Hewlett-Packard chairman John Young. Congress, meanwhile, was disinclined to wait for any commission's report. By year's end it was at work on at least seventeen bills to establish industrial policy institutions, many of them geared toward an aggressively interventionist approach organized around a "National Industrial Development Bank" or some similar reincarnation of the Depression-era Reconstruction Finance Corporation. Economist Paul Krugman predicted in late 1983 that "in the next decade, the United States will probably adopt an explicit industrial policy."[9]

Krugman issued his prediction with more confidence than relish; all but a few academic economists opposed most industrial policy proposals. Economists felt that the industrial policy advocates were untutored in theory, cavalier about the quantity and quality of economic data required for strategic interventions, and blind to the dismal record of economic planning, or anything that looked like economic planning, elsewhere in the world. Even if sound industrial policies could in principle be formulated, economists cautioned, special interests would hijack the policy process. Alan Greenspan, then a private financial expert, said in 1983 that if "you strip away the philosophical paraphernalia, industrial policy is a mechanism by which the politically powerful get their hands in the till."[10] Nobody schooled in the ways of Washington, Greenspan and others warned, could expect decisions with such weighty economic consequences to be made free of political pressures and gamesmanship. Yet the national industrial policy debate roiling Washington in the early 1980s was soon to be stilled not by theorists' disapproval, but by the fatal vulnerabilities of a concept delivered unformed into the policy arena, and by an economic turnaround that seemed to settle the issue of what ailed America.

There had never been a single definition of industrial policy, and specific proposals spanned the range from subtly nudging the market to unblushingly detailed industrial planning. As the issue gained prominence, it lost focus. With no organized group of advocates, opponents could select the most half-baked specimens from a large and unruly array of proposals, to be displayed at the "industrial policy agenda," ridiculed, and readily annihilated.[11] At the same time, "industrial policy" became a voguish new label to paste onto various odds and ends of the traditional left's economic agenda—guided capital allocation, trade protection, vast public works programs, public ownership of corporations. Industrial policy was far too frail a conceptual vessel to serve as a lifeboat for so many stranded policy proposals. As they crowded aboard, the craft foundered. By mid-1984 it was nearly impossible to say with confidence—even to the roughest degree of approximation—what adopting the industrial policy agenda would mean for the American economy. Reich observed that the term had "moved from obscurity to meaninglessness without any intervening period of coherence." Meanwhile, the long-heralded Reagan economic revival finally, and dramatically, arrived. Economic growth accelerated from –2.2 percent in 1982 to 3.9 percent in 1983, and then to a dazzling 6.2 percent in 1984 as civilian unemployment declined from 9.7 percent to 7.5 percent.[12] The long-term assessment of the deficit-fueled recovery would remain a matter of dispute, but it unquestionably silenced the industrial policy debate.[13]

Yet as industrial policy faded away in Washington, it triumphed—though usually under other labels—in the states. Several factors were at work: The Great Society surge of intergovernmental spending programs boosted the professionalism, and the administrative sophistication, of state governments, and much of that new capacity remained even when the grants ceased to flow. The New Federalism of Nixon and, especially, Reagan encouraged state activism across the policy spectrum. Economic turmoil put pressure on governors to do *something* to ease the pain of adjustment. Even amid the general prosperity of the post-1983 Reagan era, many state economies, especially in the "Rust Belt," continued to suffer. Assurances that macroeconomic policy would do the trick, effective in turning aside pressures for *national* action, carried less weight at the state level.[14] And finally, the venerable American aversion to open intervention—evident ever since Alexander Hamilton's grand agenda met popular skepticism and political defeat—applies chiefly at the federal level, while lower-level activism has long commanded more legitimacy.[15]

FROM "STATE MERCANTILISM" TO THE "THIRD WAVE"

State-level development policy has a long history, and contemporary approaches display affinities with much earlier interventions. In 1791, for example, the New Jersey legislature chartered the "Society for Establishing Useful Manufactures," granting it privileged access to real estate, state tax exemptions, and extensive water rights, and created what one writer has called "the nation's first industrial park" on the banks of the Passaic.[16] At around the same time Massachusetts was using direct public subsidies to encourage the production of sailcloth, twine, beer, and other goods, sometimes spurred by rhetoric that would sound eerily contemporary two centuries later. (When the Newburyport Woolen

Company sought subsidies from Massachusetts it argued, much as Chrysler would in 1979, that government support was warranted since "the discharge and dispersion of the workmen would be a Public detriment.") John Adams, among others, favored programs of selective assistance for manufacturers to prop up the economic viability of vulnerable communities.[17]

The new nation's shortage of finance capital, and the reluctance of international (mostly British) lenders to issue credit to *private* entities, encouraged the states to become conduits for development lending.[18] Historian Harry N. Scheiber uses the term "state mercantilism" to describe a pattern of highly competitive, sometimes quite creative state economic policies in the first half of the 1800s. Just as European nation-states in the previous century had struggled for economic primacy, "so did the state governments of ante-bellum America compete with one another for the available investment capital, labor, and other resources that could foster economic development."[19]

A backlash against overly ambitious and underanalyzed infrastructure projects, in combination with the centralizing trend of the Reconstruction era, led to an ebb in state development efforts. There have been episodes of activism in every subsequent period as particular state officials acted on the basis of special opportunities, exceptional pressures, or their own heightened ambitions. But the ferment of state-based strategizing that typified the 1820s and 1830s subsided somewhat, with one categorical exception. That exception was the South. Long after the Civil War and Reconstruction, the states of the old Confederacy remained relatively poor, dependent on agriculture, and meagerly endowed with capital. Southern states, at least prior to the 1980s, have been pioneers in almost every tactic of economic development policy, from cut-rate loans to Tokyo trade missions. One of the first high-level state industrial policy agencies was Alabama's Department of Commerce and Industries, established in 1923. North Carolina founded its Commerce and Industry Division two years later, and other Southern states were early movers in the development-agency trend. Mississippi was the first state to use industrial revenue bonds, which allow states to subsidize private investment (at federal taxpayers' expense).[20] Mississippi had this lucrative innovation to itself for twelve years before other states—mostly Southern—began issuing such bonds. Southern states actively experimented throughout the 1920s and 1930s with a variety of other tax incentives meant to promote investment.[21]

The ravages of the Great Depression, overlaid onto the slow structural decline of the cotton industry, motivated Mississippi's launch of the "Balance Agriculture with Industry" program in 1936. This enterprise—sometimes considered the first modern state development program—used marketing, tax exemptions, subsidized financing, and state-funded site and infrastructure improvements to entice out-of-state industry to locate in Mississippi. "Balance Agriculture with Industry" had considerable success in attracting branch plants to Mississippi, and quickly spawned imitators, especially among the other Southern states.[22]

Following World War II, interventionist state development policies became less of a Southern specialty, as other states shaped their own policy responses to their own economic pressures and goals. In 1956, for example, Pennsylvania established its Industrial Development Authority to subsidize investment in regions left stranded by shrinkage in the coal, textile, and railroad industries, and other Northern states soon followed suit. Many states set up an economic development office of some sort by the end of the 1950s, but most of these were relatively small affairs (again, except in the South), claiming little gubernatorial attention and enjoying limited visibility. In 1957 fewer than 1,650 people in all states *combined* worked for state economic development agencies, and development budgets nationwide totaled less than $30 million. In 1990 the average economic development appropriation for a single state would exceed that sum.[23]

Accompanying this surge in scale was a shift in mission. Early state development efforts have been commonly (and not inaccurately) characterized as "smokestack chasing." The goal was straightforward. The tactics—low taxes made lower by special breaks for new investors; cheap labor kept cheap by weak labor laws; abundant factory sites made more appealing with subsidized preparation and improvements, with all these inducements marketed aggressively—were frequently effective, for a time. But several factors undercut what has since been termed the "first wave" of state development policy. As long as good jobs were plentiful in the Northeast and Midwest, losing a few factories seemed of limited consequence. But as overall growth slowed and economic mainstays wobbled, the established industrial states began to counter such "poaching" with rising determination.[24] As global markets became more integrated and poor countries gradually industrialized, plants that had moved from Massachusetts to South Carolina in search of low taxes and cheap labor proved able to move again for the same motives, this time from South Carolina to Malaysia. Meanwhile, the increasing economic sophistication of state development officials and the emergence of a sort of professional solidarity rendered briefly unfashionable at least the cruder forms of smokestack chasing.

The "second wave" of economic development theories exhorted state officials to cultivate their own gardens.[25] Instead of seeking to lure jobs from elsewhere, according to the new doctrine, states should seek to identify their own unique economic strengths, and craft policies to make the most of them. States sought to discover which industries, both established and emerging, best suited their particular endowments of natural resources, labor force, location, and industrial history. Consultants fanned out across the country, brandishing blueprints for industrial audits, business incubators, development finance institutions, trade promotion schemes, training programs, and other devices for identifying state strengths and building on them.

In a steady trend commencing prior to 1980, state development policies became more ambitious, more interventionist, more deliberately structured. But the national industrial policy debate accelerated and altered the direction of this gradual evolution. In the early 1980s the arguments and proposals of the industrial policy advocates, though cast in terms of national problems and national institutions, had more immediate effects on state policies. Washington's anthems to the unfettered market sent a strong signal to states struggling to adapt to a changing economy: They were on their own. Late in the decade the term "third wave" was applied to the increasingly aggressive development strategies forged in response. The distinguishing features of "third wave" development thinking, as it was originally framed, were institutional reform and a special respect for market institutions. In a textbook example of the "laboratories of democracy" scenario, some significant innovations in finance and technology programs emerged (most strikingly, perhaps, in Michigan) and were widely emulated. Within a few years, however, the term lost much of its precision.[26]

While "third wave" strategies have never been uniform across states—and indeed seldom constant from year to year in a single state—three common elements are efforts to improve access to credit; measures to promote exports by state-based firms; and industrial technology programs.

Finance Programs. A large and important category of state development programs consists of financial interventions. Such initiatives—industrial authorities, venture funds, development banks, small business lending agencies, and so on—originate with policy-makers' conviction that capital markets suffer serious and definable flaws. Perfectly efficient capital markets require abundant, readily verified information, calculable risks, easily accomplished transactions, and a sufficient number of potential investors who are willing (in exchange for a fair return) to fund enterprises no matter what their size, riskiness, or timing. Perfect capital markets, by these exacting standards, don't exist now, never have, and never will. But economists typically argue that capital markets are quite good, on the whole, while their imperfections tend to be the kinds of complex flaws that defy successful intervention. State officials have frequently reached different conclusions, and crafted programs aimed at bridging perceived "gaps" in the capital markets. Some target small business, following arguments that commercial banks balk at small-scale lending, or that small firms are especially rich sources of jobs.[27] Other programs are inspired by claims that very large, or risky, or long-term projects can't be covered by private capital; still others concentrate on particular classes of potential entrepreneurs—immigrants, or women, or racial minorities—or on businesses located in especially distressed areas.

The instruments of state finance programs are similarly diverse, including direct loans with lower interest, longer terms, or more broadminded credit standards than private financial institutions offer; loan guarantees, where the state's own credit backs up that of targeted borrowers and expands access to commercial credit markets; tax incentives meant to tilt the calculus of risk and reward to favor certain borrowers, usually at the expense of the state or federal treasury; equity and quasi-equity investments, where a state agency takes a direct stake in private endeavors in exchange for returns that depend on the ventures' success; and an array of exotic or hybrid approaches, such as schemes for pooling and reselling private loans, industrial mortgages, seed-money grants, "steered" pension fund money, and so on.[28]

Export Promotion. Despite a surge of activity led by the late Commerce Secretary Ron Brown, the United States is still conspicuous among industrialized countries in its lack of a strong national organization for facilitating export trade. What trade promotion efforts exist in

Washington are scattered among the Export-Import Bank, the Agriculture Department's Foreign Agricultural Service, the Small Business Administration's Office of International Trade, the Commerce Department's International Trade Administration, and many smaller or more specialized institutions.

State export promotion programs have grown sharply, however, with the average budget nearly quadrupling between 1982 and 1992.[29] The leading tactic in state-level export promotion is the trade mission, where a governor (reinforced by aides and business people) roams the globe as a sort of salesman-in-chief. There are other approaches as well: A National Governors' Association audit found that in 1985, thirteen states helped arrange translation and other services for potential exporters, twenty-two conducted (or subsidized) studies of foreign markets to guide in-state producers, forty participated in trade shows to showcase state products, forty-five had offices to disseminate market leads to state manufacturers, and all but one paid for export-related education or exhortation for small businesses. At the end of the 1980s, forty-one states maintained one or more state business offices abroad— with Tokyo the most common site.[30]

Industrial Technology Initiatives. While colonial Massachusetts used bounties to spur investment in glass production, hollow-ware manufacturing, metals processing, and other high-tech industries of the day, the emergence of contemporary state technology programs can be dated to around 1960. New York, North Carolina, California, and a few other states formed gubernatorial commissions on how to bring the wonders of modern technology to bear on conventional governmental problems like crime control, transportation, and health care.[31] (Governors typically sold these early programs to legislatures as opportunities for getting some mileage out of their expensive state university systems.[32]) In the late 1970s and early 1980s, however, technology programs proliferated, and their mandates became at once more urgent and more narrowly economic. Between 1980 and 1983 the number of states with industrial-technology promotion programs went from eight to twenty-two, and by decade's end every state had at least one such initiative, and most had several.[33] After a surge in the 1980s, technology *finance* programs have been scaled back or abolished in many states, but industrial extension programs have proven more durable.[34] Extension programs provide technical information directly to state-based firms—

free or subsidized, in printed or electronic form or through on-site, personal advice—or, less ambitiously, broker the connection between companies and other sources of technical information. Perhaps the most visible instruments of state technology policy are the various applied research centers, science parks, and high-technology business incubators that have proliferated since around 1980.

The industrial policy paradox—in Washington, bipartisan rejection of strategic intervention; in the states, a pattern of bipartisan enthusiasm for economic strategy—turns on an implicit judgment that activism is a game with better odds at the state level. This is an important proposition, and a complex one. Assessing its plausibility requires taking into account, simultaneously, the dynamics of the market, calculations of nonmarket benefits from industrial development, and the qualities of political processes at state and national levels. It is difficult to calibrate the comparative odds of successful intervention across levels of government unless we know what success looks like. As a simple organizing device for this inquiry, consider Figure 4.

Figure 4

Characteristics of the Candidate for Intervention:	Meets Test of Market Profitability	Fails Test of Market Profitability
Yields Net Social Benefits	*Profitable* and socially beneficial	*Socially beneficial, but not profitable*
Imposes Net Social Costs	*Profitable, but not beneficial*	*Unprofitable, and undesirable*

Figure 4 begs a great many questions. The horizontal dimension, on market profitability, calls on the special competence of economists as well as experts in marketing, accounting, and law. The vertical dimension, on social benefits, collapses into a simple "yes-no" query several library shelves of economic theory, along with the work of other social scientists, philosophers, and politicians. To be useful in practice, appraisal must be infinitely more specific and fine-grained. But the present purpose is to show the structure and sequence of assessment, and stripped-down simplicity aids that effort.

Companies and individuals, pursuing their own interests by means of resources under their own control, bring into existence a staggering array of enterprises. The nice thing about capitalism is that a great many of the activities undertaken with no other guide than the search for profit turn out to be beneficial by any reasonable measure of social value. An activity that meets both tests—market profitability and net social benefits—falls into the northwest quadrant of Figure 4. The mirror image—an activity that is both *un*profitable and *un*justified by other metrics of common benefit—falls into the southeast quadrant. Here too, happily, that which is commercially unrewarding and that which is socially noxious tend to overlap.

These polar categories—undertakings that *pass* both the market and the social test, and those that *fail* both tests—are opposites in most respects but share one crucial characteristic: Neither calls for governmental intervention, beyond setting the basic rules that make up the market. For both the northwest and the southeast quadrants of Figure 4, markets get it right and government should leave well enough alone.

In a world of ideal wealth distribution and perfectly functioning markets, commercial profitability and social desirability would always and everywhere coincide. That world is not our world, unfortunately. Many of us tend to feel that the current distribution of wealth is flawed (though we often differ on the proper arrangement). Property rights are often incomplete or ambiguous. Information is missing, or misleading. And many classes of potential transactions are difficult to arrange or enforce. The other two corners of Figure 4, accordingly, require our attention. In the southwest quadrant are activities that the market rewards but that turn out to generate net social *costs*. And in the northeast quadrant are activities that promise net social benefits but fail to meet the market test. Both of these categories invite arguments for intervention to bring social and market criteria into alignment. Where markets don't deliver what efficiency (rightly measured) requires, the predicate exists for public *promotion*. Where markets deliver what they should *not* deliver, there is a case for interventions that *discourage* such private activities. Figure 5 presents the four basic cases and the policy stance implied.

Figure 5

Characteristics of the Candidate for Intervention:	Meets Test of Market Profitability	Fails Test of Market Profitability
Yields Net Social Benefits	**LEAVE ALONE**	**PROMOTE**
Imposes Net Social Costs	**DISCOURAGE**	**LEAVE ALONE**

The southwest quadrant—where market incentives lead to wasteful or damaging undertakings—is the realm of *regulation,* and is little dealt with here. For the remaining three quadrants, the trick is distinguishing between the two cases where intervention isn't needed and the one case where it is. The search for the right pattern of intervention recalls the "triage" system developed by battlefield surgeons in wartime. Casualties reach field hospitals with different degrees of damage and varying prospects for recovery. Some, lightly wounded, will recover even without treatment. Others are doomed no matter what is done to save them. And others can be saved by proper treatment but will die without it. Triage refers to the practice of dividing the wounded into these three categories and concentrating the medical team's attention on the third group of patients, where it can do some good. It may seem cruel to make such distinctions. But crueler still, when time and attention are scarce, would be failing to focus on the cases where it's possible to make a difference.

The metaphor transfers to the assessment of economic interventions. Governments can veto almost any judgment about value that the market makes, as long as constituents are willing to pay the price. But intervention is only *efficient* when it makes a reality of some valuable possibility that market forces, on their own, would have left languishing. The generic formula for successful intervention follows the logic of triage: First, predict what the market will, and won't, accomplish on its own. Second, determine where the public interest lies. Third, steer resources selectively into only those socially valuable endeavors that the market misses.

If there is a single formula for success, there are two ways to fail. One is second-guessing the market when the market gets it right; call this a Type I mistake. The other is pushing public money where private money would willingly go; call this a Type II mistake. A Type I mistake means intervening to overrule the market's adverse judgment on a venture that turns out, in fact, to cost more than it is worth—even by a comprehensive reckoning of cost and benefit. A Type II mistake means encouraging what needs no encouragement. Both errors are wasteful. But they are wasteful in different ways. Type I mistakes alter, for the worse, the pattern of economic activity, diverting resources into relatively low-value uses. Type II mistakes leave the economy's structure intact, but they squander the government's authority and administrative capacity, enlarge public spending needlessly, and displace or enrich private players in economically arbitrary and morally random ways. Type I mistakes typically became rather obvious, while Type II mistakes can be exceedingly difficult to discern.

Industrial policy opponents warned that any attempt at forging national adjustment strategies would be perverted by politics into a disastrous sequence of Type I errors. Public resources would be squandered to counter the market's judgments not in the name of broad public benefits, but to prop up interests whose political influence exceeded their economic productivity. Even if intervention could *in principle* fine-tune market forces, in practice it would prove impossible to resist demands to veto the perfectly valid, but locally painful dictates of the market. The logic has not really changed since 1792, when Senator George Cabot of Massachusetts called for federal subsidies on cod fishing (in part to offset another intervention, tariffs that raised the cost of salt used for curing cod). "Establish the doctrine of bounties," warned Hugh Williamson of North Carolina, and "all manner of persons—people of every trade and occupation—may enter at the breach, until they have eaten up the bread of our children."[35]

The critics, on balance, were probably right, at least about the more exuberant industrial policy proposals. The federal government features too many points of access, too many interlinked agendas, too many opportunities for disguising or shifting or delaying the costs of gratifying a powerful constituency to justify much confidence in Washington's capacity for surgical interventions. Are the states better at intervention? Our policy choices tacitly imply that they are; many voices have made the claim explicit.[36] Yet states are demonstrably not immune to Type I errors. Consider public programs meant to fill gaps in the market for finance capital. Success for such programs means tilting resources toward worthwhile endeavors that the market, for whatever reason, would oth-erwise neglect. Type I errors are readily defined: financing an enterprise that fails to survive, or survives but fails to produce benefits sufficient to offset its inferior financial performance. Capital markets, after all, ne-glect some enterprises for excellent reasons.

Examples of this sort of error are legion. The wave of disastrous state investments in mid-1850s transportation infrastructure—canals made obsolete by railroads before they were finished; railroads to nowhere promoted by swindlers and funded by naïfs—can be seen as the para-digm case of Type I errors. A national investigation of twenty-seven university research parks, state-funded efforts to attract and support high-technology firms, discovered that only six could be reckoned suc-cessful. Ten of the twenty-seven, in fact, had failed to find a single commercial tenant in a decade or more of operation. Another study found that only four of fourteen research parks had *ever* managed to transfer technology from the university into a viable commercial opera-tion.[37] Turned down by both private investors and the U.S. Small Busi-ness Administration, the inventor of a new brake technology for shopping carts finally received assistance from a state technology-pro-motion program. It is at least conceivable that the private sector and the SBA were correct in their assessment that the world's consumers were not clamoring for a new shopping-cart brake. Another entrepre-neur enjoyed state assistance as he struggled to perfect his product line of sauces and condiments for household pets weary of unadorned dog and cat food.[38]

There is nonetheless a reasonable argument to be made that states are less prone than Washington to Type I errors, where an honest read-ing of cost and benefit does not justify countermanding the market. With a smaller number of players, a less overloaded agenda, and some-what more straightforward issues, there may be less risk of burying analysis under a cloud of complexity and confusion.[39] Interventions can be crafted to suit local conditions, avoiding the waste of uniform na-tional solutions.[40] There is less opportunity at the state level for shifting the burdens of intervention onto less organized or less alert interests than there is in the national arena. While states are fully capable of senseless interventions, in short, they are arguably at less risk than the national government of committing enduring, epic-scale blunders.

What of Type II errors, where government intervenes to bring about a desirable result that market forces would have accomplished on their own? Such errors squander public resources, but quietly. It *seems* as if the intervention is successful: Government is acting in the name of industrial development, and industrial development is taking place. These errors of intervention are more dangerous, because less visible, and account for much of the damage done through ill-advised micro-economic policies. Type II errors certainly happen at the federal level: Companies collect tax credits for hiring many mildly disadvantaged workers they would have employed in any event; Agriculture Department marketing programs cover the overseas advertising costs of companies that would be able and willing to pay for their own commercials absent subsidies. But the risk of Type II errors is probably *higher*, not lower, in the states.

Interest-group politics is different at the state level, but not necessarily more conducive to rational microeconomic policy-making. Business lobbyists are disproportionately numerous and powerful in the states, and far more likely than their national counterparts to represent a single firm or narrow industry.[41] Industrial and occupational interests can work the state capitals with less interference from labor, consumer, and other organizations than they typically encounter in Washington.

The consequences are mixed. On the one hand, the gridlock of equal and opposing forces is less common in the states, and reasonable deals are more readily arranged. On the other, it is more likely that a locally powerful industry or occupational interest can engineer a special tax break, preferential loan, or program to promote exports or industrial research and development that is justified in the name of economic development but has the effect of substituting public dollars for private.[42] The states with the strongest traditions of activist development policies generally have a small number of politically powerful industries; more diversified economies with less concentrated interest groups have been generally less interventionist.[43] No one who has walked down Washington's K Street (where lobbyists' offices cluster) can dismiss the clout of special interests in the District of Columbia. State-level special interests, however, may be fewer but locally stronger. Recall that shifting public deliberations onto a larger stage, where narrow interests can cancel each other and the broader interest can emerge, was a key theme of the thinking that informed the Constitution.

In Iowa, for example, where meat-processing interests are politically potent, the legislature budgeted $10 million for an agricultural biotechnology development program.[44] While this was not *necessarily* pork (in the metaphorical sense), there is certainly cause to suspect a Type II error. Massachusetts's two Dukakis governments developed a network of nine public financial institutions—a questionable tactical emphasis in a state with one of America's best-developed systems of private venture finance.[45] Economic intervention, in short, is not less error-prone at the state than at the national level, but rather prone to somewhat different kinds of errors. And the lower profile of the Type II errors in which states are likely to specialize may well account for at least part of their reputation for better-aimed interventions.

At the federal level, the election of Bill Clinton did not greatly raise the stock of industrial policy, despite the fact that the President had been a famously activist governor and that his first administration was staffed by some of the intellectual architects of earlier industrial policy ideas.[46] In part this was because budgetary pressures precluded much activism, but the causes went deeper. In the decade or so between the heyday of industrial policy proposals and Clinton's first inauguration, it became clear that promoting the development of American *industry* was not sufficient, and perhaps not even necessary, for advancing the economic interests of American citizens. As capital became more mobile and corporations less rooted to any single nation, the skills and adaptability of a country's workforce became (in fact, and in perception) increasingly central to national prosperity. Among many earlier industrial policy advocates, interest had shifted away from technology extension programs, export promotion, and overcoming capital-market imperfections, and toward education, training, and workforce adjustment policies. The shift was best symbolized, perhaps, by Robert B. Reich's appointment as Clinton's first Labor Secretary.

In the states, meanwhile, the "third wave" of economic development thinking crested and broke. As American firms shook off the perceived competitiveness crisis of the 1980s, the case weakened for shoring up companies through cut-rate capital and help with exports and technology development. Early-1990s financial crises in many states constricted economic development spending; the average state's development budget shrank by 23 percent between 1990 and 1992.[47] The new development doctrines celebrating the cultivation of indigenous strengths, and discouraging zero-sum interstate competition, simultaneously began to buckle under the pressure of economic development *realpolitik* as smokestack-chasing swung back into fashion.

CHAPTER SIX

The Courtship of Capital

States have attempted for so long and by such diverse means to improve their economies that virtually any plausible approach has been tried, pursued to excess, ridiculed as wrongheaded, dismissed as obsolete, and then at some subsequent point resurrected (usually with a revised label) as the latest new idea. But even if true novelty is rare, there are some signs that a very old game—interstate competition for mobile business—is taking some new turns.[1] Just as development theorists were celebrating the conversion of state officials to the cause of cultivating their own economic gardens, bidding wars for business were once more rising in prominence. The weapons deployed include all the economic development programs mentioned in the last chapter, but with the important supplement of stepped-up efforts to lure businesses by lowering their tax liability.[2]

Consider a few examples.

• When Sony prepared to build an electronics plant to serve both U.S. and Japanese markets, its location consultants recommended a Tallahassee site. The Alabama Development Office staged a last-minute intervention, sending a state airplane to collect Sony executives for a tour and sales pitch including exemptions from property taxes and from sales taxes on equipment and construction materials. "We made Florida pretty mad," recounted an Alabama official after Sony opted for an Alabama site. "We were taking everything Florida could get."[3]

• Alarmed in 1991 by hints Northwest Airlines might relocate—and pressed by both Governor Arne Carleson and eighteen thousand Northwest workers—Minnesota offered the company a deal including state-backed bonds to build two maintenance centers and $320 million in subsidized long-term debt to cover loans from a late-1980s management buyout and to help offset operating expenses.[4]

• A mid-1980s "non-aggression pact" among New York, New Jersey, and Connecticut broke down almost immediately, and the region once again became the scene of heated competition for business. Neighboring states sought to lure away the highly desirable (and highly mobile) financial operations that underpinned New York City's economy as Chase Manhattan collected $235 million to stay in the city and the New York Mercantile Exchange received construction subsidies worth $184 million to forswear a planned move to Jersey City.[5]

• A major change in Massachusetts tax law was triggered in 1995 when Raytheon—a pillar of the Boston area's manufacturing base—announced its willingness to move in search of lower-cost locales. The new tax law, structured to encourage in-state employment and out-of-state sales, paralleled Nebraska legislation that had been known as the "Conagra Bill" and Iowa legislation called the "Maytag Bill," after similar manufacturing mainstays. The tax breaks for manufacturing meant an estimated annual $110 million to $160 million reduction in state revenues. Months later neighboring Rhode Island enacted a comparable tax break for mutual-fund companies and trumpeted the relocation of a major financial operation. In another turn of the spiral, the Massachusetts legislature once more revised its tax code to match the competition, paring another $45 million from annual revenue streams.[6]

Such stories are utterly commonplace in the business and state-government press, and comparable examples could be listed almost endlessly. On occasion they emerge as high-profile public traumas, as when a major employer or beloved sports team abandons a state that fails to match the inducements offered elsewhere. More often the deals are of modest scale and quietly accomplished, little noted outside a small circle of officials and consultants.

The lack of reliable statistics on the magnitude of location incentives makes it hard to track trends with much precision. No standardized measure of business-attraction spending exists. A periodic tally by the National Association of State Development Agencies, while useful within the trade, is based on ambiguous survey responses to ill-defined categories.[7] Beyond the gap in recordkeeping, there is a general tendency for states to obscure the details, and sometimes the very existence, of incentive packages. "Most of this is done in a clandestine nature," in the words of a leading consultant to firms seeking incentives, "and the specifics are left to negotiation."[8] Even if meaningful statistics *did* exist, moreover, gauging the priority states place on attracting investment by looking at their economic development budgets would be like attempting to measure a young man's interest in the opposite sex by calculating what he spends on flowers. The priority is reflected, in subtle ways, throughout state policy.

These limitations aside, there *appears* to have been an intensification in interstate competition for business investment. A 1997 study by Dun and Bradstreet found that more than 56,000 establishments (accounting for over 1 million jobs) moved from one state to another between 1991 and 1995.[9] The issue surfaces in the popular press with growing frequency. The average number of incentive programs offered by an individual state—a coarse measure of intensity, to be sure—rose from eleven in 1975 to twenty-four two decades later; 150 new business tax incentive programs were introduced nationwide in 1995 alone.[10] A burgeoning industry of consultants has emerged to help firms strike the best deal with rival governments; consultants to government, in turn, both sell their services retail and package their expertise in books.[11] A survey of 203 tax and finance executives at major American firms found that 73 percent perceived incentives to be more freely available in 1995 than they had been five years earlier.[12] Fully 79 percent of the respondents reported that their firms were currently collecting location incentives—most commonly property tax rebates (51 percent), income tax credits (48 percent), and rebates or exemptions on sales taxes (35 percent).

One factor behind the rising salience of interstate business competition, both in the public consciousness and on the agendas of state offi-cials, was a surge of investment from overseas, sparking in each state an eagerness to attract its share. The term "multinational corporation" came into common use only in the mid-1960s, and it was not until the 1970s that investments from abroad drew a great deal of notice.[13] The proportion of Americans working for "foreign" firms doubled in the decade after 1977 as foreign direct investment grew explosively, fueled by macroeconomic factors specific to the 1980s and by broader forces as well.[14]

This was seen at the time as a remarkable, even shocking, new trend. State officials commonly used the term "reverse investment" for establishments originating outside the United States, signaling their sense that U.S.-controlled capital, whether deployed at home or abroad, was the norm. But the rise in foreign investment in fact marked a return to normalcy for a country that had become accustomed to de-cidedly abnormal degrees of industrial hegemony. Multinational capital had shaped the American economy from the earliest days of explo-ration and settlement.[15] Foreign firms played major roles in the devel-opment of the U.S. cattle, mining, insurance, chemical, processed food, and mortgage industries during the country's first 150 years. The petro-leum industry was launched in Pennsylvania by a British company; one player in the early oilfields was an operation called Union Petroles d'Oklahoma. Beyond serving the classic economic imperative of mix-ing capital and expertise from more sophisticated economies with American natural resources, overseas firms invested in the United States to be close to a growing market; or to bypass trade restrictions; or to gain local patent protection; or to meet local-content standards re-quired to sell to government; or to benefit from state and local boun-ties, tax exemptions, grants of land, and other inducements.[16] What broke up this pattern were the two world wars as wartime damage and postwar expropriations and reparations dealt setbacks to most non-U.S. economies. By the time European and Asian corporations once again began to operate globally, and the United States again played both home and host country to multinational corporations, the period of dominance had lasted so long that "reverse investment" seemed like something new and strange to many Americans.[17]

Depictions of business as rootless and cosmopolitan are common, and not only in our own day. "Merchants have no country," Thomas Jefferson bluntly declared in 1814.[18] A hundred years later Thorstein

Veblen argued that the "new industrial order necessarily overlaps national frontiers,"[19] and in the 1960s the international economist Charles Kindleberger pronounced that the "nation-state is just about through as an economic unit."[20] The courtship of capital is certainly not limited to the American states. East Asian economies are at least as eager as the hungriest state to accommodate investors, and European nations scramble to attract job-creating businesses. As Russia struggles to engage the world market, its regional leaders are employing the classic tactics of business attraction, including overseas missions, glossy brochures, tax breaks, and subsidized inputs. (An official of Togliatti, in Russia's Samara region, made a pitch to the Western press in 1996 that eerily echoed the generic marketing script of U.S. development officials, extolling Togliatti's business-friendly government, its cosmopolitan population, and its young, well-educated workforce.[21]) Empirical research finds that American-based corporations playing the role of "global capital" on the European stage are more responsive to location incentives than are domestic corporations.[22]

Does a firm's "foreignness" matter today in how one looks at interstate competition for business? Or is capital simply capital, whatever its provenance? By one metric, bidding wars for foreign firms are different because any resources that states surrender are lost to the domestic economy, while payments to U.S.–based firms are merely moved from one set of American pockets to another set.[23] But ambiguities over where the benefits of location incentives ultimately lodge—"foreign" firms often have U.S. stockholders, employees, and customers—makes this a blurrier distinction than it might at first appear. Foreign-based firms could differ consistently from U.S.–based firms—offering better jobs, or worse jobs; delivering collateral benefits in the form of new technologies, management approaches, global linkages, or imposing hidden costs on the U.S. economy.[24] But while there are ample anecdotes, and even some formal evidence, to support such generalizations, there are few consistent distinguishing features of foreign firms, beyond the obvious facts that weak firms seldom expand internationally, and that corporations tend to carry elements of their home country's business culture along with them.

The conclusion that capital has become entirely cosmopolitan is premature. Most corporations and investors retain some residuum of national identity, and for many purposes the distinction between foreign and domestic capital remains an important one. But not, at the end of the day, for present purposes. Interstate rivalry for business investment differs in some significant details, but not in anything fundamental, when the prize is an enterprise with roots overseas. Non–U.S. firms are overrepresented among high-profile bidding wars for a simple reason: Branch-plant expansions are rare, and relocations rarer still. U.S.–based firms, by definition, are already rooted in some American locale. Overseas firms contemplating U.S. investments are seldom so strongly anchored to any single state, and are more often "in play."

NINE DEALS THAT CHANGED THE AMERICAN AUTO INDUSTRY

Nine massive transactions undertaken since 1980 have moved motor vehicle production in the United States away from the Big Three and the Midwest, and toward German and Japanese "transplants" located mostly in the South. Reasonable people can differ about precisely why this occurred, and about whether it was, on balance, a good thing. But it is incontrovertible that the eclipse of the Big Three and the proliferation of Japanese and European transplants constitutes an economic event of considerable significance, in which state officials were passionately engaged and Washington largely passive.

- *Honda in Ohio* The first of the Japanese auto companies to make its U.S. move was Honda. Following quiet negotiations with Ohio—where it was already making motorcycles—Honda announced in January 1980 that it would build a plant in Marysville, to employ about 5,300 workers. The state incentive package was apparently worth about $20 million, which comes to less than $4,000 per job.[25] The deal worked well for both parties. Honda's share of the U.S. market soared—helped in part by advertisements emphasizing the cars' Ohio origins—and new investments followed the first. By the late 1980s Honda workers were collecting pay comparable to that of employees at established U.S. automakers, and superior health, pension, and vacation benefits. The county containing the Honda plant registered the highest average income in Ohio.[26]

• *Nissan in Tennessee* Honda had chosen a location in the midwestern "auto alley" that held most Ford, Chrysler, and General Motors plants. Nissan broke the pattern (and set what would become a new norm) by building *its* U.S. plant in the South. Thirty-nine states submitted proposals to Nissan, but the final selection was between Georgia and Tennessee. While Japanese auto plants were new to the old Confederacy, foreign investment wasn't. Nearly a fifth of the capital expenditures made in the Southeast between 1969 and 1973 was a result of foreign investment, and Georgia, as Nissan pondered its options, was already home to eighty-five Japanese firms.[27] The choice this time, though, went to a site in Smyrna, Tennessee, following an incentive deal (including road improvements, waste-water treatment facilities, water and rail links, and commitments of job-training funds) worth a reported $66 million, or around $17,000 per job.

• *Mazda and Ford in Michigan* Mazda Motor Manufacturing, in partnership with Ford, considered eleven states as possible locales for its new assembly plant before a site in Flat Rock, Michigan, was announced in late 1984. A state incentive package worth an estimated $14,000 per job included $9 million in infrastructure improvements, a $21 million loan, and $19 million in training funds.[28] In addition to these direct financial incentives was a large tax subsidy—a near-total tax abatement for twelve years—negotiated by state officials, but with the cost borne by local government.[29]

• *Saturn in Tennessee* Saturn was not a foreign firm, but a separate new division of General Motors—the first in decades—heralded as a fresh start for American automaking, an all-new car to be made in an all-new factory with the world's most modern techniques and management methods. Nearly every state vied for the prize. Seven governors appeared on the Phil Donahue Show to pitch their states as the site for Saturn.[30] Tennessee, a newly emerging presence in the U.S. auto industry, won the competition with a package worth about $27,000 per job, including $50 million for infrastructure and $30 million for worker training.

- *Mitsubishi and Chrysler in Illinois* When an alliance between Mitsubishi and Chrysler—named Diamond-Star, after the two corporate logos—sought a site for its manufacturing plant, political sensitivities constrained the site search. Chrysler had recently been saved from bankruptcy through a rescue effort including Midwestern state governments, so the serious contenders were limited to Indiana, Ohio, Michigan, and Illinois. The most ardent suitor turned out to be Illinois, and when Diamond-Star's consultants identified the Bloomington-Normal region as a possible site, the Illinois Department of Commerce and Community Affairs was tasked with closing the sale. Bloomington-Normal boasted excellent transport links and a thriving white-collar industrial base dominated by insurance and higher education—an oasis of growth within a troubled Illinois economy.[31] The eventual package included nearly $100 million in promised incentives from Illinois, including the standard elements of site and infrastructure improvements and the earmarking of worker-training funds for the new plant's employees, but also the designation of the plant site as an Enterprise Zone under a 1982 Illinois law meant to steer capital to blighted areas (which Bloomington-Normal, by most metrics, was not).[32] The cost per job for the state's share of the incentive package was reckoned at between $33,000 and $40,000.[33]

- *Toyota in Kentucky* Japan's largest automaker announced in the mid-1980s that it would join its rivals and begin U.S. production. Two-thirds of the states entered the bidding, and Georgia, Indiana, Kansas, Missouri, and Tennessee sent teams to make their case in Japan. Kentucky persuaded Toyota to choose a site in Georgetown with a headline-making incentive package worth around $50,000 per worker. At first, Kentucky was jubilant over the deal. But as details on the incentive package became public, opinion grew more divided. Small business interests led a coalition calling for renegotiating the deal with Toyota, and there was talk of impeaching the officials who drafted it.[34]

- *Fuji-Isuzu in Indiana* As the Toyota deal took shape Fuji-Isuzu— a second-tier Japanese motor company perhaps best known for an advertising campaign whose cheerfully mendacious spokesman, Joe Isuzu, became an icon of the 1980s—announced that it would be building trucks in the United States. The sites on the short list were in Illinois, Kentucky, and Indiana. The ardor of two of the contenders was cooled somewhat by recent success—Diamond-Star for Illinois, Toyota for Kentucky—and Indiana was determined to land a Japanese plant to compensate for the setbacks it had suffered as U.S. automakers lost market share. Indiana won the bidding with an incentive package valued at about $51,000 per job by *Automotive News*.[35] But the site for the Fuji-Isuzu plant was not Kokomo, Anderson, or any of the other blue-collar cities laid low by the eclipse of the Big Three, but instead a prosperous college town, Lafayette.

• *BMW in South Carolina* In the 1990s German auto firms followed the same path of U.S. assembly plant investments that the Japanese had tread in the 1980s. Their motives were comparable, but not identical, to those of their Japanese counterparts. Nissan, Fuji-Isuzu, Mitsubishi, Toyota, and Honda had opened U.S. plants largely as strategic moves against U.S. protectionism.[36] The German firms were driven by more conventionally economic motives for overseas investment: escaping higher labor costs at home. The first major German investment was BMW's assembly plant in Spartanburg County, South Carolina. The deal, announced in 1992, included a rich package of incentives from the state government, valued at somewhere between $65,000 and $75,000 per job—upping the ante beyond previous benchmarks set by Illinois and Indiana.[37]

• *Daimler-Benz in Alabama* The news that a new line of Mercedes sport-utility vehicles would be built in America triggered bidding by thirty states. South Carolina presented a package worth over $100 million, and even offered to buy a thousand acres of land on which to relocate eight endangered red-cockaded woodpeckers that had inconveniently built their nests near the proposed Mercedes site.[38] North Carolina, conspicuously bypassed so far by foreign automakers, made a similarly generous offer despite its tradition of disdaining bidding wars. But after a flurry of last-minute site visits, and initial expectations that North Carolina had won, the decision went in favor of a site near Tuscaloosa, Alabama. Alabama's incentive package left the competition far behind, featuring $170 million for acquiring and improving the plant site and $60 million for worker training. (Later estimates pushed the total cost of subsidies and tax breaks to Mercedes closer to $300 million.[39]) The reported cost per job approached three times the previous record.

Nearly two decades' experience with interstate competition for auto plants suggest a few general observations. First—except for their rising cost—it is remarkable how *similar* the incentive packages have been. Each deal includes subsidized site purchase or preparation and partial state funding for training, as well as exemption from various state and local taxes. This is hardly consistent with the view of states as "laboratories," testing tactics for accommodating capital at the smallest sacrifice of public resources. Nor is there much to support the scenario of distinctive states and distinctive automakers working out the best fit between locale and enterprise. The pertinent metaphor is neither the laboratory nor the dating game, but simple supply and demand.[40] As long as state officials perceive auto assembly plants as desirable, and as long as many states can offer acceptable sites from which to serve the American marketplace, there will be a seller's market for automaking jobs. As early deals revealed states' willingness to pay—and shortened the list of foreign car companies still to build a U.S. plant—the cost climbed from the $4,000 Ohio paid for each Honda job to the $168,000 per job Alabama paid for Mercedes.[41]

Second, there is little evidence that the price paid for foreign auto jobs buys a rational pattern of intrastate development. The best economic argument for location incentives is based on steering employment opportunities to areas that need them most. In the six earliest auto investments analyzed by two scholars in 1989, the winning bids came from *states* suffering above-average unemployment. "Creating jobs" was a plausible political imperative for state officials. But in every case but one, the specific area in which the plant located suffered from less joblessness—sometimes very much less—than the state overall. (See Figure 6.)

The third observation concerns *national* policy on the automobile industry—the dog that didn't bark. The plight of the Big Three and their mostly Midwestern dependents weighed heavily on national politics in the late 1970s and early 1980s. Rescuing Chrysler from bankruptcy had imposed on Washington considerable risk, plus the

Figure 6[42]
State and County Joblessness at the Time
Major Auto Deals Announced

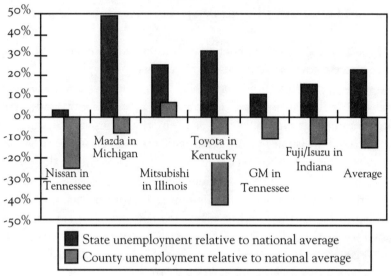

Source: Data from Milward and Newmand, Tables 5 and 6

ideological discomfort of so bluntly flouting laissez-faire conventions. Negotiating "voluntary" auto import quotas with Japan to lessen the pressure on domestic automaking had cost both bargaining chips and free-trade bragging rights. And the nation's foreign policy, including expensive commitments in the Middle East, reflected the imperatives of a car-based culture. Some observers (this author included) have questioned the logic of straining to preserve the American auto industry in its mid-1970s form.[43] But even if one feels that national policy had been wrongheaded, it is no less interesting to see it so completely undone with the active, and expensive, help of state officials. The table on page 103 tracks the shift in U.S. auto production patterns between 1982 and 1994. Michigan's share of total output dropped, Ohio's surged, Missouri's slipped—and three other states dropped from the list, to be replaced by Kentucky, Tennessee, and Illinois as production got underway at the new transplants. Total production grew by nearly 80 percent over the period, and only California decreased its output in absolute terms. Even so, this represents a stark and rapid rearrangement, with scant national debate, of an industry that had so recently dominated the policy agenda. And it illustrates the degree to which Americans' engagement with global capital is now orchestrated by the states.

States with Over 5 Percent of U.S. Motor Vehicle Output

1982		1994	
State	**Share**	**State**	**Share**
Michigan	33.7%	Michigan	28.0%
Ohio	11.4%	Ohio	14.5%
Missouri	8.3%	Missouri	7.5%
California	5.5%	Kentucky	6.5%
Delaware	5.1%	Tennessee	5.9%
Georgia	5.1%	Illinois	5.6%

(Source: Calculated from *Ward's Automotive Yearbook* 1983 and 1995)

Do Incentives Affect Location Decisions?

Are states simply throwing their money away on incentives to firms that actually decide on wholly independent grounds where to site their investments? Or do policies meant to attract business really affect private-sector location decisions? To some extent, logic insists, they must: Other things being equal (the theorist's ritual incantation) lower rates of taxation, special tax breaks, customized infrastructure, subsidized inputs, and other such inducements will raise the expected return on investment in a state and thus make it a more attractive locale. The problem lies in determining the practical effect of such policies when other things are *not* equal. Factors under state control form only one dimension of business location decisions, and it is no simple matter to isolate their effect. Add to the issue's empirical complexity the political voltage associated with matters concerning "business climate" and it is not really surprising to discover that the debate is characteristically deficient in both candor and clarity.[44]

Ten or fifteen years ago, economic development conferences where practitioners and academics mingled would usually reenact the exchange between two uneasy partners in rebellion, Glendower and Hotspur, in Shakespeare's *Henry IV, Part I*. State officials, convinced of their incentives' potent effects on business location decisions, would borrow Glendower's dialogue: "I can call spirits from the vasty deep." The academics, dubious that policy could matter much amid the economic fundamentals, echoed Hotspur's retort: "Why, so can I, or so can any man. But will they come when you do call for them?"[45] Within academia, one could burnish a reputation for sagacity by explaining that states were powerless to alter business location decisions, and then sadly noting the naiveté (or worse) of politicians who insisted on acting otherwise. Many researchers considered state officials too dim to understand the evidence; or cynically willing to exploit popular credulity about the power of "job creation" policies; or complicit with business interests hungry for subsidies however economically sterile; or (most charitably) engaging in a kind of Pascal's wager—skeptical that their efforts to lure business had much impact on how the state economy fared, but unwilling to abandon the enterprise because of the awful consequences of being proven wrong.[46]

Academic opinion has shifted in recent years, however, and scholars have become somewhat more respectful of the view that states can attract (or repel) private-sector investment through the policies they deploy. There is still no uniform consensus that state policies matter much more than they used to for business location decisions, and indeed some researchers argue the opposite.[47] But the view that public policies affect a state's appeal to mobile investment capital is discernibly gaining credence among empiricists. (The Appendix surveys some of the extensive literature examining state policy's leverage on business location.)

Intuition, as is sometimes the case, accords with the trend in expert opinion. There are abundant reasons for firms to be more footloose today, and hence more readily swayed by state policies, than they were as recently as two or three decades ago. National (and international) markets are becoming more integrated. The gradual shift within manufacturing toward goods with high ratios of value to weight; along with improvements in transportation; along with new communications technologies that make services much easier to export, all tend to render any one spot on the map an increasingly acceptable substitute for any other spot on the map. Once-dominant factors like proximity to inputs and markets carry diminishing weight. Mergers and acquisitions have shrunk the number of firms anchored to a particular locale by family or cultural ties. Foreign firms launching American operations start with a clean slate, and can consider cost factors without the constraints of sunk investments in any state. (In recent years a number of companies, including London Fog, Scott Paper, and W. R. Grace have proven sufficiently rootless to relocate near the homes of senior executives, offering some informal evidence that the economic inertia which once blunted the effect of business-attraction policies has weakened.[48])

While technological and market trends make it increasingly *possible* for companies to base location decisions on cost factors affected by policy, intensifying competition and pressure on profit margins makes companies more sensitive to taxes and hungrier for subsidies. The perception within the business world that everybody else is collecting location incentives renders firms more determined to get their share, lest they suffer a competitive disadvantage.[49] State taxes on business income are now 16 percent of the federal-state total, moreover, raising the appeal of exemptions and abatements.

How Should States Respond?

Not long ago, theorists debated why states persisted in behaving (in defiance of the evidence) as if they had much leverage over private investment. Today's question is considerably more interesting: If reality *has* caught up with state officials' eternal faith that taxing and spending policies weigh heavily on business location decisions, what should states do about it? There are four generic options.

1. **Refuse to Play.** The conclusion that states *can* affect investment decisions by no means justifies every action undertaken in the name of creating jobs; even if the game isn't futile, it remains possible to lose. State officials can still conclude that the odds aren't worth the ante. This position can find support in both history and theory. In late-eighteenth-century Massachusetts, according to Oscar and Mary Handlin's first-rate account, tax exemptions to spur investment first expanded and then "came to be reckoned poor fiduciary practice. . . .

The whole technique, therefore, fell into disuse."[50] Alan Altshuler and
Jose A. Gomez-Ibanez have marshaled evidence and logic to suggest
that local officials often overestimate the revenue benefits, and under-
estimate the public costs, of new commercial development, calling
into question the rationality of most cities' development hunger. State
officials may be similarly myopic when reckoning the net benefits of
industrial investments.[51]

The mainstream view among economists remains that states ought
to concentrate on the economic fundamentals, instead of fiddling with
special lures to attract companies. A coalition of economists issued a
1995 resolution calling for an end to targeted business incentive programs.[52] Some politicians, such as Alabama's James Folsom, have faced
a political backlash for courting capital with too much ardor and too
little discretion. Others, such as Republican State Senator Charles
Horn of Ohio, have decried rivalry for business as "a zero-sum game
with no wealth creation." Horn was unusual but not unique among officials in his confidence that "Ohio can show economic gains by unilat-
erally disarming in this war among the states."[53] A report by the
Economic Policy Institute argues that tax-break competition is irrational for both state officials and, in the long run, for business leaders as
well, and calls for states to come to their senses and abandon development rivalry.[54]

Yet few governors were willing to forswear competition even when
most theorists argued it was futile, and the trend today is toward more,
not less, interstate rivalry for business investment. North Carolina, for
example—which had long stood out among the Southeastern states for
its attention to education and infrastructure and its reluctance to offer
location incentives—adopted 1996 legislation to meet the competition
by loosening limits on bidding for business.[55]

The economist's admonition to avoid narrow business-attraction
programs in favor of sound overall economic policies is hard to dispute
in theory. But in practice the distinction tends to break down. Seldom
does competition for investment take the form of one-time-only exemptions from the rules that apply to other firms. Instead, interstate rivalry both affects how general policies are interpreted and applied, and
alters the evolution of those general policies. Changes in the Massachusetts tax code in the mid-1990s have been depicted as enlightened
fiscal policy reforms, for example, but were demonstrably crafted to pre-

vent Raytheon and Fidelity from moving operations to more accommodating states. Whether the policy shift constitutes a targeted, tactical
intervention or a general revision of the state's economic strategy is
thus open to debate.

Most important, it is far from clear that to stay above the competitive fray would turn out to be prudent policy, even if governors could be
persuaded to do so. New Zealand dismantled its extensive array of investment incentives in the mid-1980s, as part of a reform campaign, including a wide range of tax reductions, and saw its fiscal position
improve with no discernible loss in investment. But if the economic
fundamentals are such that an enterprise finds New Zealand an appealing location, it is relatively unlikely to be lured away by more generous
incentives offered elsewhere, since there are few close substitutes
nearby. The individual states (though not necessarily the country as a
whole) operate in different settings than does New Zealand. With the
exception of Alaska and Hawaii, every American state has contiguous
competitors. (Interestingly, one empirical study found that Alaska and
Hawaii started the 1970s with a relatively small number of business incentive programs and—unlike almost all other states—saw the number
decline over the course of the decade.[56]) The Constitution affords firms
located in any state the full benefits of American corporate citizenship.
So while most enterprises still determine their location choices among
countries on the basis of cost factors beyond government's control, the
fundamentals far less frequently dictate the choice among *states*.

The stakes for states can be high. Consider Alabama's expensive efforts to lure Mercedes—perhaps the most widely cited recent instance
of foolishly overbidding for business. The deal was undeniably expensive, and helped cost Governor Folsom his job. Yet it passes the first
hurdle for counting subsidies a success: It almost surely altered Mercedes's decision. Of sixty-two sites the company considered before the
states began their bidding, none was in Alabama.[57] While the Mercedes
plant represents a large net deficit for Alabama's state treasury, tax revenues are only one ledger on which the advantages of investment are
reckoned, and arguably not the most important to voters.

Auto assembly jobs are highly desirable, especially as the number of
jobs paying middle-class wages to workers without advanced training
continues to dwindle elsewhere in the economy. The wage benefits of
attracting Mercedes are substantial. At least one thousand of the initial

twelve hundred jobs are expected to go to Alabama citizens, and the payroll is expected eventually to expand to as many as ten thousand. The jobs start at $12.80 an hour, and rise to $17.50 within two years—double the state average—while offering uncommonly rich benefits. Suppose Alabama citizens end up with two thousand Mercedes jobs—allowing for *some* growth, but heavily deflating published expansion projections—and suppose the wage premium over alternative jobs is $8.75 an hour. For a full-time worker (not counting overtime) that means an *annual* wage premium of about $18,000. For two thousand workers, that sums to about $36 million per year. Over the course of ten years, even at a discount rate of 7 percent, this comes out to a present value exceeding $250 million in higher wages—considerably more than the initial estimates of the deal's cost to Alabama's treasury, and probably more (in present-value terms) than the higher revised cost—without assuming *any* wage or tax benefits from suppliers, invoking any kind of "multiplier," or taking into account any increase in state and local revenues due to the new investment. This calculation is rough, certainly, and a cheaper deal (if attainable) would surely have been better.[58] But it is hard to argue that Alabama would have been wise to reject the Mercedes deal as offered.

Timothy Bartik has estimated that, on average, it costs about $4,000 per year to create a new job through incentive programs or tax reductions. If any but a small fraction of the people who end up holding the jobs are state residents who would otherwise have been unemployed or underemployed, this is not a bad deal. It presents some complications that the costs are borne by the state treasury, and the benefits come largely in the form of premium wages. And it would be far better, of course, to have good jobs locate within a state without having to pay for them through tax breaks or subsidies, as was once far more common. But one hesitates to counsel politicians that the proper posture is standing aloof from the competition for capital.[59] Most state officials are convinced that forswearing location incentives means shrunken opportunities for their constituents. In a great many cases, they are correct. "It seems difficult to imagine that any company would undertake a major new investment," concludes a 1995 report by the Competitiveness Policy Council, "without first attempting to extract benefits from the state in which it proposes to invest." The council notes with particular concern that "this gradual change in the expectation of business . . . seems to have infected even home-grown corporations," citing successful efforts by Sears, Pratt and Whitney, IBM, and McCormick and Co. to use the threat of relocation to obtain new concessions from government.[60] If enterprises—even those with deep roots—are gradually becoming more responsive to subsidies, refusing to play can quietly become a losing strategy.

2. Play Smart, and Play to Win. The states' second option is to accept that competition for investment is the name of the game, and play the game to win. This is the strategy that the typical official finds most congenial. For aggressive and astute negotiators—and how many officials fail to consider themselves aggressive and astute?—the potential upside from entering the competitive fray is to claim for one's state a disproportionate share of the nation's more desirable jobs (and the accompanying electoral credit). Officials often see the downside to competition as limited, in part because of the optimism that characterizes most politicians, but for other reasons as well: The direct budgetary cost of even the most ambitious economic development programs is seldom large, relative to other direct-spending programs. Subsidies tend to gratify influential constituencies whether or not they influence location decisions. When tax reductions, rather than spending programs, are the main weapons of interstate rivalry the costs seem even smaller, since they tend to fall in future years, take the less-tangible form of revenues forgone, and can be minimized by contending that *without* competitive cuts the tax base would shrink so much that the subsidies (in whole or in part) "pay for themselves." Aggressive bidding for business is frequently defended as the means by which regions less favored by history, geography, or demography level the playing field, and economic development competition can thus be justified on egalitarian grounds.[61]

The coauthor of a tract that casts interstate business rivalry as "The New Art of War" urges officials to structure their economic policies to "capitalize on the vulnerability of opponents"—that is, other states. Tax breaks and other incentives "are a cost of doing business. They can and should be managed so as to maximize upgrades to and synergies in the local/regional economy, while ensuring acceptable rates of return to taxpayers."[62] Observers less inclined toward martial metaphors often endorse interstate competition as well, but call for it to be channeled into more constructive forms.[63] The Competitiveness Policy Council, while deploring simple bidding wars, supports heavy state spending on training, research, and physical capital, even when such investments are packaged to suit a particular firm.[64] The Corporation for Enterprise Development, which has long experience in these issues, has articulated principles for business-attraction policies based on incentives that differentially attract the most desirable firms, or deliver collateral benefits to the local economy, or both. Unlike financial transfers, they write, such business-friendly policies as "investments in training or physical infrastructure accrue to the broader community and remain in a community."[65] An assessment of North Carolina's economic development strategy in the early 1980s related how the state had learned to minimize tax incentives and "put much more emphasis on assistance in financing and in creating appropriate facilities and infrastructure" as well as supporting worker training and promoting first-rate research facilities, most famously Research Triangle.[66]

Campaigns to cut business costs frequently gain state officials the applause of academic economists, as long as the cuts come in the form of general policy changes instead of one-time deals. Many economists, and not just conservatives, dispute the logic of taxing corporations in the first place. Theorists are dubious about attempting to tax mobile resources, predicting inefficiency as enterprises deform their activities to escape taxation, and warning that in the long run it isn't possible to tax purely mobile capital, which will either flee the jurisdiction or pass the burden down to more rooted suppliers, workers, or customers.[67] Far from being alarmed at the prospect of downward pressure on corporate taxes, economic theorists often wonder how state-level business taxation has survived as long as it has.

And it is important to retain some perspective on this point. Until recently, at least, there has not been the collapse of corporate tax revenues that a diagnosis of unbridled interstate competition might predict. State taxes on corporate income *have* fallen as a proportion of total state revenue.[68] But as a fraction of pretax corporate income they have actually *risen*, from an average of about 4.2 percent over the 1970–73 period to an average of about 5.5 percent over the 1990–93 period, as the overall burden of government has shifted toward the states.[69] There are some early indications, however, that the erosion of state business taxation is accelerating; recent state tax cuts fall disproportionately on the corporate side.[70]

The happy warriors face, moreover, must face up to some worrisome complications. Competitive pressures are driving states to develop increasingly expensive ways of delivering benefits to mobile businesses. Michigan passed legislation in 1995 granting firms that post substantial employment increases *refundable* credits on their corporate tax obligations, based on the personal income taxes attributable to new jobs. New Jersey offers "Business Employment Incentive Grants" to companies adding at least seventy-five jobs (or fewer in designated urban areas), likewise based on state income taxes withheld from new employees. Kentucky goes a step further, giving selected companies the right to charge their employees "job assessment fees" amounting to up to 6 percent of their gross wages, which the employee can subsequently recoup from the state in the form of personal-income tax credits.[71] A business tax rate of zero, in other words, need not be the limiting factor in interstate rivalry.

"The task for state officials," writes one champion of economic development competition, "is to practice 'discrimination' by offering extra sweeteners only to new firms, or those existing firms that present a realistic threat of leavings, avoid violating state laws and constitutions, avoid subsidies that cause distortions and still portray their state as generally hospitable to business."[72] This sort of strategically targeted business assistance is an admirable goal, but it is often elusive in practice. One can think highly of state officials while still fearing that they may be outgunned in negotiations by their corporate counterparts. And even if state officials were all black-belt negotiators, they would be hampered by legal prohibitions against precisely the sort of "discrimination" that is so appealing in principle. In the early 1980s, New York City granted a $2 million tax abatement to the Helmsley Palace hotel. When it resisted demands for a $20 million tax break for Trump Tower, on the grounds that no similar public purpose was served, a state court declared that Trump was entitled to equal treatment.[73] After Alabama passed new tax laws tailored to lure Mercedes, Trico steel (a partnership of LTV, Sumitomo, and British Steel) applied for and got its own $85 million tax break for a Decatur plant; and a competitor, Gulf States Steel, claimed $30 million in tax incentives. Neither firm gained competitive advantage—nor did Alabama, as other states quickly matched its new tax incentives. But revenues available for other public purposes dwindled.[74]

Calls to minimize blunt financial inducements and concentrate instead on "positive-sum" incentives such as assistance for training and infrastructure seem sensible but tend to exaggerate the distinctiveness of such deals.[75] This argument's key vulnerability turns on what economists refer to as "appropriability," and is best illustrated by reference to employee training. A state training program that helped corporations develop their workers' *general* skills—that is, skills that boost productive capacity in a range of alternative occupations, and not just with their current employer—would indeed provide payoffs extending beyond the firm receiving the immediate benefits. On the other hand, state-subsidized training in strictly firm-specific skills—that is, skills with few or no alternative uses—is essentially equivalent to a simple grant, as long as the company would have had to provide such training itself in the absence of state assistance. Neither the workers, nor the wider state economy, gain much from such training. The two kinds of training are likely to look much the same from the outside.[76] Similarly, state assistance in site preparation or infrastructure development is only "positive sum" when the investments are broadly useful, rather than customized to the needs of a single firm.

While it is in the interest of states to craft packages of subsidized training, research, site preparation, road and sewer development, and other forms of in-kind assistance in ways that deliver broader benefits, it is usually in the interest of the company to push in the other direction—toward more narrow assistance that substitutes directly for items that would otherwise have to be paid for with the firm's own resources. The resolution, logic suggests, will usually be in the company's favor: The distinction between general and specific assistance is seldom obvious. Officials can often satisfy the political imperative to point to "partnerships, not giveaways" while simultaneously satisfying firms' more focused interest in assistance that goes directly to the bottom line. It is somewhat inconsistent, moreover, to conclude that states are compelled by competitive pressure to accommodate business demands for incentives, yet are in a position to stipulate the form those incentives will take.

Well-trained workers, top-flight infrastructure, a high quality of life, and all the rest might be very nice, but firms may still have an appetite for tax breaks, direct financial incentives, and targeted training and infrastructure subsidies—and the leverage to insist upon them. A report done at the behest of Raytheon—but done by a team of distinguished researchers, with reputations to defend—conceded that Massachusetts in the mid-1990s already boasted many of the advantages (world-class research universities, cultural amenities, an educated workforce) that many states were scrambling to develop under the banner of positive-sum competitive strategy. But "other states have been moving aggressively to implement a wide array of incentive and cost-cutting programs. On balance, therefore, and despite the recent improvements in the general business climate, it is difficult to avoid the conclusion that the competitive environment for manufacturing industries in Massachusetts compared with other states is less favorable today than it was ten years ago." Despite its outstanding performance on several dimensions, the report concluded, if the state hoped to brake "the loss of good manufacturing jobs it cannot afford significant deficits in any aspect of industrial performance. The competition is simply too strong."[77] It is no doubt wise to be strategic when structuring business-attraction policies. But the best strategy can be undercut by a crumbling negotiating position. Companies in a position to insist on incentives as a condition of creating or preserving jobs, in short, are often in a position to specify their form.

One might be skeptical, for similar reasons, about states' ability to impose conditions that succeed in steering firms to areas especially plagued by poverty or unemployment. Many observers, recall, endorse location incentives conditionally, as long as the subsidies move opportunities toward disadvantaged areas instead of merely moving them around from one state to another. The best available research, however, has revealed that "incentives do not level the playing field," and the researchers find it "difficult to argue that two decades of competition has produced a more efficient pattern of location inducements."[78] This should not be surprising. If firms are convinced that tax breaks and other incentives are ubiquitous, so that their rivals are already advantaged by location inducements—as were four out of five of the corporate officials responding to a 1995 Peat-Marwick survey—they might reckon that their own subsidies do no more than level the playing field, and understandably refuse to take on any extra costs (such those attendant on locating in economically disadvantaged areas) as a condition of receiving such assistance.[79]

3. Forge Alliances. Mobile firms and the citizens of states vying for investment share many interests. Both want good education and training policies, reliable roads and bridges, clear-cut rules fairly enforced, and government that is well-run and no bigger than it has to be. But there are undeniable differences at the margin, including priorities for public investment, workplace rules, and how the burden of government is allocated. The resolution of these issues depends on bargaining leverage, which (as the next chapter discusses in detail) in turn depends on mobility. If factories, offices, and machinery were infinitely mobile, one pattern of resolution would prevail. If investors and entrepreneurs, on the other hand, somehow lost all ability to relocate, there would be a different configuration of burdens and benefits.

Economic and technological trends of the past few decades have generally increased the relative mobility of capital, shifting the balance of leverage. Changes in the publishing business offer an analogy. Not long ago, the major book houses commanded clear advantages in their dealings with scattered retailers. But as book distribution becomes more concentrated and chains replace corner bookstores, leverage shifts toward the retailers. The national retail chains increasingly demand, and get, up-front payments from publishers as a condition for putting books on display.[80] Such transformations are hard to evaluate by conventional metrics: If the only effect is to alter the division of benefits among the parties, and there is no material impact on efficiency, the economist has little to say.[81] Some observers, of course, will be less detached when the rearrangement of bargaining power means that states must begin paying for the privilege of business investment.

If the individual states are losing leverage to increasingly mobile and increasingly demanding businesses, one obvious remedy is to seek strength through unity. Workers fortify their bargaining power by forming unions. Corporations (when unchecked by antitrust laws) gain power by forming cartels. Similarly, states can forge alliances with other states, constructing a united front against business demands. Such an alliance would have little power over companies that can operate just as easily from Indonesia or Paraguay as from Indiana or Pennsylvania, of course. But for enterprises with good reasons to be located within the United States but whose economic fundamentals permit a multitude of alternative American locations—criteria that define a large and important class of businesses—interstate alliances have great potential for tilting the terms of location deals in states' direction.

Interstate agreements to curb competition are frequently proposed, and sometimes even implemented. Some are coalitions of contiguous states—in the industrial Midwest or the greater New York region, for example—that are especially good substitutes for one another, and so have special reasons to avoid dissipating their leverage through competition. Other coalitions feature less detailed agreements but broader scope. The National Governors' Association adopted nonbinding "guidelines for the de-escalation of interstate bidding wars" in 1993, including provisions for the exchange of information among states on the incentive packages offered and explicit criteria for "positive-sum" development efforts.[82]

Alliances of this sort, however, are inherently fragile. For an individual state, the best of all possible worlds is one in which all *other* states abstain from offering business location incentives, thus bridling competition and letting the holdout state lure firms cheaply. The scenario is a classic "prisoners' dilemma"; states do better collectively if they keep up the common front. But each state does best if it alone defects from the coalition while the others stick together. And keeping faith while *others* defect brings disaster. The natural trajectory is for such arrangements to break down. In the case of state agreements to limit business competition, defection is especially likely because the cast of characters changes frequently, and a pact signed by one governor may be renounced by her successor. Moreover, since business incentives come in so many different forms—some obvious, some covert; some clearly cast as location lures, others plausibly depicted as general economic policy reforms—it is relatively easy to defect with impunity. It is hardly surprising, then, that most alliances of this sort either collapse amid recriminations or are (by tacit consensus) rendered dead letters not long after their ratification.[83]

4. Federal Action. One objection to ad hoc interstate alliances is that they are unworkable. Another is that they are unnecessary, since an alliance already exists with the admirably descriptive title, "the United States of America." To conclude that competition for investment is individually irresistible but collectively perverse is to lay the predicate for national action. The Framers perceived the states as squandering their economic leverage in the 1780s through divided dealings with trading partners and arranged in the Constitution for a unified front on commerce. If investment competition presents similar problems and justifies similar remedies, such action could take several forms—none of them inconceivable, none of them uncontroversial.

Even though the European Union falls well short of "nationhood" by most measures, it maintains tougher limits on internal competition for investment than does the United States. The Treaty of Rome forbids member states to offer firms subsidies, grants, or preferential tax rates except to steer development to blighted regions or in service of union-wide (not merely national) economic goals.[84] The European Commission reviews state aids and, in principle, can invoke sanctions against policies meant to tilt investment toward some single nation's economy. Curbs are less stringent in practice, as might be expected in an imperfect union of nations addicted to industrial intervention. But the provisions are by no means toothless, and in many ways Italy and Ireland are more restricted than Iowa and Illinois in their efforts to outmaneuver their neighbors. Over the 1985–87 period alone, the commission required member states to unwind twenty-two separate subsidy deals.[85]

The simplest federal restriction on interstate competition would be to declare investment, like trade, a federal responsibility and preempt state efforts to lure capital. This might concievably work for *foreign* investment.[86] Yet the majority of state concessions go to U.S. firms or to organizations with mixed or ambiguous parentage, diluting the analogy to trade policy. And even if it proved possible to develop legislation establishing federal authority, policing a regime of national investment policy would be extraordinarily difficult. Legitimate preemption requires a precise and bounded assertion of federal authority that is hardly compatible with the vast range of policies that can be deployed to attract investment. The pure preemption approach—certainly in matters concerning *domestic* investment—would likely be either ineffective or nightmarishly intrusive (and quite possibly both).

An alternative approach would be national legislation that instead of preempting state business-attraction policy would blunt or nullify its effects and thus dampen competition. Two officials at the Federal Reserve Bank of Minneapolis have called on Congress to define state location incentives as taxable income for companies receiving them, and to tax that income at a 100 percent rate. Rendering incentives useless to firms, they argue, would cut off destructive interstate competition at its source. Similar effects could be achieved by restricting state debt's exemption from federal taxes to states that refrain from aggressive business-attraction efforts, or by reducing federal grants proportionately as the sum of investment subsidies rises.[87]

There is a certain elegance in subduing interstate competition by simply negating incentives. The proposal is complicated, however, by the requirement of a clean distinction between targeted incentives and general economic policies. The Federal Reserve officials, like most

economists, make more of the distinction than may be warranted. As
states scramble to match or beat their neighbors' tax-break offers, they
write, the "competition has simply led states to give away a portion of
their tax revenue to local businesses; consequently, they have fewer resources to spend on public goods, and the country as a whole has too
few public goods."[88] Firm-specific subsidies *do* have the special problem
of altering the comparative payoff to different kinds of activities in
ways that are economically random or perverse. But specific and general incentives alike drain resources from state treasuries. More practi-
cally, federal action to deter specific incentives would require some
procedure to determine precisely *which* policies should be counted as
targeted incentives, and which should be construed as benignly general
policies. This process would presumably involve some combination of
federal bureaucrats, lawyers, and judges, attempting to make fine distinctions on complex issues where billions of dollars depend on the decision. Similar processes under existing law—for example, the
determination of appropriate "transfer prices" for reckoning the base
cost, and hence the taxable profit, of a multinational firm's internal
transactions—seldom present very edifying spectacles. If legislative
changes succeeded in snuffing out interstate bidding wars, these deter-
minations would have to be made with decreasing frequency. But for
some time, at least, such administratively painful and substantively debatable distinctions would be indispensable.

Federal action to limit competition could come in the quite different form of legal prohibitions, rather than legislative penalties. The
higher courts traditionally take a hard line against anything that can
be construed as hindering interstate commerce. In cases offering partial precedents over the past decade or so, however, the Supreme
Court has proven reluctant to limit business rivalry, finding in 1985
that "a State's goal of bringing in new business is legitimate and often
admirable" and in 1994 that a "pure subsidy funded out of general revenues ordinarily imposes no burden on interstate commerce, but
merely assists local business."[89] But a number of legal scholars are convinced that location incentives are far more vulnerable to legal attack
than the record to date suggests. Tax-based incentives may be challenged by parties who claim they bear more than their share of the
burden because of provisions favoring mobile capital. Perhaps more
fundamentally, tax schemes that reward local production and penalize
firms with most of their employment and capital based elsewhere

could be attacked as impediments to trade among the states. The legal theory remains untested in the courts, but a few experts now see "a constitutional cloud over all state tax incentives."[90]

Any legislative approaches to federal action would have to pass *political* feasibility tests, even if their practical difficulties could be overcome. (And to the extent that "the Supreme Court follows the election returns," as the adage goes, so would the legal approaches.) Most mobile companies and their advisers, of course, bitterly oppose federal action to curb interstate competition. More interesting is the *broader* resistance to federal restraints. "States would be well served," conclude economists Paul Krugman and Edward Graham, "if their power to grant investment incentives were simply abolished."[91] The states, in the main, beg to differ. When the notion of international treaties limiting location incentives was briefly floated in the 1980s a Louisiana official declared "this unfair and impractical idea is opposed by state commerce and development directors and also their governors."[92] The General Accounting Office surveyed state officials about potential curbs on location incentives, limiting the restrictions to bidding wars for *foreign* investors, where the zero-sum argument is strongest. Of the forty-eight states responding, thirty-one were "strongly opposed, eight were "opposed," another eight were "neutral," and only one was mildly in favor of the idea.[93]

What motivates such thunderous opposition? State officials may anticipate awkward, intrusive federal control and conclude that the cure of coordination would be worse than the disease of division. Or, governors may be convinced that even if interstate competition brings losses for the United States *in general*, their own state is well-positioned to gain. (The status quo of interstate rivalry, moreover, tends to draw into state politics people who believe in competitive development strategies.) Another potential explanation involves warped incentives on the part of *current* governors, who reap the credit for job creation while their successors deal with the longer-term consequences of neglected alternatives and shrunken revenues. Perhaps the simplest motive is the primal desire of officials at any level to retain their power.

An alternative reason, of course, is that governors oppose limits on interstate investment competition for sound substantive reasons. Officials may reject the metaphor that we're all in the same boat and will do better in the global economy if we all pull together. They may find shipwreck a more realistic metaphor and object to being tied to forty-nine other flailing survivors. If a political consensus in its favor were to develop, federal action to curb economic development competition is almost certainly possible. Analysis (and experience) could soften the defects of the approaches sketched out here. But the tenor of the times is deferential to state prerogatives, and hostile to central solutions. Whether limits on interstate bidding for business are eventually seen as desirable, in short, will depend on how the broader debate over interstate rivalry plays out.

CHAPTER SEVEN

Commonwealth and Competition

As the states grow in authority, autonomy, and reliance on their own resources, one of the main effects (whether intended or not, whether advertised or not) will be to raise the intensity, and the stakes, of interstate competition. Understanding the coming era of devolution requires predicting the consequences—across a range of public policies—of stepped-up rivalry among governments.

Whether states ought to compete with one another, when cast as an absolute, is a silly question. They always have and always will. Our earliest days as a nation were marked by fevered struggles among Virginia, New York, and Pennsylvania over the location of the capital city.[1] New York dug the Erie Canal in 1817–25 explicitly to claim for the Empire State the lion's share of Western-bound commerce, sparking desperate efforts by Pennsylvania to build its own gateway, and canal and railroad initiatives by half a dozen other states. "It is hard for a later age accustomed to a comparatively mild chamber-of-commerce mentality," wrote Louis Hartz, "to appreciate the intensity of the passions which the regional rivalries of this period evoked."[2] The question for today is to what extent, and in what realms of policy, interstate competition works to improve government and where, conversely, a stronger sense of commonwealth (or, if you prefer, collusion) would better serve citizens' interests. The issue is a good deal subtler than is generally conceded.

Few propositions are saluted so uniformly—and with such good reason—as the precept that *business* competition is a good thing. Competitive markets promote efficiency as calibrated by the theorist's specific metric: minimizing production costs, and balancing the worth of the resources that go into the marginal increment of production with the value consumers place on that increment. Beyond technical efficiency, business competition affirms and promotes broader values—choice, flexibility, inventiveness, accountability—that are cherished by a growing share of the world's population.

An instinct prevails (especially but not exclusively among economists) that it must be possible to extend to the public sector these same benefits of competition. The theoretical literature on intergovernmental competition centers on a brief 1956 article by an economist named Charles Tiebout.[3] "Just as the consumer may be visualized as walking to a private market place to buy his goods," Tiebout wrote, so does each person survey the alternatives in the governmental bazaar in which "the prices (taxes) of community services are set. Both trips take the consumer to market." The richer the diversity of competitors in a private market and the more intense their rivalry, the more likely is the consumer to get the right deal at the right price. So, too, with government, Tiebout wrote, the "greater the number of communities and the greater the variance among them, the closer the consumer will come to fully realizing his preference position."[4] People can sort themselves out among communities based on their tastes and their pocketbooks, and public officials must manage adroitly—minimize taxes, weed out waste, keep a keen eye on citizens' priorities—or lose constituents to other locales.[5] This article has become one of the most famous publications in modern economics, and the theme of marketlike efficiency through intergovernmental competition can be telegraphed, among the cognoscenti, by merely mentioning Tiebout's name.

A teeming chorus echoes the theme, though often with most of the caveats and conditions stripped away.[6] "The choice of locations that our competitive governmental structure presents to individuals and businesses constrains the range of policies government can adopt because, over time, individuals and businesses can 'vote with their feet' and move to other jurisdictions," reads a 1991 report by the Advisory Commission on Intergovernmental Relations. "Just as market competition produces an economic system responsive to consumer needs, interjurisdictional competition can produce a government system responsive to voter desires."[7] The authors of a standard public finance text present as self-evident the notion that interjurisdictional competition "is a spur to efficiency because it forces government officials to keep benefits in line with taxes paid."[8] Paul Peterson—a political scientist, and not one who habitually defers to economists—writes that "states and localities . . . have one great advantage over the national government: they constitute a multiplicity of decisionmakers, each constrained by a competitive market consisting of other state and local governments."[9] Nobel-winning economist Gary Becker has suggested that competition among the former components of the Soviet empire could be "the most significant and lasting gain from the collapse of the Soviet Union"— high praise indeed, considering the other contenders for top honors in this particular contest.[10] Even the Progressive intellectual Herbert Croly, generally seen as an ardent Hamiltonian centralizer, was enthusiastic about "the merits of a system of generous competition" among jurisdictions.[11]

Making the public sector more "businesslike" through competition has tremendous intuitive appeal. The cost of government is a chronic grievance for American voters. If competition could wring out waste and tighten up management, citizens could get better value for their money—tax relief, a more ambitious government, or both. Beyond raising efficiency, expanding citizens' choices through rivalry among states might boost the legitimacy of the public sector. This is no small virtue in an age when a few citizens lash out violently against a government they view as arrogant and unaccountable, and when many more turn to the quieter secession of cynical disengagement. The ballot box has its limits: Citizens get to choose only at long intervals, from a restricted list of options and must ally themselves with a majority (or at least a large bloc) of others to make their voice effective. "Voting with your feet" among competing jurisdictions gives the individual power over government that can be exercised on the citizens' terms, on their own initiative, at any time. If public authority is pushed down to levels where choice and competition can operate, every citizen can stage a personal revolution armed with only a moving van.

It is important to observe at the outset, however, that in the private sector—the home turf of the efficient competition model—the textbook ideal of market rivalry is only a rough approximation of reality. Even in theory the merits of competition are hardly unalloyed. In summarizing the virtues that economics perceives in competitive markets, F. M. Scherer and David Ross note that these advantages apply "under certain conditions"—conditions that hold closely enough, frequently enough, to justify the fact that market competition "is held in such high esteem by statesmen and economists alike."[12] Objections, which Scherer and Ross find weighty but not so grave as to upend the presumption of efficiency, include reservations about the enthronement of customer choice as the only metric of value; the inconvenient fact that costs will sometimes continue to fall as scale increases, so that the motivational advantages of competition clash with technical economies of size; and the Schumpeterian notion that a degree of market power, rather than quelling ambition, forms part of the motive to innovate.[13]

In practice, the private sector displays competition and coordination in an almost infinite range of mixtures. Different industrial conditions establish different incentives for business people to compete, collude, or combine. Changes in policy orthodoxy, or in the political climate, can alter the government's desire and capacity to counter those incentives. Review the classic depiction of market competition, for example, then consider the economic arrangements that characterize professional sports. The National Football League and Major League Baseball are not generally considered institutions for saints or socialists, and the profit motive of players and owners alike has been convincingly demonstrated. Yet a large fraction of the revenues that teams reap from most sources goes into a common pool, to be shared among the teams in the league irrespective of performance.[14] The rationale for this arrangement is that if financial success and ballfield success were too tightly linked, high-earning teams would have the resources to outbid others for top players, while losing teams could afford only second-rate athletes. As superiority becomes self-reinforcing, soon every season would be so predictable that fans would lose interest. Financial competition is bridled, in other words, in the name of sustaining athletic competition—and thus the institution's collective financial interest.

Not long ago health care was a fragmented industry. Patients seldom paid for their own treatment, and the insurers, employers, and government agencies who *did* pay were largely unorganized. The provision of health-care services was similarly decentralized; doctors were usually bound to hospitals and to other professionals, if at all, by loose alliances. (This old arrangement was no textbook case of market exchange—due to third-party payment and the information edge of providers, among other complications—but it did feature autonomy and rivalry on the part of suppliers.) In recent years, governments and employers have sought bargaining leverage through preferred-provider plans, health maintenance organizations, and other institutional devices to gather or exploit market power. Among other things, this has meant shrunken earnings for medical institutions and health-care workers, including physicians, whose average incomes declined (even before adjusting for inflation) in 1995.[15]

In response, hospitals and doctors have begun to develop their own strategies for strength through unity. Some of the Boston area's most prominent medical institutions have forged a joint holding company to meet purchasers with a common front. Physicians are turning to practice-management companies to help deal with the pressures of the modern health-care industry. In 1996 two of these companies—Medpartners/Mulikin and Caremark International—merged, giving some seven thousand physicians a unified agent in bargaining with purchasers.[16] One of the more startling developments is the stirring of trade unionism among physicians. The first national physicians' union was launched in late 1996—explicitly aimed at countering the market power of HMOs—when American podiatrists declared the formation of an AFL-CIO affiliate to be called the First National Guild for Health Care Providers of the Lower Extremities.[17] Beyond conventional trade unionism in an unconventional trade is a range of other experiments in organization among physicians. In the words of a Florida doctor who helped to organize nearly one-fifth of the private practitioners in Brevard County: "The managed care organizations have economic power. And we have the power of our group."[18]

The reigning orthodoxy in defense procurement policy as recently as the 1980s centered on enforcing relentless competition among separate suppliers to drive down the costs of weapons systems. But as procurement budgets shrank and overseas competitors gathered strength, the Pentagon and the Justice Department looked with more favor on large-scale suppliers. Between 1992 and 1996 a $40 billion merger wave (which played out with the federal government's consent, and in many cases at its explicit behest) shrank the number of players in the weapons industry and left only a few "national champions" standing.[19]

Unity empowers; division enfeebles. The organized prosper at the expense of the disorganized. This is not the end of the story: Unity also complicates; division also clarifies. But the power of unity is the point of departure for a large proportion of economic and political theory—and practice as well. Strength through union is one of the principles on which our constitutional system was constructed. The Framers were even inspired (if only in part) by blunt market power calculations of the sort that any industrial organization theorist or corporate acquisitions manager would find familiar. Alexander Hamilton, exasperated by the inability of the Confederation states to counter Britain's aggressive trade policies, argued in Federalist 11 for a constitution that would "oblige foreign countries to bid against each other for the privileges of our markets."

> Suppose, for instance, we had a government in America capable of excluding Great Britain . . . from all our ports; what would be the probable operation of this step upon her politics? Would it not enable us to negotiate, with the fairest prospect of success, for commercial privileges of the most valuable and extensive kind in the dominions of that Kingdom? . . . Let the thirteen States, bound together in a strict and indissoluble Union, concur in erecting one great American system superior to the control of all transatlantic force or influence and able to dictate the terms of the connection between the old and the new world![20]

The particular rules that prevail in each setting determine who is allowed to organize, and who must act alone. Profound consequences often follow. Market competition is so central to the American system, and its results so broadly benign, that we forget it is simply one special case of the general truth of power through union: Consumers benefit by denying producers the right to organize. There are other imaginable ways to set the rules, other ways to allocate the power of unity. The Communist societies of the Soviet Union and its satellites granted *producers* the advantage of coordination, and forced *consumers* to compete with one another for scarce and shoddy goods—a brutal and stupid way to organize an economy, to be sure, but (except in the long run) not an impossible way.

Until recently colleges and universities, especially in the Ivy League, routinely practiced collusion: Instead of competing for promising freshmen by dangling the richest aid packages in front of the brightest prospects, schools allocated most aid according to financial need, and used lures other than tuition discounts to attract top students. The Ivy League schools and a few other selective universities met four times yearly to (in essence) fix prices, going so far as to equalize aid offers to individual students who had been accepted at more than one school. This has changed. An antitrust case brought by the Justice Department forced the schools into a 1991 consent decree to forswear collusion. Meanwhile, the demographic cycle has made schools hungrier for top students. As colleges and universities lose the power of combination, leverage has shifted to parents and students—particularly those academically desirable students with the means to pay for their own education. By 1995, nearly one student in ten was collecting aid paid out with no reference to family finances.

Is this rearrangement of leverage a good thing? University budgets are tighter than they otherwise would be, arguably bridling waste and frivolous spending. Well-off families with bright children pay less than they otherwise would for college educations. And average students from less affluent families have worse prospects for financial aid. If one views this pattern of changes as an improvement, on balance, one would applaud the end of financial aid collusion; if not, not.[21]

A fundamental misconception is at work among many who look to intergovernmental rivalry as a remedy for the ills of America's public sector. In the business world, the main engine of administrative efficiency is not so much competition, but rather the rights to residual revenues that give owners (or those answerable to owners) highly concentrated incentives to wring out waste. Private-sector monopolies, even when undisciplined by competition, don't usually display egregious administrative slackness. The rich profit margins that monopolies enjoy result from keeping costs at or near the competitive norm, while selling at prices well above what a competitive market would permit.

The consequences of operational inefficiency are graver in a competitive industry, to be sure, and private-sector rivalry, on the margin, motivates better management. But spurring ever-greater efficiencies in a given line of enterprise is not the only effect of business competition. Rivalry also drives resources out of endeavors that can no longer be pursued with profit, and into more promising fields. The owners of a

neighborhood grocery confronted with competition from a new super-
market *may* respond with ever-greater diligence in running the same
kind of store in the same locale. But the limits of that strategy are
reached rather quickly. The more promising response is likely to be targeting a narrower market, or becoming a different kind of store, or perhaps closing down and redeploying the capital into an entirely different
business. Dwindling profitability didn't force buggy-whip makers into
stellar feats of productive efficiency; it steered them into other lines of
work. As investors and entrepreneurs scan the economic terrain—
across the economy, within an industry, within a single market—they
look for lucrative opportunities not yet too crowded with competitors.

Competition isn't necessarily what forces firms to do things right—
that spur also comes from profit-minded owners to whom managers
must answer—but it forces them to think very hard about the right
things to do. Good management is necessary but not sufficient; competitive success *also* requires targeting the right market with the right
product. Consider (from a medical entrepreneur's point of view) the
recent surge of interest in moving Medicare patients out of fee-for-ser-
vice health care and into health maintenance organizations. The potential market is enormous, and there is a great deal of money to be
made. The Health Care Finance Administration recently calculated,
however, that 10 percent of Medicare patients account for 90 percent
of the cost.[22] While it will never be possible to predict perfectly which
patients will turn out to be among the sickest 10 percent, getting good
at such predictions—and good at configuring marketing, facility locations, and service packages to attract the healthiest elderly and discourage the sickest—will greatly improve the competitive prospects of
a health maintenance organization. Herculean efforts to streamline
procedures, keep down supply costs, and minimize waste will almost
surely have less impact on the bottom line than whether an organization's patient mix averages half as sick, or twice as sick, as the overall
population.

Something similar will be true of intensifying competition among
the states. It can no doubt motivate instances of greater efficiency, in
the obvious sense of doing the same things better. But imagine that
competitive pressures inspired cost reductions averaging 10 percent for
state activities—one out of ten steps cut in the process of getting a dri-
ver's license; one out of ten Medicaid forms abolished; one out of ten
vehicles eliminated from the motor pool. If interstate competition were

governors' chief motive, this kind of administrative reform would soon be seen as the hard way to gain a competitive edge—too laborious, and too little targeted. Reconfiguring their state's portfolio of activities to present a more appealing package to the right constituents would promise a bigger impact.

There is little evidence to support the notion that competition gives state governments a systematic edge in operational efficiency over the monopolistic federal government. (Nor, indeed, do citizens seem to expect this: "Better management" ranked second to last among the six reasons respondents favored state over federal government in a 1995 poll.[23]) Reagan-era block grants, as noted earlier, led to administrative savings in the range of 3 to 5 percent,[24] while aggressive managerial improvements in Michigan's exemplary welfare reform efforts in the mid-1990s were predicted by state officials to pare costs by something under 1.5 percent.[25] Both federal and state governments run correctional facilities with roughly comparable missions, contexts, and constraints, permitting some meaningful managerial comparisons. John J. DiIulio, Jr., has found wide variance in management quality across prisons, but the differences depend on specific managers, not the level of government. There is no tendency for state institutions to outperform federal institutions, and considerable evidence that Bureau of Prisons operations are better-run than their state-level counterparts. He sketches an extreme reform scenario of centralizing American corrections under the Bureau of Prisons, calling it "not a completely crazy idea"—from the judicious DiIulio, a fairly optimistic assessment.[26] Another veteran observer of administrative behavior throughout the public sector, David Osborne, concludes that the "typical state bureaucracy performs a little better than the typical federal bureaucracy—but not much."[27]

The handicaps of scale, complexity, and attenuated accountability that afflict the federal government plague the states as well. While vigilant management can limit waste, a degree of administrative inefficiency is all but inevitable in public undertakings, at whatever level. Where tasks are sufficiently clear-cut, mandates sufficiently simple, and competition sufficiently robust, public tasks can be accomplished more efficiently by delegating them to private suppliers. Where privatization is not possible or prudent, there is little reason to expect state governments to be much (if any) less subject than the federal government to administrative inefficiency. Moving the center of gravity in public policy-making from Washington to the states, in sum, will probably improve the administrative efficiency of government somewhere between a little bit and not at all.

A rather more plausible benefit of greater interstate competition is a stepped-up pace of policy innovation. The stagnation or shrinkage of the federal workforce in recent years (and civil service rules that prevent pruning deadwood or infusing fresh blood) contrasts with a sharp expansion of most state governments over the same period. Despite the Clinton Administration's much-touted—and mostly serious—efforts to "reinvent government," so far federal agencies only occasionally have either the statutory running room or the staff creativity to start afresh.

One needn't romanticize state government—which suffers from its own variants of bureaucratic sclerosis and inertia—to recognize that the odds of a new idea arising and surviving to implementation are higher, on average, at the state level. Even if state and national governments were identically staffed, and constrained to comparative degrees by legal limits on bureaucratic creativity, state-dominated policy is likely to be more innovative, on balance, for the simple reason that there are fifty opportunities instead of one to engage a problem creatively. A home run *somewhere* is more likely, in other words, with fifty batters swinging, even if no one among them is a superstar and each has only three strikes. Taken together, the factor specific to late-century America (state vitality and federal fatigue) and the factor that's more fundamental (the rising odds of success with multiple tries) suggest that devolution will intensify policy innovation.[28]

New ideas, however, are only one ingredient for better government, and diversity is not an unalloyed virtue. It is no insult to state policymakers as a class to point out that they will produce not just insightful breakthroughs, but some ghastly mistakes as well. The adage that if a sufficiently large number of monkeys bang on keyboards for a sufficiently long time, eventually one will type out *Macbeth* is plausible (if not, to my knowledge, empirically verified). But the process just as surely will generate every single *Gilligan's Island* script. Multiplicity, in short, is not enough. Proliferating alternatives only lead to progress if the alternatives are judged, if the judgments are informed by the right criteria, and if choices made in the course of judgment shape subsequent practice.

The ballot box gives officials potent motives to seek out good ideas and put them to use, and it is debatable whether interstate competition can provide much extra inducement to innovate. There are certainly reasons to doubt that states uniformly adopt best practice once experience has revealed it. A total of nineteen states, anxious to reduce labor costs but reluctant to simply fire workers, structured early retirement programs between the early 1980s and early 1990s. But the programs actually increased the burden of retirement programs, on average: Pension costs were higher than expected, the more productive workers left while their less talented colleagues stayed, and a high fraction of early retirees ended up being replaced. The errors were not particularly subtle, and relatively simple fixes—such as restricting eligibility for early retirement—improved the programs greatly. States adopting programs later, however, generally made the same mistakes as their earlier-acting counterparts, with little evidence of learning from others states' experience.[29] New Jersey has retained since the Depression the same rickety system of local financial accounting, restricting audits to a few specialized firms, despite ample examples of superior systems in other states and the existence of a Government Accounting Standards Board dedicated to setting and promulgating best practices.[30]

Such anecdotes, though, cast little light on the overall pattern of innovation and diffusion of good ideas. Whether Americans will be well-served by the multiplicity of approaches unleashed by stepped-up devolution depends on state governments' capacity and inclination to adopt valuable innovations and to abandon errors. And this, in turn, depends in part on how rivalry with other states—as a supplement to periodic rivalry with other candidates for public office—will affect the incentives, the agendas, and even the identities of state officials. Which brings us to the central question of interstate competition.

Exit, Voice, and Loyalty, a luminous little book published in 1970 by Albert O. Hirschman, examines alternative devices communities can deploy to enforce accountability.[31] Government and business are not the same. The efficiency of market competition requires some conditions that may be impossible, or difficult, or undesirable for the public sector to meet.[32] People come to government with somewhat different motives, to satisfy somewhat different kinds of needs, than they bring to the private marketplace. Hirschman suggests that "voice"—the ballot box, the press, the right to assemble, petition, and protest—is the characteristic instrument of accountability in the public sector, while "exit"—the right to sell one's stock, change suppliers, or switch to a different brand—characterizes private markets. Neither mechanism is exclusive to its home sector. Stockholder meetings, suggestion boxes, and complaint desks, for example, give "voice" a role in business, and the call to expand the rights of corporate "stakeholders" other than investors and customers is essentially a proposal to augment "exit" with "voice" in the private sector. Interstate competition, by comparison, can be thought of as amplifying the importance of "exit" in government.

Two distinguished conservative thinkers have used precisely this terminology in elevating interstate competition as one virtue, and perhaps the central virtue, of America's compound republic. "The principle of federalism," writes James Buchanan, the Nobel-laureate patriarch of public choice economics, "emerges directly from the market analogy. . . . [P]ersons retain an exit option: at relatively low cost, at least some persons can shift among the separate political jurisdictions. Again analogously to the market, the separate producing units (in this case, the separate state governments) would be forced to compete, one with another, in their offers of publicly provided services."[33] The judge and scholar Frank Easterbrook, after invoking the bumper-sticker version of the Tiebout theorem—"people may vote with their feet as well as with the ballot," suggests that "because the feet respond to self-interest more reliably than the ballot does, competition among political bodies may be more important than elections in driving the political system." Easterbrook entertains no doubt about whether this is a good thing: "The question is not whether the availability of exit puts pressure on jurisdictions," he writes, "but whether it puts enough pressure."[34]

Economic theorists take care to specify that the efficiency of intergovernmental competition required that any policies related to *distribution* be handled separately. Redistribution remains the main disability of competitive regimes, and the residual justification, in theory, for some overarching government. This is sound, but unduly narrow. More accurately, to the extent competition serves as the instrument of accountability in the public sector, *any* dimensions of value that distinguish government from business (not just distributive criteria) are drained of force.[35] The "price" of government (chiefly taxation, but also any other burden such as mandates, regulation, or uncongenial legal codes) cannot exceed benefits received. In the words of Wallace Oates, whose *Fiscal Federalism* has become a classic text, "the outcome under interjurisdictional competition is identical to the outcome that would emerge if one were to replace local governments with perfectly competitive firms that supplied local public goods to firms and households at marginal cost."[36] There is little that purely competitive jurisdictions could do that private firms cannot do, and firms have some abilities that governments lack. (For example, they aren't bound by the antique borders of existing cities or states and can be bigger or smaller than their public-sector antecedents, as scale economies dictate.)

The literature on intergovernmental competition recognizes that constituents vary in their preferences, their endowments, and the priorities they place on alternative public policies. (Indeed, it is such differences that make competition among heterogeneous governments so intellectually attractive to economists; if preferences and endowments were uniform there would be less payoff from diversity.) But two of the most important dimensions along which constituents differ are too often slighted: first, in their relative *mobility* from one state to another, and second, in their relative *desirability* as constituents, from the perspective of officials in competing states. These differences make interstate competition a less benign force, even in theory, than it seems at first blush.

Retreating (for the moment) into a set of sharper distinctions than the real world typically displays and setting aside some important complications that we will take up soon, consider Figure 7. Suppose individuals and institutions were either entirely mobile, or entirely immobile, instead of being spread across the infinitely varied range we actually see. Suppose, too, that potential constituents could be categorized as either desirable to state officials (by whatever criteria the officials hold dear) or flatly undesirable. Then competitive state policy-makers' generic strategies could be summarized along the lines of Figure 7.

Figure 7
Constituents' Characteristics
and Competitive State Strategies

	Mobile	Immobile
Desirable	ATTRACT	EXPLOIT
Undesirable	REPEL	NEGLECT

To the extent competition for constituents is the central force behind officials' deliberations—an important qualification—then policies will be crafted to *attract* individuals and institutions that are both desirable and mobile. Competition-minded officials would find it rational to *exploit* constituents who are desirable but *not* mobile. They would seek to *repel* mobile, less desirable constituents. And the basic stance toward less desirable, immobile individuals and institutions would be *neglect*. With the understanding that pure cases are seldom seen, consider how this framework applies to some contemporary policy issues.

MOBILE AND UNDESIRABLE

Perhaps the purest example of the southwestern quadrant of Figure 7—policies structured to repel constituents whom state officials, for whatever reason, consider undesirable, but who can move across state borders—is the frequently invoked prospect of becoming a "welfare magnet." Paul Peterson and Mark Rom have mapped out the dynamic by which state officials frame welfare policies with an eye to the reactions of needy individuals, officials in *other* states, their own taxpayers, and political rivals. Each state "fears to provide full services lest it become attractive to poor people. Since every state makes a similar calculation, redistribution levels do not reach the level that would probably be set by the national government." As one item of evidence, they note that state-set AFDC benefits fell by 35 percent, on average, between 1970 and 1985, while federal food stamp benefits rose by 31 percent over the same period.[37]

Warnings of a precipitous "race to the bottom" in welfare policy, however, have been (in a very precise sense of the term) premature. Benefit levels have not in fact converged in a common downward spiral; they varied as much among states in 1985 as they had in 1940, as Peterson and Rom observe. (Indeed, President Clinton cited this range of variance in justifying his decision to sign the 1996 welfare reform legislation, dismissing the significance of dismantling the national system since "there's not really a national guarantee that amounts to much now."[38]) The poor, by and large, have not been roaming America in search of richer welfare benefits; the anchors of family and culture have generally outweighed the lure of more generous public assistance regimes. Before the mid-1990s, researchers found little evidence that differences in state welfare systems strongly affected migration patterns, and critics have sought to dismiss the "welfare magnet" scenario as empirically repudiated.[39]

But even if the evidence were strongly against the hypothesis that generous welfare programs lure the poor—instead of merely ambiguous on the point—that would not be fatal to the argument that interstate competition will drive down benefits, for two quite different reasons. First, it matters considerably less whether poor people actually *do* move in search of higher benefits than whether voters and state officials *believe* they do, and governors demonstrably base policy changes on the "welfare magnet" scenario.[40] Second, the partial dismantling of federal welfare policy—which occurred, officially, in October 1996 but whose full effects will take several years to emerge—radically changes the incentives of both needy citizens and state officials in ways that make a "race for the bottom" far more probable than it ever was in the past.[41]

Federal funding for needy families now comes in the form of block grants to the states, with no *individual* entitlement to assistance of any sort, and only whatever level of federal-to-state funding Congress chooses to provide for antipoverty programs. The initial block-grant budget, $16.4 billion, is based on state welfare caseloads from the early 1990s, and stays the same until 2002. Since the baseline was set during an era of relatively high spending, most states collect slightly more in block grants than they would have under the old system—until inflation erodes the grants' real value, or until a recession hits, or unless they configure their policies in a way that increases the number of jobless beneficiaries. The big change in state officials' incentives comes from the fact that federal grants no longer rise and fall in line with state spending. In the past an extra dollar spent on benefits, or a dollar saved through more stringent rules, had less (often much less) than a dollar's impact on the state budget. With block grants, every dime devoted to poor kids now means less for roads, schools, prisons, and economic development. There's a much bigger bottom-line payoff from cutting benefits.

Beneficiaries, in turn, may well confront intensified incentives to migrate. In the past, the poor could count on *some* floor under benefits no matter what their home state. But now, states can opt for welfare regimes harsh enough to motivate at least some of the needy to search elsewhere. And that possibility—especially if it is exaggerated in the minds of state officials—sets the stage for competitive cuts in benefits. But, to be clear, it only sets the stage. Whether the players follow that particular script depends on the economic conditions and the political climate prevailing in the late years of this century and the early years of the next, and projections are inevitably speculative.

Some commentators flatly dismiss the possibility. Mississippi Governor Kirk Fordice, for example, rejects as a "disgusting elitist argument" the claim that unbridled state control will mean harsher treatment for the poor, countering that state officials are no less humane than their federal counterparts, which is no doubt true.[42] Mickey Kaus writes that governors "will be competing for the national prominence that will go not to the cruelest state, but to whoever figures out how best to get welfare recipients into the workforce."[43] Indeed, some states are embarked upon precisely such paths of reform. Michigan and Wisconsin, for example, have developed ambitious efforts to move people from dependency into the workforce—plans with tremendous potential for producing new approaches, albeit at a substantial cost. Other states may adopt these models, and the pioneers may continue to improve them through the end of the century in a "race to the top" unhindered by budgetary pressures or economic downturns—in which case I will happily accept indictment as an alarmist.[44]

Or things might turn out otherwise. Imagine it's 2001. Inflation has shriveled the real value of welfare block grants, and Congress is in no mood to bail out the governors by voting bigger budgets. A stubborn recession has swollen benefit claims, while unskilled jobs for former welfare recipients have evaporated. The evening news in Michigan, Wisconsin, or another pioneering state is full of stories about the ragged families streaming across the border for a chance at job training and the kind of support that boosts the odds of getting and keeping a decent job. In the statehouse briefing room, a grim-faced official takes the podium: "We don't want to be brutal. In a better world, we could continue our experiments with training, job-search help, and child care. But work-based reforms would strain our means even if we only had our own poor citizens to worry about. This state can't solve the problem of American poverty alone. It would be unfair to our kids and our businesses if we go broke trying. The only responsible choice is to match what other states offer—no more, and maybe even a little less." It is easy to picture a lot of decent politicians making that speech. It is somewhat harder to imagine states raising tax money (year after year, in good times and bad) to pay for costly welfare-to-work experiments, when the prize for success is a higher share of the nation's poor.[45]

MOBILE AND DESIRABLE

The most obvious intersection of mobility and desirability consists of the footloose firms that states court with intensifying ardor. Officials value the employment opportunities, economic dynamism, tax revenues, and campaign support that businesses offer. Communications and transportation advances make states increasingly good substitutes for one another across a range of economic activities, and make capital more mobile in response to economic differentials among states.

Competition for capital not only makes states reluctant to tilt their tax burdens toward corporations, or to pursue spending agendas at odds with business priorities. It also imposes barriers to other policies perceived as inconsistent with corporate interests. California's Governor Wilson, for example, has twice vetoed bills that would require large manufacturers to police their subcontractors' compliance with immigration and labor laws. (The bills' supporters argued that otherwise firms have an incentive to accept low bids made possible by corner-cutting—or worse, as revealed by 1995 factory raids, slave labor in the garment industry—while turning a blind eye to suppliers' infractions.) Wilson based his veto on the not-unreasonable claim that requirements imposed by California alone would drive manufacturers to choose other states.[46] Amendments to the Taft-Hartley Act in 1947 gave states the option to outlaw "union shops," where workers were required to join or contribute to unions within a certain period after being hired. Twelve states passed such legislation almost immediately, and by 1976 twenty states advertised as lures to business their laws deterring labor organization.[47]

This category—mobile and desirable—contains other examples beyond footloose capital.[48] The childless are at once more mobile, on average, than families with children and more likely to present public officials with a bonus of tax revenues in excess of the cost of services. As people with small stakes in quality schools seek out low-tax locales, and as officials are tempted to cater to their special priorities, political support for public education weakens.[49] Consider, too, the well-off elderly. Liberated from work and family obligations that previously anchored them, many are free to scan the country for the most attractive state in which to retire. As long as their incomes and insurance coverage moderate the burden they present to state services, they are desirable recruits for retirement havens.[50] A regression study that controlled for climate and other factors found that states without personal income taxes attract a disproportionate share of retirees. (The absence of an income tax apparently is worth an extra twenty-five sunny days as a lure to migrants over age sixty-five.[51]) Some suggestive evidence comes from Australia, where the federal government has a monopoly on income taxation but where states once levied "death duties" that accounted for nearly 8 percent of state revenue in 1971. Queensland phased out death duties in the late 1970s, leading to a spike in migration from other states as the elderly sought to preserve the values of their estates. Within six years, Australia's other six states had abolished death duties as well.[52] (Here, as in other cases, "exit" and "voice" work in concert. Political activism rises with both age and income, and the well-off elderly wield other weapons beyond the threat to move, so causal factors are particularly hard to isolate.)

IMMOBILE AND DESIRABLE

The northeast quadrant of Figure 7, where desirability intersects with immobility, presents state officials with incentives to exploit. This is an unduly loaded word, perhaps, to summarize a common phenomenon. A fundamental precept of tax policy, for example, calls for taxing those individuals and institutions least able to take evasive action (since tax-avoidance maneuvers distort the workings of the market). If taxes must be paid, the logic goes, they should be levied on those who have no option but to open their wallets. Any other approach to taxation, in principle, is both economically disruptive and likely to yield meager revenues. Theoretical economists find it utterly predictable that states target their tax cuts to mobile firms, and are only puzzled that taxes on capital did not long ago disappear.

Economic theory, moreover, predicts that the real burden of taxes will fall on immobile factors, even if the bill *appears* to be paid by others.[53] But even if everything (except land) *is* mobile in the long run, over the short run in which we all live resources differ considerably in their mobility and in their exposure to exploitation. Major transportation projects provide one illustration. Once financial capital is embodied in the form of toll roads, subways, or railroads the investors lose the leverage of the exit option. The once-private New York subways were regulated into bankruptcy and taken over by government early in this century; new private toll roads being built today in Texas, California, and elsewhere might someday confront a similar hazard. Owners of immobile assets often seek protection through legal codes, political activism, or appeals to higher levels of government, and there is a rich history of federal judicial action to shield fixed investments such as railroads from exploitation by the states.[54]

Electricity utilities offer a notable contemporary example. Power companies must install expensive equipment that is difficult or impossible to move. Since power supply has traditionally been a "natural monopoly"—a status that is just now beginning to change—states normally regulate power companies to hold down the rates consumers pay. But the lack of an exit option for capital, and the volume of the political voices calling for low electricity prices, can tempt regulators to exploit utilities by keeping profits unreasonably low. The value of investments made by utilities, in other words, can be appropriated by customers, with regulators acting as their agents. The annual real return on new utility investments between 1974 and 1987 was less than 2 percent—far below the norm for more mobile forms of investment.[55] Richard J. Zeckhauser and Glenn Blackmon, who have studied this dynamic, argue persuasively that such regulatory expropriation turns out badly for ratepayers, since the defensive stratagems utilities devise to limit their vulnerability result in needlessly high generation costs that consumers ultimately must pay. But the downside is subtle, and often delayed until long after current regulators have left the scene. (Utilities are themselves altering their pricing in the face of new competitive pressures—with state regulators' concurrence—to favor the footloose at the expense of the rooted. In Michigan, CMS Energy's residential customers saw an 8.2 percent increase in their rates in 1996, while all nine thousand industrial customers got a 4.2 percent rate *reduction*, and some of the biggest firms had their rates reduced 20 percent. Boston Edison offered 20 percent discounts for up to four years to major companies threatening to move out of state.[56])

IMMOBILE AND UNDESIRABLE

Few constituents are entirely immobile, to be sure, and few are entirely undesirable. But there are certainly individuals and institutions whom state officials—if driven by competitive motives—find it safe to neglect. Many small businesses, for example, are rooted in a single state, and generate no great surplus for the state treasury. But the most important category of candidates for neglect, if we count on "exit," instead of "voice," to guide policy priorities, is the broad middle class. The average family is unlikely to pull up stakes and move in response to any single state policy, and (even if it did) would only galvanize policy-makers' attention if that family formed part of a mass exodus.

Unemployment insurance is a distinctively middle-class program, open only to those with a well-established habit of working, but of small importance to anyone wealthy enough to weather unaided a few weeks or months without a paycheck. The system is a complex amalgam of state and federal responsibilities. Franklin Roosevelt's powerful Committee on Economic Security argued during the early New Deal that programs to insure workers against the income risks of joblessness—with the premiums paid, at least in the first instance, by their employers—could only be mounted nationally, since "so long as there is danger that businesses in some states will gain a competitive advantage through failure of the state to enact an unemployment insurance law, few such laws will be enacted."[57] Roosevelt was reluctant to push for full federal responsibility. But his administration structured the system so that states without their own unemployment insurance provisions would be covered by an expensively ambitious federal alternative. As a result, states opted to enact their own policies, which they maintain to this day. Yet states retain great discretion over eligibility rules that govern the program's scope and expense. These rules have been tightened progressively—with the costs to employers correspondingly shrunken—so that a falling fraction of workers find that they are actually able to collect unemployment benefits when they lose their jobs. A 1995 staff report for the Advisory Council on Unemployment Compensation argued that "competition among the states to attract and retain employers and jobs may put states under considerable pressure to have smaller UI programs than they would choose to have in the absence of competitive pressures."[58] Canada established a similar unemployment insurance system at roughly the same time as did the United

States. But Canada's system is mostly administered and financed centrally, and the provinces have little incentive or opportunity for competitive benefit reductions, producing much wider coverage and higher benefits than America's state-driven system.[59]

The burden of state taxation falls in a pattern that reflects relative mobility, weighing most heavily on the middle class. Thirty years ago a leading theorist predicted that competition would tend to "produce either a generally low level of state-local tax effort or a state-local tax structure with strong regressive features."[60] The prediction has been amply realized. While it can be a complex matter to pinpoint just how progressive or regressive a tax code is—that is, the degree to which the burden of taxation rises, or falls, with income—analysts display uncommon consensus that state taxes are regressive.[61] States rely far more than does the federal government on the consumption taxes that disproportionately affect families of modest means. Income taxes, which are moderately progressive at the federal level, are far less so in the states. Six states had no personal income tax in 1994, while thirty-four states had either a flat rate for rich and poor alike or a top rate that kicked in at a level somewhere below $50,000 in annual income (and sometimes as low as $3,000). Only nine states had top brackets above $50,000, and only three increased tax rates as incomes passed $100,000.[62]

Amid cyclical ups and downs, moreover, the regressive tendency of state taxation appears to be deepening. Personal income taxes contribute about one-third of state tax revenue. While reforms in the early 1990s boosted the progressivity of a few states' income taxation systems, tax codes have generally lost progressivity in recent years.[63] Between 1980 and 1994 *total* consumption taxes remained relatively stable at just under half of all state tax revenue. But within that total, there has been a marked shift away from selective taxes on gasoline, tobacco, and other specific items, and toward general sales taxes that can be avoided only by shrinking consumption overall. *Corporate* income taxes as a share of total state tax revenue have dropped by nearly a third from their 1980 peak of 9.7 percent.[64]

Most telling, perhaps, have been the priorities for tax relief in 1995 and 1996—the first consecutive years of state tax reductions since 1979–80. As economic expansion swelled revenues and political trends highlighted tax relief, few state legislatures failed to enact at least some kind of tax cut. In total, 1995–96 legislation delivered state tax cuts worth around $2.9 billion, relative to the baseline of previous law. (Offsetting tax increases made the net reduction about half this large.) But the cuts were far from uniform. Corporate income taxes accounted for less than 7 percent of 1994 state tax revenue—but claimed 28 percent of the tax cuts enacted in 1995 and 1996. Personal income taxes, which accounted for 32 percent of 1994 revenue, claimed 41 percent of the 1995–96 reductions. General sales taxes (33 percent of 1994 state tax revenue) and special sales taxes on tobacco, gasoline, alcohol, and other specific items (17 percent of revenue)—which tend to fall most heavily on middle-class taxpayers—were each actually *increased*, on balance, by the mid-decade wave of state tax law changes.[65] Indeed, the average state sales-tax rate reached a record 5.13 percent in 1996.[66] Despite the populist rhetoric accompanying tax-cutting campaigns in many states, the long-suffering middle class was last in line.

The logic of relative mobility makes this less surprising than it might seem in light of electoral calculations alone. Individuals are less likely than capital, in general, to migrate to a state with more appealing policies, and thus less able to influence governments with the threat of exit. It is true that migration to escape objectionable policies or seek out better ones is by no means unknown. Indeed, migration is routine among alternative locales within a single region, and at the local level claims of efficiency gains through intergovernmental competition have considerable credibility. But mobility is an unworkably blunt instrument for disciplining *state* government.[67] Just as some might argue that divorce is the final solution to irreconcilable differences or suicide to an unbearable life, in the extreme the right to switch states can certainly matter. The notion also has a special appeal in this land founded in part by religious deviants "voting with their feet" against European polities that did indeed push them to the extreme; the postwar exodus of blacks fleeing both political repression and economic stagnation in Southern states recalls that earlier migration. Yet while the American right to migrate from one state to another is a precious option, it is an extraordinarily awkward tool for communicating or giving force to policy preferences.

State policies come packaged together, and it is notoriously difficult to signal through the ballot box the precise nature and intensity of one's interest in a particular issue—but a good deal easier than through migration. Beyond the multiple dimensions of state policy is the extraordinarily high cost of personal mobility as a political tactic. The roots of family, home, friends, job contacts, culture, and history make migration a prohibitively expensive way of disciplining state government in any but the most extreme circumstances. An analogy from economic theory can clarify this claim. Since consumers differ in the value they place on a particular good or service—and hence the price they would be *willing* to pay—everybody but the marginal customer (who is indifferent between buying or not buying at the going price) is getting a bonus of value in excess of cost. Economists call this bonus "consumers' surplus." Increasing this surplus—even though it shows up nowhere in national economic statistics—is what defines a good economy.

Similarly, in any reasonably healthy commonwealth, rarely will citizens be at the point where one extra dollar of taxes or one extra disappointment with public services will inspire them to pack their bags. Nearly everyone enjoys a substantial measure of what might be called "citizens' surplus" in excess of the cost of remaining in a state. Even if a citizen is contemptuous of state government's competence, or convinced she gets little in return for her taxes, or greatly impressed by the heads-up public management practiced in some other state, these concerns are unlikely to outweigh the familial, cultural, and economic factors anchoring her to her home state. When she *does* move, the odds are very long that it will not be in response to any identifiable act of state government. If we had to rely on migration to keep state officials accountable, in short, the reins would be exceedingly loose.

Individuals differ, moreover, in their responsiveness to state benefits and burdens, and in the strength of their attachment to a particular place. Those with tight family ties are more anchored than those without; the gregarious and the engaged are more anchored than the loners; those bred to a particular culture are more anchored than the more cosmopolitan. Income matters as well. Adults with family incomes over $50,000 are about 25 percent more likely to move interstate than those with incomes in the $25,000 to $50,000 range.[68] The richest (adults with personal income exceeding $85,000) and the poorest (with income under $15,000) were *both* about one-third more likely to move across state borders between 1993 and 1994 than those earning middle-class incomes between $30,000 and $85,000.[69]

Competitive anxieties make states timid about health, safety, workplace, and environmental regulations; about workers' compensation; and about unemployment insurance and other policies that shield citizens from the global market's harshest excesses and truncate the extremes of wealth and poverty. The point here is not to defend all such interventions, or to deny the merits of reform, but rather to highlight the biases one must anticipate from any reform effort that is undertaken with an anxious eye toward mobile corporations, and toward the fortunate fraction of citizens who are most sensitive to taxes and best able to buy their own way out of economic risks and the costs of communities in decline.

Competition for constituents is not the only factor motivating state officials, or even the major factor. "Voice" often works to counter "exit" as an influence on policy-makers, and the immobile have the greatest interest in developing their political voices. At the same time, "exit" and "voice" interact. Interstate economic competition conditions, constrains, and even distorts ballot box competition. In the current environment of shrinking federal grants and rivalry for investment, only a small-government platform is very plausible. The agenda of a present-day Edmund Brown, Bob Lafollete, or even Frank Sargent would be so manifestly unrealistic that such candidates would have small hopes of winning office. Candidates with a talent for shrinking government and a taste for the accompanying politics, conversely, find the times in their favor, and frequently meet with success.

Competition *over* government—electoral rivalry to earn citizens' confidence and the loan of their ultimate authority—is an important virtue of our political system. Indeed, it is *the* important virtue. But competition *among* state governments is a far different thing, and most of its apparent virtues dissolve upon inspection. The larger the role of interstate competition as a guiding force within American government, the more "exit" will ascend and "voice" be muted. It is by no means clear that this will turn out to be a good thing.

CHAPTER EIGHT

The Stewardship of Skills

The gravest potential consequence of the trend toward competitive state autonomy may be a diminution (or a distortion) of public spending on education and training. State and local governments dominate education as they do few other major policy areas. It may seem far-fetched that the states' growing importance can do anything but strengthen their stewardship of skills, especially as competition hones their performance. Education reform, after all, has become a high-profile crusade in state after state. But a closer look reveals cause for concern.

No policy prescription, perhaps, appeals to so wide a spectrum of political convictions, or follows from such disparate economic diagnoses, as does the call for better education and training. Skills are increasingly pivotal to raising growth rates *and* lowering economic inequality, making skill-building an urgent concern spanning some otherwise divergent agendas.

The central productive role of "human capital" is certainly not new; research by economic historian Claudia Goldin documents the role an earlier surge of secondary education played in the twentieth-century income growth.[1] But the significance of skills, relative to other elements of the economic equation, has grown in pace with technical change and the integration of the world economy. Competition from labor overseas, or from smart machines domestically, erodes the earning power of unskilled workers. Fewer and fewer jobs require only a strong back or a large capacity for boredom. New occupations generally call for advanced skills, and even traditional occupations are being redefined in ways that heighten the importance of human capital. A voluminous empirical literature confirms the impact of worker skills on productivity and wages.[2]

The paycheck penalty a changing economy imposes on the unskilled has grown sharply in recent decades. Between 1979 and 1993, average weekly earnings for men with less than a high school education *fell* by 26 percent, once inflation is taken into account, while male college graduates enjoyed a 5 percent increase in their average earnings. Female high school dropouts saw their average inflation-adjusted earnings fall by 9 percent, while women with some college education gained 8 percent, on average, while college-educated women gained 23 percent.[3] Family income shows a similar trend. Between 1973 and 1993, families headed by high school dropouts had a 30 percent fall in real income (adjusted for family size.) Families gained 17 percent over the period, on average, if headed by someone with three or four years of postsecondary education, and 31 percent if the family head had a college degree or further formal schooling.[4]

Both within and across nations, the growing importance of human capital has contributed to a widening of income inequality. Even as the supply of educated workers has surged, their earnings premium, remarkably, has held up or widened; the payoff to education is growing faster than education differentials are narrowing.[5] Since income inequality is mostly a matter of differences *among* workers—rather than a shift in the division between profits and wages—the gap in workers' earning power is the primary source of economic divisions among Americans. Aggressive measures to increase educational attainment among the less affluent constitute just about the only strategy consistent with American values for blunting the trend toward inequality. Our culture recoils at simple redistribution. But public spending to build up willing workers' earning power commands popular legitimacy.

Boosting human-capital investment, moreover, is a far more promising approach to securing middle-class prosperity than the business promotion policies that figured in the national industrial policy debate and that typify many states' economic development strategies. Even if public efforts to increase research and development, or promote exports, or improve access to capital *could* raise the profitability of American business (at a reasonable cost to the public), workers would not necessarily share in the gains if their own contributions to productivity failed to increase. And even if existing American firms falter, cutting-edge skills can make American workers attractive to new companies or foreign-based firms. Skill-building, in short, augments earning power directly. As a bonus, adopting a skill-based economic strategy doesn't require resolving the intellectually vexing and politically incendiary issue of whether it is trade or technology that is causing such turmoil in the workplace. The same broad prescription—more and better education and training—follows from either diagnosis.

Education is a *policy* issue, summoning questions of collective choice. This is less true in America, perhaps, than in other countries where education at all levels is overwhelmingly public. But even in this country, the public sector accounts for roughly 70 percent of measured spending on education.[6] How we allocate responsibility for education and training across levels of government—and the implications of that allocation for both the level and the nature of human-capital investment—ranks high among the most consequential policy issues facing America. This chapter explores two aspects of the issue: first, the division of responsibility for job training among the federal government, state governments, and individuals; second, the future of state education spending in a context of growing need, tighter budgets, and the pressures of interstate competition.

DUELING JOB-TRAINING REFORM PROPOSALS: DEVOLUTION, OR VOUCHERS?

Of all the components of the skill-building system—including primary and secondary schooling, higher education, and early childhood programs such as Head Start—the least glamorous is perhaps the array of vocational institutions, community college curricula, and other programs gathered together under the label of job training. Twenty or thirty years ago job training might have been reckoned not just least glamorous, but least important, relevant only for the disadvantaged, or for the handful of workers unlucky enough to be displaced from the stable jobs that then seemed an American's birthright. That has changed. As more workers confront mid-career transitions, and as the content of even the most traditional occupations gains in complexity, job training beyond the conventional sequence of formal schooling is becoming the norm. Federal Reserve Chairman Alan Greenspan—not known for his vulnerability to policy fads—observed in congressional testimony in 1996 that because of rapid technological change and economic restructuring, "job skills that were adequate only five years ago are no longer as relevant. . . . We need to improve the preparation for the job market our schools do, but even better schools are unlikely to be able to provide adequate skills to support a lifetime of work."[7]

The postwar history of American job-training policy features arpeggios up and down the scale of federalism. Through the 1950s and (especially) the 1960s older manpower programs expanded and new ones proliferated to produce a confusing array of efforts run by different agencies, for different clienteles, with different permutations of federal, state, and local funding and authority. The norm, however, was substantial federal funding (since adult job training, especially where it had some remedial component, tended to be a weak claimant for state and local education resources) but state or local administration (since the federal government lacked the administrative capacity to deliver services) under federal guidelines and oversight.

The awkwardness inherent in this fragmentation of funding, authority, and street-level delivery became growingly apparent by the early 1970s. Dissatisfaction with the system inspired the Comprehensive Employment and Training Act of 1974, consolidating programs into block grants.[8] The devolutionary theme of CETA, however, was muffled as its vast public employment component came to dominate the program in the Carter Administration. CETA was abolished in 1982 amid scornful tales of sterile make-work, and replaced by the Job Training Partnership Act. The new training legislation was described by its architects (chief among them Senators Dan Quayle and Ted Kennedy) much as CETA had once been hailed—as the consolidation of an unruly intergovernmental enterprise. JTPA *was* different, however, in a greater role for the private sector. Decisions about local training programs were to be made by a business-dominated "private industry council." Performance standards set expectations for trainees' subsequent employment and earnings and (in principle at least) imposed penalties on states and local programs for falling short. JTPA also greatly strengthened the authority of the *state* and diminished that of local government. Federal grants went to governors; cities and their mayors became, for the most part, just one among many classes of claimants.[9]

The Job Training Partnership Act has failed to live up to its billing. The much-touted performance standards turned out to be laughably easy to meet in JTPA's early years, as local programs and training providers proved adept at selecting the more promising candidates from among the broad group of eligible potential trainees. Suspicions of poor performance remained unconfirmed, however, until 1993. The Labor Department had commissioned a massive long-term study of the impact of JTPA participation. As social program evaluations go, this study was remarkably scrupulous about scientific method, and its conclusions are correspondingly compelling.[10]

The results were mixed, but broadly discouraging. Adult women trainees saw a 15 percent increase in earnings, relative to women who didn't get JTPA training, while men gained about 8 percent. These earnings improvements were statistically significant, and (while small) exceeded by a bit the modest cost of JTPA services. But for young people, the evidence suggested JTPA did little or no good.[11] (New legislation in 1992 tightened the rules somewhat, but doubts remained.) Other studies point to unspectacular results from many federally funded, state-run job-training programs.[12]

Training reform rose on the policy agenda in the mid-1990s as both the Clinton Administration and the Republican-led Congress declared their disenchantment with the status quo. Senator Nancy Landon Kassebaum of Kansas, the widely respected chair of the Labor and Human Resources Committee in the 104th Congress, had long decried the muddled complexity of job-training policy. She proposed legislation to consolidate virtually all federal training and employment efforts into a single block grant to each state, stripping away the rules and restrictions and leaving states free to tailor programs to suit their own conditions. Governors could use the funds as they saw fit (as long as at least one-quarter went for some kind of employment programs and another quarter went for worker education, broadly defined). Up to half of the funding, in fact, could be used for economic development instead of job training if states decided business promotion was the best way to improve workers' prospects.[13] The federal government would lose all direct authority over training programs. Instead, the Secretaries of Education and Labor would join nine other members of an oversight board that would negotiate performance "benchmarks" with each state. If a state fell short of the performance standards it had previously agreed to meet—and if a majority of the diverse board could come to consensus on the need for sanctions—the harshest possible penalty would be a temporary 10 percent reduction in the block grant. The weak provisions for oversight reflected Kassebaum's conviction that federal involvement (beyond sending money) did more harm than good, and her faith in state governments' ability and incentive to make the right choices for their citizens.

The administration's rival proposal took a sharply different approach to reform. Instead of altering the balance of authority between federal and state agencies, it sought to dilute the role of *any* public agency while elevating individual choice, and competition among training institutions, into the main engines of accountability for job-training policy. This was a fairly startling departure from Democratic orthodoxy. It had been controversial within the administration, and flatly heretical to some congressional leaders. Many legislators—a number of whom claimed paternity for one or more of the existing programs—were reluctant to see special programs for military veterans, or workers who lost their jobs because of new trade agreements, or the disabled, or laid-off lumberjacks, or ex-offenders, or Native Americans subsumed into a single system.

While some were motivated by simple turf-consciousness, others were convinced that the disadvantaged would inevitably be short-changed in any market-oriented training system. Even those with no great affection for the status quo were often skeptical about the workability of a system based on consumer choice, and were unpersuaded by provisions for testing and counseling potential trainees and for disseminating data about which skills were in demand and which training institutions had the best track records. The "private industry councils" that ran local programs under existing law, while of mixed operational effectiveness, were populated by politically influential business, labor, and government leaders. Public-employee unions and community groups—dependent on the institutions that would be dismantled, bypassed, or forced to compete—mounted an impassioned assault on the more ambitious reform proposals. Job training was a presidential priority, and the administration earmarked funding increases for training reform even while cutting other popular programs, but budget pressures

precluded adding the flood of new resources that would have been required to bypass or buy off the opposition.

The administration's tentative proposals during its first two years,
accordingly, had been a mixture of sensible but minor refinements to
existing programs, and muted versions of the choice-driven approach
aired during the campaign.[14] The 1994 elections changed the terrain.
With Congress controlled by Republicans, many of whom were deeply
hostile to any kind of federal job-training effort, constituencies that
had been battling centrist Democrats' restructuring proposals suddenly
faced much more alarming prospects. The best odds for preserving
funding for workforce development now lay in presenting a compelling
reform package with which to deflect calls to abandon federal training
policy.

Augmenting human capital investments in ways that minimized
bureaucracy and maximized individual choice, accordingly, became the
focus of the administration's first policy response to the loss of Congress. President Clinton devoted much of a special televised address in
the waning days of 1994 to a proposed "Middle Class Bill of Rights."
Two of its four elements—expanded individual retirement accounts
and tax credits for families with young children—were variants of ideas
the Republicans had already advanced. But the other two were distinctive. One was to make the costs of education or job training beyond
high school tax deductible, which was both a deft way of delivering a
modest middle-class tax cut and a spur (if a minor one) to postsecondary education.[15] The other element, labeled the "G.I. Bill for America's Workers," was the administration's revised training reform
proposal. It was informed by a symmetrical skepticism about federal and
state bureaucracies. Despite respectful nods in the direction of "state
and local flexibility" it emphasized markets far more than devolution.
Individual choice, market information, leaner government, and private-sector involvement were the central themes. Authority would
flow toward individuals, rather than state governments, as many training programs were abolished in favor of "skill grants"—vouchers that
could be tendered at community colleges, proprietary schools, or whatever institutions proved able to meet workers' needs.[16]

The proposal fell short of a pure voucher approach, in part because
the market information needed to inform choice would remain inadequate for some time to come; in part because the voucher model was

less convincing for young people (and for some disadvantaged adults with little work experience) than it was for most adult trainees; and in part because of lingering reluctance to antagonize certain constituencies with stakes in specific programs. But it represented a remarkable shift toward choice and competition.

Equally remarkable, perhaps, was the alignment of political forces that brought the Clinton Administration and the Republican-led House of Representatives together, for a time, into an alliance against the Republican-led Senate. The "empowerment" faction of the Republican Party was enchanted with voucher schemes, and no more enamored of state-level bureaucracy than were the administration reformers. Differences over funding levels, among other issues, made the alliance an uneasy one, but the administration generally endorsed the House of Representatives' training-reform legislation as a reasonable facsimile of the president's proposal. The House bill cut programs and stressed vouchers. It also echoed the administration's concerns for curbing the diversion of training money into economic development activities, and for ensuring that *local* governments, not just states, had a voice in how the remaining governmental role played out.[17]

Deepening partisan rancor, however, eventually eroded the odd alliance and ended the potential for training reform in the 104th Congress. The Senate held fast to its doubts about vouchers and its insistence on putting state governments firmly in charge.[18] As the 1996 presidential election approached, the administration's erstwhile allies in the House were not anxious to give Clinton the occasion for a bill-signing ceremony. Voucher-based training reform had been trumped, for a time, by the state-centered status quo, and by the rival reform idea of preserving public training programs under strengthened state control.

EDUCATION IN AN ERA OF DEVOLUTION

By longstanding custom the federal government maintains a subordinate role in American education. Public funding for primary and secondary education reached about $260 billion in total for the 1993–94 school year. The federal share was just over 7 percent of this. (See Figure 8.) Local government accounted for the largest fraction (about 47 percent), with state spending only a little lower.[19]

Figure 8
K-12 Education Funding 1993–1994
(Total Public Funding: $260 Billion)

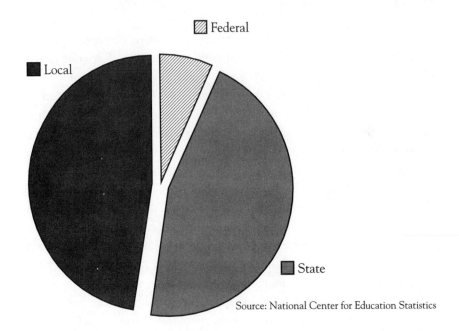

Source: National Center for Education Statistics

For *higher* education, government overall accounts for about two-fifths of total resources (with tuition and private grants covering most of the rest.) About 65 percent of this public share is from the states.[20] Of the $212 billion in total state spending on education in 1992, 56 percent was in the form of aid to local school districts, 36 percent went to state colleges and universities, and the remainder was divided among scholarships, aid to private schools, primary and secondary education programs run directly by the states, and administrative costs.[21]

Public education presents a sobering story to prophets of decentralized government's superior efficiency. Few major endeavors within the public sector are so heavily weighted toward state and local authority; none, perhaps, has fallen so short of citizens' legitimate expectations. A reform commission warned of a "rising tide of mediocrity" throughout American education in the 1983 report titled *A Nation at Risk*. A few years later, President George Bush summoned the governors to an intergovernmental summit meeting—only the third such meeting in American history—to discuss the crisis in education. Both Bush and Clinton gave rhetorical prominence to education that was echoed, at least in part, in budgetary priorities; federal spending on education rose from about $55 billion in 1988 (expressed in constant 1995 dollars) to $65 billion in 1992 and $74 billion in 1995.[22]

Neither president, though, challenged the states' dominance of education policy. While Clinton's "Goals 2000" initiative—largely a continuation of Bush Administration efforts—was sometimes pilloried as an attempt at centralizing control over the schools, its national standards are almost entirely voluntary. Nor was Clinton, who had made his national reputation as a governor crusading for school reform, much inclined to encroach on state autonomy even had the political climate permitted. In a 1996 address to the National Governors' Association Clinton declared (accommodatingly, if erroneously) that "the governors . . . have constitutional responsibility for the conditions of our public schools."[23]

Decentralized education policy is not enshrined in the Constitution (although President Clinton is by no means the only one to harbor illusions on this point.) It is rather a matter of tradition, political preference, and the accumulation over time of institutional capacity. Calls for greater centralization of curriculum, finance, or (most rarely) management are occasionally heard. But the federal government commands neither the popular legitimacy nor the capacity to take operational responsibility for American education. There is room for more ambitious and better targeted federal efforts to supplement state and local education activities. A serious case can be made for national standards that go beyond the exhortations and voluntary options of current practice, and indeed Clinton endorsed a version of such standards in his 1997 State of the Union address. More promising, however, are innovations like charter schools that dilute the influence of both state and local government through augmenting the authority of citizens themselves. The federal government already gives moral support and limited financial reinforcement to the charter school movement. More tangible aid—including large-scale financial support—is certainly conceivable. But the future of American education—at least the *immediate* future— will be set for the most part in the state capitals. The states' incentives and capacities to fund education adequately, and to manage it well, become correspondingly important.

The skill-building challenge is growing not just in urgency, but also in scale. Primary and secondary school enrollment, after declining through the 1980s and increasing slowing in the early 1990s, is expected to surge as the baby-boom echo works its way through the schools, from roughly 45 million students in 1995 to around 50 million in 2005.[24] Education Secretary Richard W. Riley warned in mid-1996 that enrollment increases would require the construction of six thousand new schools over the following decade (at an average cost of $10 million) in addition to the $112 billion in unmet construction needs the General Accounting Office had identified in America's eighty thousand existing schools.[25] This implies a reversal of recent trends. While *per-pupil* expenditures increased in recent years as enrollments fell, education spending as a share of total state expenditure declined slightly, from around 34 percent in 1980 to 30 percent in 1992.[26]

Will the states prove to be faithful stewards of American education as challenges mount? The question will not really be resolved until after the turn of the century, when enrollments peak amid the budgetary pressures of a devolutionary era (and after a recession has reality-tested budgetary expectations). There is certainly a plausible case for optimism. Education is among the most popular public undertakings in almost every state. Some governors are clearly making education—or at least some parts of the education agenda—an exception to their reigning themes of austerity. Consider some governors' 1996 budget plans: In Maryland, Governor Glendening's proposed budget called for a decline in inflation-adjusted state spending, but a large increase for community-college construction and renovation.[27] New Jersey Governor Whitman's austerity budget included stagnant or reduced higher-education funds, but a sharp increase in primary and secondary education spending. (Court judgments requiring parity in education spending among districts doubtless affected Whitman's priorities.[28]) Massachusetts Governor Weld accompanied his call for additional tax cuts with a declaration that "in the long run, nothing is more critical than education and training." His budget proposal did indeed preserve resources for primary and secondary education reform (though higher education budgets were cut sharply).[29]

Economic development imperatives are conventionally thought to ensure states' emphasis on education and training. Governors, legislative leaders, and their advisers are fully aware of the links between skills, productivity, and earning power. In the words of one observer of state policy trends, "state leaders now believe that failure to educate children and prepare them for work will undermine the competitiveness of the entire state economy."[30] Corporate CEOs attending the 1996 Governors' Education Summit committed themselves to "considering the quality of a state's academic standards . . . as a high-priority factor in determining business location decisions."[31] (The executives did specify that school quality was only one factor among many, and that others could carry greater weight.) Companies care about schools both as the sources of their future workers' skills, and because bad schools make it hard to hire and keep good workers. Empirical research has shown that productivity levels differ substantially from state to state, and that the skill level of a state's workforce is a significant determinant of productivity.[32] Prudent states, then, might be expected to sow the seeds of future prosperity by investing heavily in education and training.

America's history also offers a comforting example of states and localities stepping up to an educational challenge comparable in some respects to today's. The expansion of high school education that fueled economic growth and narrowed earnings inequality earlier in this century was orchestrated and paid for by lower-level government. States and cities did *not* seem to be motivated solely by concern for their own economic futures (or if so motivated, they were often disappointed). Rich agricultural states with weak prospects for manufacturing—including Nebraska, Nevada, and Kansas—plowed revenues originating on the farm into high school educations for their young citizens, research by Claudia Goldin reveals. But rather than reaping the benefit—more productive populations, faster economic growth, and higher revenues—these areas "exported" their human capital (in the form of educated migrants) to faster-growing manufacturing regions.[33]

Optimists can argue from economic, political, and historical grounds that states will shoulder their responsibilities for education and job training. Yet the upbeat examples have their darker counterparts. As Weld, Whitman, and Glendening were releasing 1996 budgets that enshrined education as a priority, for instance, California Governor Pete Wilson's budget proposal featured large tax cuts along with inflation-adjusted declines in per-pupil primary and secondary education funding.[34] New York's Governor George E. Pataki's budget proposal called for additional rounds of tax relief and, among the offsetting budget cuts, large reductions in state aid to the City University of New York and the State University of New York, and the diversion of $100 million in lottery proceeds from school funding to tax relief. Pataki also called for diluting the compensatory theme of New York's education policy by inaugurating a new state scholarship for the brightest students—regardless of financial need—while cutting off all state aid to students with grade-point averages below a C.[35] Pataki's proposals were amplifications of a general trend: Tuition increases at state colleges have been accelerating through the 1990s as state government covers a shrinking share of education costs.[36]

Education austerity is sometimes linked directly to business-attraction campaigns. This seems puzzling on its face: Shelves are clogged with blue-ribbon commission reports declaring education the most vital investment for the information age, the key to economic development, the gateway to the middle class. Such conclusions have become clichés, transcending partisanship. They also happen to be the simple truth. Why, then, would states under competitive pressure neglect investments in human capital?

Most businesses *are* in favor of better education (not least because most business leaders care about their communities). But business tends to be *directly* interested in a narrow segment of the education system, affecting their employees' children and their own specific human-capital needs. And prudent firms, no matter what their stakes in good schools, will always prefer that they themselves, and their key employees, pay as small a share as possible of the costs.

In 1995 Cleveland announced that budgetary pressures would force it to close eleven schools—just as it was offering to spend $175 million on stadium improvements in hopes of dissuading its football team's planned move to Baltimore.[37] The Albuquerque suburb of Rio Rancho lured the world's largest chip-making operation with a $114 million incentive package tailored to meet the list of priorities Intel had circulated to officials in several states. The package included publicly funded training, subsidies for relocation costs, reductions in corporate income taxes, and a thirty-year exemption from property taxes—the source of school funding. Despite a 64 percent increase in *individual* property taxes, the school district proved unable to fund school construction to meet swelling enrollments. As production got under way at the new Intel plant, most primary and middle school students attended school in trailers or in classrooms packed to double capacity, and plans to build the first high school for the 44,000-resident town were derailed by shortfalls in property tax revenue. (When a front-page *Wall Street Journal* article linked the Intel incentive package with Rio Rancho's

foundering school system, Intel agreed to provide special support for local education.[38]) After luring Mercedes in 1993 with a package of tax
incentives and direct subsidies, Alabama had trouble coming up with
the funding. Governor Fob James, Jr., attempted to divert funds earmarked for education, but backed down after the Alabama Education
Association prepared a legal challenge.[39] Education officials called for
changes in the Kansas statute on tax abatements after International Paper was granted a 100 percent, two-year tax abatement with no review
of the impact on schools.[40]

These disquieting anecdotes could be dismissed as aberrations,
rather than portents of future trends, if there were broader grounds for
confidence in states' incentives to give education its proper weight. But
there are a number of depressingly logical reasons for beleaguered state
officials to skimp on schools. The most obvious is that education is usually a long-term investment. If a governor raises taxes to build skills,
most of the benefit (higher productivity, incomes, and revenue) will be
realized in future administrations. Even when officials are utterly convinced of the merits of education and training, they may be reluctant to
fund education at the expense of short-term tax relief, or of competing
spending with a more immediate payoff.

Timing aside, moreover, people aren't fixed assets. After all, the case
for any public spending on education and training—instead of leaving
skill-building to the market—is based in part on the mobility of human
capital, which weakens businesses' willingness to invest in worker skills.
But mobility also dilutes the incentives of *states* to invest in education.
Workers educated at the expense of one state can move away and apply
their productive skills elsewhere. Roughly 3 percent of Americans relocate from one state to another each year. The more educated the individual, in fact, the more likely he or she is to leave the state. Consider the
Census Bureau data for people age twenty-five or older (to avoid the bias
from newly minted college graduates heading off for their first jobs). Only
1.6 percent of high school dropouts moved interstate each year—based
on the 1981–94 average—compared to 2.2 percent of high school graduates; 2.9 percent of workers with some postsecondary education; and 3.9
percent of college graduates.[41] In other words, if a state ensures that a
worker gets a college degree, instead of dropping out of high school, part
of the reward is doubling the probability of losing that worker to another
state. Ballot box pressures will partly counter this narrow economic calculus, to be sure. And both interstate mobility and the differential between more- and less-educated workers in the propensity to move, have

been declining in recent years.[42] But the mobility of human capital clouds confident predictions that development-minded states will emphasize education.[43]

Perhaps the most serious cause for doubting the long-term durability of states' commitment to skill-building, however, is that education and training policy has a distributional element—an element that becomes more important as economic inequality deepens. In an earlier era of human-capital development, according to Claudia Goldin and Lawrence Katz, publicly funded education "enabled those from less fortunate circumstances to enter the higher-paying occupations of the early twentieth century."[44] The political climate prevailing in those days proved hospitable to aggressive state and local spending on education—even though some of the benefits fell to other jurisdictions, and even though the wealthy often carried a disproportionate burden of paying for the schools that mattered most to their less fortunate fellow citizens. The politics can play out differently, as Thomas Jefferson learned in pre-Constitutional Virginia. Education was close to Jefferson's heart; he directed that his epitaph record his founding of the University of Virginia, rather than his presidency of the United States. One of Jefferson's earlier forays into education reform, however, foundered on the politics of inequality. Jefferson had proposed for Virginia a public education system modeled on innovations in New England. But the initiative failed in large part because "the Virginia elite, on whom the bulk of the taxation would fall, had no intention of paying for the education of their poorer neighbors' children."[45]

The political tension inherent in taxing the mobile, the well-off, and the childless to pay for education spending that matters most to the less skilled, the less affluent, and those with large families could quite plausibly lead states to scale back their overall commitment to human-capital development.[46] Still more likely is a selective retreat, paring back the redistributive aspects of education and training, and concentrating on what concerns businesses and more mobile individuals. The starkest pressures, in any case, remain to be faced, including the full effects of anticipated tax cuts and the fiscal damage that an economic downturn or two will inflict on state budgets. The jury is still out on whether officials will preserve the priority of broad-based education and training. But the stakes are high enough to render discomforting the risk that the states will falter as stewards of skill-building in the coming devolutionary era.

CHAPTER NINE

The Endless Argument's Next Stage

America confronts three subtly related challenges in the century's waning years. First is to mitigate the cynicism that has soured our politics for a generation. Second is to narrow the chasm between the benefits citizens expect from government and their willingness to endure taxation. Third is to contain pressures toward economic inequality and reverse the erosion of the middle class. If the public sector's center of gravity continues to shift toward the states, there will certainly be *some* advantages; no change of that scale can fail to register on both the credit and the debit side of the ledger. But on balance, devolution will prove to be a detour, a disappointment, or a misstep toward engaging these fundamental problems.

DISTRUST OF GOVERNMENT

Alienation from government has become an American epidemic. Attitudes about the public sector have deteriorated well past the point of

healthy skepticism, becoming a reflexive cynicism about the possibilities of collective action. As we saw in Chapter One, Americans retain
more trust in state and local government than in Washington, and advocates of devolution advertise the potential for restoring confidence
in the public sector by shifting authority to levels of government held
in more esteem. A well-founded promise of renewing citizens' trust in
their public institutions would be enough on its own—even in the face
of major objections on other grounds—to convert many to the cause of
devolution.

One way devolution could repair confidence in government, of
course, is by making government work better. But superior performance
isn't strictly necessary. Citizens might be more accepting of state-dominated government if the process of policy-making seems more familiar
and less mysterious. States might also benefit from a psychological phenomenon by which individuals are often contemptuous of a general
category while exempting from scorn their own member of the class. A
great many people see car mechanics in general as inept and dishonest,
for example, but revere their own mechanic; others lament the sorry
state of public education while giving their children's school high
marks; and still others cheerfully reelect their congressman while
damning Congress as a cesspool of corruption and foolishness. Devolution might put this tendency to work shoring up American attitudes toward government, even if performance stays the same—and if
performance improves, so much the better.

But states enjoy greater public esteem in part because the federal
government has been responsible for some of government's more
thankless tasks, including welfare, immigration, and Social Security's
massive transfer from workers (who resent it, and doubt they'll get
their turn) to retirees (who view their benefit checks as no more than
their due). Federal taxes actually cover over one-fifth of state and local
spending, distorting perceptions of which level delivers the most value
for taxes paid. Citizens tend to identify Washington as "the government" and vent their dissatisfaction accordingly, absolving states and
cities as junior accomplices. But as the states take on more responsibilities they will draw a corresponding share of public hostility unless
they prove markedly better at earning public esteem through efficiency. Antipathy toward government will thus be rearranged—but
not diminished.

Popular support for state government, moreover, is a relative thing.

Only 25 percent of Americans surveyed for a major 1995 study trusted the federal government to always or usually "do the right thing." But citizens' confidence in their *state* government was only modestly greater—35 percent instead of 25 percent. A renaissance of American commonwealth arguably requires something more impressive than earning the trust of one citizen in three, instead of one citizen in four.[1] The defects of size, complexity, and opacity that alienate citizens from the federal government are attenuated only slightly in the states. Indeed, rather than striking a happy balance between local impotence and federal paralysis, for some important governmental functions states may be poised at just the wrong level of aggregation—too small to engage global challenges or take proper account of national consequences, but too large for the civic intimacy that can cement citizens' trust. Worse, if the ascendancy of the states leads to disappointing performance, or a tilt toward policies inimical to many citizens' interests—as is more than plausible—then devolution will *deepen* disillusionment with politics, and propel another turn in the spiraling decline of trust in government.

GOVERNMENTAL EFFICIENCY

There is an alluring a priori case for predicting that public-sector efficiency will increase as responsibilities flow to lower levels of government. Yet this *potential* advantage largely fails to pan out; there is little evidence of a significant or systematic state efficiency edge. The states share with Washington the basic operational handicaps of the public sector.

The devolution debate, moreover, is almost wholly irrelevant to the debt service and middle-class entitlements causing most of the strain on citizens' tolerance for taxation. It is safe to assert that the ascendancy of the states will have, at best, a limited impact on the cost of American government. This is not an argument based on ideology, or economic theory, or learned predictions about comparative administrative behavior. It is a matter of arithmetic. In 1996 total public spending came to about $2.3 trillion. State and local activities, funded by state and local taxes, *already* accounted for about one-third of this total. Another one-third consisted of check-writing programs like Social Security and Medicare. National defense (12 percent of the total), interest on the national debt (10 percent), and federal grants to state and local governments (another 10 percent) accounted for most of the remaining third of the public sector. All other federal domestic undertakings, taken together, claimed between 4 and 5 percent of total government spending.[2] Suppose every last thing the federal government does, aside from running defense and foreign affairs and writing checks (to entitlement claimants, debt holders, and state and local governments) were transferred to the states—national parks and museums, air-traffic control, the FBI, the border patrol, the Centers for Disease Control, the National Weather Service, student loans, the space program, and all the rest. Suppose, then, that the states proved able to do *everything* that the federal government used to do a full 10 percent more efficiently. The cost of government would fall by a little under one-half of one percent.

Beyond the low ceiling on cost savings—and more pertinent to the hidden issue of the *quality* of government—is the similarity between most federal agencies and most state agencies on the core characteristics of scale, complexity, and administration by legislative statute and formal rules. It is rare that economic or managerial imperatives will call for the reassignment of authority away from central government, but then stop at the states. State boundaries have been drawn by a capricious history, and only occasionally (and then by accident) does a state constitute the most logical economic unit for either making policy or delivering services. The coalition between the state-sovereignty constitutionalists and the efficient-scale decentralizers is based on a misunderstanding, and will break down as soon as it begins to succeed.

More promising strategies for improving the efficiency with which public purposes are pursued usually involve going *beyond* devolution to the states. The array of options includes privatization, to enlist private-sector efficiency advantages in the service of public goals; vouchers, to assign purchasing power while letting individuals choose how to deploy it; and the empowerment (through authority and resources) of levels of government smaller than the state, including cities, towns, and school districts. None of these strategies is without its risks and limits, but together they form a far richer menu of reform possibilities than the simple switch from federal to state bureaucracy.

Devolution is often, though misleadingly, cast as a way station toward such fundamental reforms. Its popularity among those convinced of American government's shortcomings, and committed to repairing them, diverts reformist energy that could be put to better use. State governments are only slightly, if any, less bureaucratic than Washington, and no less jealous of power or resistant to change. Power dislodged from federal bureaus is likely to stick at the state level instead of diffusing further. The characteristic pattern of American intergovernmental relations is rivalry between state and local officials, and Washington more often acts as local government's shield against state hegemony than as the common oppressor of cities and states. The ascendancy of the states is thus unlikely either to liberate local governments or to unleash fundamental reform in how government operates.

RISING INEQUALITY

It is by no means certain that America will prove able to reverse growing economic inequality and the erosion of the middle class, no matter how we structure our politics. Devolution, however, will worsen the odds. Shared prosperity, amid the maelstrom of economic change tearing away at the industrial underpinnings of middle-class culture, is an artifact of policy. Policies to shore up the middle class include work-based antipoverty efforts that become both more important and more expensive as unskilled jobs evaporate; relentless investments in education and job training; measures to strengthen employees' leverage in the workplace; and a more progressive tilt in the overall burden of taxation. The individual states—each scrambling to lure mobile capital, fearful of losing businesses and well-off residents to lower-tax rivals, anxious to minimize their burden of needy citizens—will find such policies nearly impossible to sustain. As Washington sheds responsibilities and interstate rivalry intensifies, only a small-government agenda becomes realistic.[3] But even for principled small-government conservatives, devolution is likely to prove less satisfying than many expect. Since it has been justified in terms of improving, not shrinking, government, the ascendancy of the states represents no conclusion to the debate over the public sector's proper size and scope.

Like the run-up in federal debt in the 1980s and early 1990s, devolution short-circuits (rather than settles) deliberation over government's purpose by making activism impossible—for a time. America's federal system is sufficiently resilient that unless citizens are convinced of small government's merits, the tilt toward the states that suppress public-

sector ambition will eventually be reversed, though only after an unpre-
dictable price has been paid. The conservative intellectual Herbert
Storing has argued that a strategy of crippling the activist impulse
through devolution, instead of discrediting it through reasoned appeal,
was "not only contrary to the best conservative tradition but also hope-
lessly unrealistic."[4] By attempting to enthrone the states as the sole locus of legitimate government, conservatives muffle their own voices in
the conversation over the country's future.

By the standards of those who credit any diagnosis of what ails
America *other than* "big government," shifting authority to competing
states is likely to solve minor problems while causing, or perpetuating,
far graver ills. As states gain a greater share of governmental duties but
prove reluctant or unable to tax mobile firms or well-off individuals,
the burden of funding the public sector will tilt even more heavily toward middle-class taxpayers. Their resentment of government can be
expected to intensify. Efforts to use state laws or regulations to
strengthen employees' leverage in the workplace will often be rendered unworkable by interstate competition for business. America's
largest source of fiscal imbalance—the unsustainability of middle-class
entitlement programs as the baby boom generation ages—will be un-
touched by devolution, feeding cynicism about the imperviousness to
solution of America's public problems. And the fragmentation of taxing and spending authority puts in peril the education and training
agenda that defines our single most promising tactic for shoring up the
middle class.

The global marketplace both gives new fuel to America's culture of
opportunity *and* allows the range of economic conditions experienced
within this erstwhile middle-class country to reflect, with less and less
filtering, the whole planet's disparate array of fates. A middle-class national economy, within a world of economic extremes, is a precious but
unnatural thing. The policies that sustain shared prosperity will be difficult, perhaps impossible, to pursue if America's center of gravity in
economic policy-making continues its precipitous shift toward the separate states. Federal officials, as a class, are certainly no wiser, more far-
sighted, or defter at implementation than their state counterparts. But
our country as a whole remains much less subject to the flight of wealth
and the influx of need than are its constituent states. Policies to shrink
the underclass and solidify the middle class are thus far more sustainable at the federal level.

Toward a New Balance

How, then, should America recalibrate its federal-state balance to meet contemporary challenges? Six broad propositions crystallize from the analysis laid out here. They will not be the final word on the proper tuning of America's federal system—as if any assessment could ever be—but are offered as a contribution, and perhaps a catalyst, to the next installment of America's endless argument.

Do Devolve—Where It Makes Sense. Underscoring devolution's limits should not be misconstrued as belittling the benefits of moving public functions as far down the federal scale as possible. Many responsibilities *do* belong at the state level. Where states vary greatly in circumstances or goals, where external impacts are minor or manageable, where the payoff from innovation exceeds the advantages of uniformity, and where competition boosts efficiency instead of inspiring destructive stratagems, the central government should stand clear—both to honor our culture's durable preference for decentralized power and to forestall federal overload. For similar reasons, Congress should avoid the inevitable temptations to circumvent post-1995 curbs on unfunded mandates. Imposing duties on lower-level governments with no reckoning of the costs (just like states ignoring the consequences of their actions for the national commons) flouts fundamental imperatives of governmental accountability. The list of public functions where Washington has little legitimate role is long and important.[5] But it is shorter (not longer) today than it was a quarter-century ago, and will be shorter still another quarter-century hence. And the impetus for decentralization should seldom stop at the state level.

Restore Federal Primacy in Antipoverty Policy. The devolution of antipoverty policy will eventually be seen as a mistake, if perhaps an inevitable mistake. The Gordian knot of the welfare status quo may have been beyond untangling by the mid-1990s. We will never know; the first Clinton Administration, in its critical early days, puts its chips on health care and gave its welfare reform plan short shrift, eventually ceding the issue to Congress. But with the first serious recession (if not before), state-based welfare policy's built-in bias toward undue harshness will be revealed. As hard times swell the ranks of needy families while hobbling job-creation efforts; as welfare must compete with every other budget item for shrinking state funds; and as taxpayers and officials ponder the prospect (always riveting, and increasingly realistic) that anything but the sparest safety net will lure the poor from other states, antipoverty programs will spiral toward the furthest degree of austerity citizens' consciences will permit.[6] Budgetary and political realities at the federal level will preclude reversing course anytime soon. Nor is there yet any agreed-upon blueprint for how to achieve the humane, work-oriented welfare policy that virtually everyone endorses in principle. We have embarked upon a period of state-dominated antipoverty policy, and may as well make the best of it by harvesting every bit of evidence state experimentation produces, to be analyzed and stockpiled for the eventual reconstruction of a national system. And we should hope that the country does not become too coarsened by what we will witness in the meantime.

Recognize the States' Limits as Stewards of Education. Chapter Eight flagged the risk that pressure on revenues, and the accumulation of competing burdens, may lead states to fumble their longstanding responsibilities for education and training—and at precisely the point in history when human-capital policy is soaring in importance. At a minimum, Washington should enlarge its role in higher-education finance, where the states are already retreating. Beyond that, previous rounds of reform suggest that state agencies have neither the capacity nor the incentives to pursue the campaign of job training required to accelerate the adaptation of America's workforce—especially not through conventional bureaucratic programs. Choice and competition, rather than devolution, should thus serve as the guiding principles for job-training reform. The federal role in primary and secondary education will, and should, remain limited, but national performance standards ought to undergird state and local reform efforts. Innovations such as charter schools can go devolution one better, meanwhile, by moving decisions a good deal *closer* to the people. And throughout, we must be vigilant against the prospect that budgetary pressures and fractious politics will lead states to abandon the campaign of sustained, universal human-capital investment that is the best hope of preserving America's middle-class culture. The odds of this surrender occurring remain difficult to gauge; the calamitous consequences should it happen are all too clear.

Curb the Courtship of Capital. Not least to lower the risk that budgetary pressures will trigger a retreat from broad-based education investment, Washington should bridle interstate competition for business. In other countries or other times, bidding wars for capital might well be benign—as a counter to antibusiness cultures and a rampant public sector, or where global capital would shun a country unless rivalry among locales forced down costs. But in the contemporary United States their chief effect is to warp state priorities, with no net national gains. Citizens would be well-served by the sturdiest curbs the Constitution will permit on state location subsidies and tax incentives. The best approach would be through national legislation that alters states' incentives to offer such inducements, or companies' incentives to accept them. An alternative championed by some legal scholars would be to challenge in court the constitutional legitimacy of inducements that (arguably) distort interstate commerce. Congress is not likely anytime soon to pass legislation bridling bidding wars, and the judicial approach could serve as a stopgap. But any remedies achieved through legal challenges are likely to be incomplete and (by any economic calculus) inelegant.

Reduce the States' Dependence on Their Own Tax Revenues. By far the most reliable effect of the states' ascendancy will be downward pressure on the size of the overall public sector. Limiting bidding wars for mobile businesses would plug only one leak in our federal system's fiscal structure.[7] American public finance requires far broader reform, unless we aim to tacitly endorse automatic austerity through fiscal fragmentation. Tax competition, as a device for disciplining government, is mostly redundant with the ballot box, and where its effects are distinctive they are seldom benign. The conceptual case for raising funds centrally is considerably stronger now than it was when the Nixon Administration first launched general revenue sharing in 1969: States have taken on new burdens and their traditional responsibilities (especially education) have surged in importance, while the "mobility gap" between capital and citizens has widened, constraining and distorting state taxation. The federal financial context, to be sure, is a good deal bleaker than it was in Nixon's day; there is no extra revenue to share, and little prospect of any on the budgetary horizon. But when we next revisit basic principles of public finance—as we likely will before the new century gets too far along—high on the tax-reform agenda should be bringing the United States closer to the model prevailing in other federal countries: subnational tax policy closely coordinated, and fiscal competition tightly circumscribed.[8]

Fix the Federal Government. The notion that devolution can spare us the chore of federal reform is a dangerous mirage. A feeble federal government served Americans badly in the 1780s, and will do far worse today. We must reconstruct Washington's often-primitive personnel and budgeting systems, build on recent improvements in procurement rules, and redouble efforts to make federal operations more efficient, innovative, and accountable. Serious federal reform may not be any gentler than devolution to the public-sector status quo. Quite the contrary—it will often involve privatization, vouchers, and more traumatic "reinvention" than Washington has seen so far. But there is no inconsistency in pursuing common goals through means that make the most of the market. Beyond such procedural improvements, we must confront the politically difficult budgetary decisions needed to rebalance federal priorities and to forestall Washington's scheduled retreat into near-irrelevance throughout much of the domestic sphere. This is a tall order, to be sure, and cannot be accomplished without at least a partial restoration of the federal government's popular legitimacy.

The embrace of devolution risks truncating a painful but vital national conversation over the scale and purpose of America's public sector. Citizens resent the cost of big government and endorse a reversal of its postwar growth, but they tend to resist giving up its benefits. For two decades the electorate has groped toward a resolution of this anguished ambiguity, harvesting hard-won lessons from each seduction by politicians promising more for less, austerity without pain, or sacrifice only for others. Happily, the debate is becoming by degrees more realistic and less specious: Many on the left now less reflexively resist privatization, work-oriented welfare reform, the urgency of productivity growth. Many on the right are becoming more candid that fiscal discipline involves sacrifices for all, not just feckless bureaucrats and the unworthy poor.

Grown-up politics, in short, just may be within our reach at last. But the federal retreat and the states' advance threaten to replace deliberation with a headlong spiral toward a single option—government that is solicitous of a few favored interests, and otherwise austere. "Shrink government" is one honorable answer to the problems that bedevil America. But it should not be the only option. Paradoxically, if we want to have a free choice over the big questions of government's scale and purpose—whether and how we intend to prepare all willing workers for rewarding roles in the world economy; the terms on which our citizens engage global capital; how we should share the risks and burdens of economic change—we must choose together, as a nation. Fifty separate choices sum to no choice at all.

We must not needlessly impose uniformity on our vast and varied nation; the vitality our diversity affords is one American trump card. But the other is national unity. Finding the right federal balance will be—as it has always been—a matter of detailed analysis and debate, policy by policy. The search for specific solutions, however, first requires debunking today's prevailing sentiment that devolution offers an easy alternative to national reform.

Enchanted by the advantages of state autonomy, we are rushing to abandon the far greater advantages of a continent-scale common front with which to face the coming century's economic pressures. Cultural fragmentation and the erosion of our sense of community are much-noted, much-lamented contemporary trends. Yet if we fail to reassert shared purpose in the *economic* realm, state boundaries may become fault lines along which the American commonwealth will fracture. If we neglect the institutional foundations of national solidarity, the strains on our culture will become all the harder to contain. And the United States' willing dis-integration, in the face of an integrating world, will be recorded as one of history's monumental follies.

Declaring devolution a false path to reform will not be a particularly popular conclusion, I recognize, in an era so skeptical about government and so dubious that Washington can ever be made to work. Fixing the federal government is an intimidating proposition, and it is all too understandable that we grope for alternatives. The trajectory of fiscal and political trends suggests that devolution will remain the focus of politicians' promises and citizens' hopes for some time to come.

But the inherent limits of a fragmented approach to national adaptation will eventually inspire America to reappraise the ascendancy of the states. Not too far into the new century we will again collect the resolve to confront together our common fate. And we will once more take up, in the two-century tradition of Americans before us, the echoing challenge of George Washington's 1796 farewell address: "Is there a doubt whether a common government can embrace so large a sphere? Let experience solve it."[9]

APPENDIX

Research on the Impact of Business-Attraction Policies

Whether or not supply-side inducements are important enough in the calculus of investment to make a difference in drawing firms and capital to a particular place," writes Peter Eisinger, "has been of such substantial importance for public policy and at the same time so intractably difficult to answer that it has generated an enormous but finally inconclusive literature."[1] This appendix surveys some of this literature and attempts—despite Eisinger's warning—to come to at least a tentative conclusion about the trajectory of expert opinion.

Researchers have employed two basic strategies for assessing business-attraction efforts—each strategy valuable, and each imperfect, in its own way. One approach for determining how government policies affect location decisions of business managers (and surely the most straightforward) is simply to ask business managers how government policies affect their location decisions. The other generic approach involves using statistical tools to isolate the effect of decisions about taxing and spending on the pattern of economic activity within a state.

172 Appendix

SURVEY RESEARCH

Before turning to surveys of business officials on the relative importance of business-attraction policies, consider briefly the other side of
the transaction—the attitude of public officials who design and deploy
such policies. Abelardo Limon, Jr., in a survey of economic development officials (urban, in this case, rather than state) discovered that a
large majority believed tax reductions and targeted financial incentives
to be "extremely effective" in attracting investment, although somewhat less important, on balance, than local labor forces, markets, and
transportation networks.[2]

Surveys of business managers similarly suggest that access to markets and inputs are the most important factors in location decisions,
but different surveys yield different conclusions on the impact of public policies. Earlier studies, interestingly, find relatively small effects.
Eva Mueller and James N. Morgan, in a careful 1962 study for the
American Economic Review, conducted extensive structured interviews
with the top managers of 239 representative Michigan manufacturing
firms. Managers of *new* establishments reported that labor cost, proximity to markets, and the availability of skilled labor all mattered more
than tax levels. Mueller and Morgan found as well that "historical accident and the personal preferences of the founders" played important,
sometimes dominant, roles in determining location, especially for
smaller firms. Only 3 percent of employers mentioned taxes or location inducements as a primary reason for choosing to invest in Michigan (although 7 percent said such factors affected the decision about
where to locate *within* Michigan).[3] Established firms considering relocation *did* cite tax levels as significant factors in choosing a new location—but only 4 percent of companies with growing sales and payrolls
reported that they were open to relocating their operations; ailing
firms were more apt to move. For companies opening new branch
plants, input costs and proximity to markets were mentioned about
twice as often as wage levels or tax burdens.[4]

The Mueller and Morgan study did not dismiss tax levels or location inducements as irrelevant. But it cast them as decidedly subordinate factors compared to access to markets and inputs (especially
labor)—at least for Michigan manufacturers in the early 1960s. Benjamin Bridges, Jr. (in a somewhat less intensive review, but one based
on broader data), reached similar conclusions from the early-1960s sur-

vey data that location incentives were "certainly a secondary factor in the choice of region and probably also a secondary factor in the choice of location within a region."[5] In the 1970s a series of informal surveys and "business-climate" rankings by consultants and business magazines sought to establish tax levels and business-friendly policies generally as major determinants of location decisions. But more scientific surveys continued to show other factors dominating site selection, while taxes and location inducements, in most cases, had little weight.[6]

While surveys suggested that taxes and incentives *did* affect the location of multinational (including U.S.–based) firms within Europe, mid-1980s studies found such factors to be minor elements in the location decisions of German and Japanese firms in the United States.[7] H. I. Chernotsky surveyed twenty-one of the 105 multinational corporations located in or near Charlotte, North Carolina—fourteen German, and seven Japanese—who reported that labor quality mattered greatly; labor cost and unionization less so; taxes were of minor significance; and firm-specific location incentives essentially had no importance.[8] A survey study by Takeshi Nakabayashi covering fifty-nine Japanese firms operating in the United States found that "factors which cannot be readily controlled or upgraded by states, such as proximity to market, productivity of labor, presence of unions and so forth, are commonly considered as being of major importance."[9] About 40 percent of the respondents reported being offered specific incentives (typically tax breaks, training subsidies, or low-interest loans) but only three of the fifty-nine respondents said they would have located elsewhere without the incentives. These Japanese managers, interestingly, invoked reasons other than financial ones in their assessment of incentives. The fact that states were willing to offer costly incentives, and that high-level officials were willing to make the offers in person, seemed to be taken as a signal of goodwill, independent of any economic significance. At the same time, many managers reported a reluctance to take on the burden of obligation—for example, to hire disadvantaged workers—that they perceived, rightly or wrongly, to go along with financial incentives.[10]

Writing against the backdrop of industrial decline in the mid-1970s Northeast, Bennett Harrison and Sandra Kanter expressed great skepticism about the efficacy of business-attraction policies. They argued that state and local taxes were too small a share of total costs (citing estimates in the range of 4 to 6 percent of sales) to matter greatly in location decisions, and reiterated the theme that economic fundamentals would usually outweigh location incentives of any feasible magnitude, rendering location policy either futile or superfluous. Harrison and Kanter reviewed survey data showing that only 9 percent of companies moving into Michigan, 15 percent of those *leaving* New York City, and 11 percent of those investing in Southern states ranked tax levels as major factors. Conducting their own in-depth interviews with officials of several firms benefiting from economic development incentives in Massachusetts, they learned that in every case "the company took actions according to its own plans, *then* learned about the existence of the tax credits and applied for them, often at the explicit urging of the state bureaucrats in charge of the program."[11]

A few years later Michael Kieschnick surveyed 337 firms in ten states, finding that very few of them (about 3 percent of new firms, 6 percent of branch plants, and none of the firms expanding operations at an existing plant) reported that they would have located in another state in the absence of tax incentives.[12] In the late 1980s a team from Arthur Andersen and Company surveyed 250 senior executives for large companies doing business in several states. Half the respondents reported making no effort to monitor the impact of state and local taxes on profit levels, and many had no idea what portion of the total tax bill state and local taxes represented. Nearly half agreed with the statement, "Compared to other issues I deal with daily, state and local taxes are of little importance to me," and 55 percent reported that the advantages of their location—including access to labor and markets—justified paying a tax premium.[13]

A 1987 review article by John Blair and Robert Premus summarized survey research on industrial location, and hinted at some subtleties that other studies may have missed. In line with the research summarized above, Blair and Premus found that surveys conducted before the mid-1970s found proximity to markets, labor, and (sometimes) raw materials overwhelmed taxes and financial incentives in business location decisions. But as markets became more integrated and transportation and communications networks improved through the 1970s and 1980s, physical proximity to customers receded somewhat in importance.

A study of 204 firms from other states (or nations) opening plants in North Carolina, South Carolina, or Virginia in the 1977–82 period found market access less important than the cost and availability of labor and land. And nearly seven hundred surveyed executives from relatively technology-intensive industries reported that they placed primary importance (in descending order) on the availability of appropriately skilled workers; the cost of labor; proximity to a university; and taxes (including personal as well as corporate taxes, an increasingly important cost factor for firms whose main productive factor was highly skilled, relatively well-paid workers). For these high-tech executives, traditional location factors like raw materials and market access mattered little—consistent with the notion that high-value, low-weight products made it cheap and easy to serve distant markets from whatever locale offered an attractive production platform.[14]

Overall, Blair and Premus's research suggested that "industrial location choices are governed to a lesser extent than in the past by access to markets, labor, transportation, and raw materials," and that state and local taxes, physical infrastructure, and the quality of the workforce—all factors affected by policy decisions—were rising in importance. Specific financial incentives, they suggested, might in principle "have a higher payoff than in the past."[15] Robert Walker and David Greenstreet, in statistical research based on survey responses from 742 manufacturers in Appalachia, found that *within* the region "incentive offerings are decisive to a plant's final choice of locality."[16] And a survey published in 1995 by KPMG-Peat Marwick offered suggestive (though not scientific) corroboration that firms were becoming less rooted by economic fundamentals, and more readily swayed by location policies. Only one-third of the 203 executives surveyed declared that they would *not* relocate their headquarters solely to collect tax incentives. While most were unable or unwilling to calibrate the scale of an incentive package that would motivate a relocation, the median dollar figure cited was $5 million.[17]

Survey research confronts inherent difficulties. Many surveys, including some cited above, are rendered suspect by problems in defining the universe to be sampled, in selecting the sample to be surveyed, or in ensuring a reasonable response rate. Even when researchers are scrupulous about designing and conducting surveys to minimize bias, their grasp on the truth can be weakened by respondents' tendency to give unreflective or flatly misleading answers. Business officials might downplay the significance of location inducements for fear of seeming too mercenary. Or they might amplify their true importance in hopes of bluffing officials into sweetening incentives or deterring burdens. Ronald Ferguson and Helen Ladd record a revealing example. When

Massachusetts passed legislation in 1983 that encouraged firms to give advance notice and adjustment assistance when closing plants, electronics company Augat Inc. declared that the burdensome new rules had inspired it to expand in Maine instead of Massachusetts. Some time later, when the legislature adopted new tax accounting rules opposed by many business groups, Augat once again called attention to its planned expansion in Maine—this time blaming the new tax law, not the plant-closing law, for forcing it to locate out of state.[18] It may have been that both factors influenced the location choice; it may have been that neither did. But even if Augat's choice had been based on factors that had nothing to do with state policy, a politically prudent business official might not lightly disclose the fact. This incentive to bluff, hedge, or dissimulate is well kept in mind when reviewing survey research.

STATISTICAL ANALYSIS

The literature on policy's leverage over business location is not limited to survey research. The other general approach is to watch what business decision-makers *do* in response to policy differences, not what they *say*—generally employing statistical techniques to impose some precision on the measure of "what they do." This typically involves assembling a large number of data points—by defining the scope of a study to include a long time period, many different jurisdictions, or both—and sifting the data through a methodological sieve (usually some variant of multiple regression) to sort out the connections between policy decisions and economic outcomes, while controlling for the ups and downs of the business cycle, long-term industrial change, demographics, and other factors aside from policy choices.

These statistical techniques can be subtle and sophisticated, and researchers often display great ingenuity in their application. Yet empirical research on economic development policies remains complex, controversial, and ultimately less than conclusive. There are many different plausible candidates for the "dependent variable"—the phenomenon to be explained—including the number of jobs in a state (all jobs, or restricted to jobs in designated sectors or exceeding certain wage levels); the average wage paid; the "gross state product" (a guage of value-added analogous to measure the more familiar national output); the unemployment rate, average family income; and so on. For each of these, one might focus on the absolute level, or on a state's rank within the nation, or on change over some period. Economic impacts might be assumed to be contemporaneous with policy changes, or "lagged" by one year, or five years, or some other interval.

For "independent variables"—the factors, including tax and subsidy policies, that are invoked to explain why the world turns out as it does—the causal impact attributed to any one variable depends on which others are included, and on the structure of the statistical model.[19] Reasonable independent variables might include distance from major markets; long-term trends in established industries; average wage levels; unionization rates; tax rates (on corporate income, personal income, or purchased inputs, as well as nontax payroll levies like workers' compensation or unemployment insurance premiums); investment in roads, bridges, and other physical infrastructure; the educational attainment of the workforce, or levels of public spending on education; the number, nature, and generosity of economic development programs; state laws and regulations governing the workplace, such as minimum wage or right-to-work laws; the state's overall level of taxing and spending; environmental regulations, and so on.[20] On independent variables as well, researchers must make choices about whether to introduce them as absolute levels, national rankings, or percentage changes, and whether to use current or lagged values and, if lagged, by how much.

Data limitations often force researchers to use models that they fully understand to be flawed. Models that include more than a handful of explanatory variables tend to collapse into inconclusive complexity, so analysts must impose an artificial simplicity. Seldom can independent variables be measured in precisely the right way. (For example, if a researcher believes that a state's stock of transportation infrastructure is an important determinant of business location, she will discover that nobody keeps track of additions to and depreciation of these assets in any systematic way, so she will turn to annual spending on roads and bridges as an imperfect proxy.) Nor are there good data on many important dependent variables. The Bureau of Labor Statistics at the U.S. Department of Labor, as well as the Commerce Department's Bureau of Economic Analysis and Bureau of the Census, collect a good deal of reliable, standardized information on employment, wages, production, and income. But data on business startups, retrenchments, expansions, and relocations—often the central object of location policies—is seldom available, at least not in the kind of consistent, standard form that makes for confident statistical inference. Private companies like accounting and consulting firms or credit agencies collect some information on business investment, as do the federal government's Labor and Commerce Departments and the Internal Revenue Service in the Treasury Department. These data are often unavailable to researchers, or available only with restrictions, or (if freely available) they prove to have been defined, collected, and organized in ways that suit their originators, but frustrate statistical research.

Some may find this litany of limitations to be exasperating, and conclude that the truth must be in the eye of the beholder. But any such interpretation would be unduly cynical; the complexity is with the world, not the statistical methods. I raise these points in part to help readers calibrate their expectations for conclusiveness, and in part as a tribute to the wit and persistence of the researchers whose work is summarized in this section. It is not at all surprising that a variety of conclusions can be found in the literature on the impact of state policies on business location decisions. And it is all the more remarkable that—while consensus is far too strong a term for what's occurring—opinion does seem to be coalescing on a view that gives more weight to state policies than was the case as recently as ten years ago.

One of the earliest econometric studies of how state policies affect economic development was done in 1959 by Wilbur R. Thompson and John M. Mattila, who attempted to test the reasonableness of state officials' "apprehension that firms are readily repelled by harsh tax treatment, and attracted by tax leniency."[21] Yet their study—ambitious by then-prevailing standards, if not by those of today—did not find differences in state taxes to be a significant determinant of employment growth in twenty-eight of the twenty-nine industries they examined. (The one exception was apparel.[22]) Jane Little found the location decisions of non–U.S. investors in the 1970s to be little affected by tax levels or investment incentives.[23] In the early 1980s Dennis Carlton undertook an intensive statistical analysis of three technology-intensive industries: fabricated plastics products, communications transmitting equipment, and electronic components. He found that a state's business climate—which he defined to include "positive" factors such as public loans for industrial investment, tax exemptions or abatements for corporate income, research and development spending, or purchases of land and capital equipment; technology promotion programs and right-to-work laws, as well as "negative" factors like state minimum-wage and fair employment laws—failed to have a discernible impact on location choice or employment levels. Nor did tax rates seem to matter significantly—perhaps, Carlton speculated, because state corporate taxes are ultimately passed on to workers and landowners, or perhaps because tax rates are very poor proxies for taxes actually *paid*.[24]

L. Jay Helms used fourteen years of data on forty-eight states to test the link between growth in personal income and a range of policy choices, finding positive and statistically significant (or nearly so) results for public spending on highways, education, and health care, but a strong negative effect of state spending on income transfer programs.[25] Thomas Plaut and Joseph Pluta constructed a massively ambitious model to explain state-by-state growth in manufacturing employment and value-added between the mid-1960s and the mid-1970s by reference to market access, the cost and availability of inputs, physical climate, and policy variables (including tax and spending levels). Their study, unlike some others at the time, found that relatively high taxes and policies perceived as unfriendly to business *did* deter investment and job growth (though they still mattered less than "traditional market factors"). Some peculiarities in their results, however, illustrate the hazards of statistical modeling. (For example, their model suggests that "industry is attracted to states with high wage rates" and to "states with a less productive labor force" and identifies a "positive relationship between welfare expenditures and industrial growth."[26])

Robert Newman sought to explain each state's job growth in thirteen broadly defined industries (relative to the national average for the same industries) from the mid-1950s to the mid-1970s in terms of only three explanatory variables: changes in each state's level of corporate taxation (relative to the national pattern); relative changes in the unionized fraction of the workforce; and whether the state has adopted right-to-work laws. By employing a fairly loose standard of statistical significance, Newman found a negative relationship between job growth and state tax levels in five of the thirteen industries, and a *positive* relationship between job growth and right-to-work laws for ten of the thirteen. The overall model gave a fairly scanty account of the national pattern of employment growth—not surprising, for so stripped-down a model—but Newman could claim with some plausibility that it lent "considerable support to the heretofore unsubstantiated argument that corporate tax rate differentials between states as well as the extent of unionization and favorable business climate have been major factors influencing the acceleration of industry movement to the South."[27] In later research with a colleague, Newman reviewed data from Pennsylvania, Ohio, Michigan, and Wisconsin to demonstrate that for some firms, at least, tax levels seemed to be important determinants of industrial location.[28]

Therese McGuire noted in the mid-1980s that "a consensus among researchers appears to be that *some* taxes do matter for *some* important decisions,"[29] while William Wheaton pored through state tax systems and concluded that "state and local taxation of businesses is not trivial anymore."[30] Leslie Papke, in a careful empirical study conducted a few years later, found that relatively high tax levels can depress the rate of corporate births in three of the five industries studied, and suggested that a "new consensus may be forming . . . which contradicts the conventional wisdom that state and local taxes have little or no effect on business location."[31] And around the same time James R. Hines employed a clever approach to test the effect of state taxes. Some countries, including Japan and the United Kingdom, let their companies subtract taxes paid to American states against any national corporate income tax they owe, making state taxes painless for British and Japanese firms. Other countries offer only partial credit, so companies from those countries see state taxes as a real cost. Hines finds that companies that pay state taxes out of their own resources are significantly less likely to invest in high-tax states than those whose home-country governments essentially absorb the cost of state taxes, suggesting that tax policy matters for those foreign firms.[32]

Timothy Bartik, perhaps the most prominent empirical researcher on the impact of state and local economic development incentives, used a variant of the standard regression approach to test how corporate tax rates and the degree of unionization of a state's workforce affected the location decisions of Fortune 500 branch plants in the 1970s, controlling for other relevant factors. He estimated that a 10 percent increase in the corporate income tax rate would shrink the number of new plants by 2 to 3 percent, and a similar increase in business property taxes would have comparable (though slightly smaller) effects. Unionization had an even bigger impact in Bartik's model; the number of branch plants in a state would shrink by 30 to 45 percent for every 10 percent increase in the unionized share of the labor force.[33] Later work—including his own new research and a careful review of nearly fifty previous studies—led Bartik to generalize his findings. While studies from the 1950s through the mid-1970s seldom found that state and local taxes depressed economic growth, Bartik concluded from his survey of the literature, more recent studies usually identified a clearer impact. The evidence suggested that a 10 percent cut in state and local taxes would lead to an increase in business activity somewhere in the range of 3 percent.[34]

The difficulty of getting clean data on taxes actually paid or subsidies actually collected, and the inferiority of proxies like the average statutory tax rate, has inspired some researchers to turn to simulations to calibrate the likely effect of business-attraction policies. James A. Papke and Leslie E. Papke built computer models mimicking the economic characteristics of some four hundred industries. Applying the specific tax rates and rules of the different states (and some individual localities) to these models, they estimate the effect that a new investment will have on the investor's after-tax bottom line—in theory, the most interesting variable to measure—across different states. After running scenario after scenario through their computers, they find that the real impact of state tax policy depends greatly on the specific characteristics of each investor and on the details of the tax code. But they find that differences across states *can* matter greatly, and conclude that "on balance, it appears that the 'revisionist' case is advancing; that is, differential tax burdens do influence investment location decisions."[35] Researchers at Vertex, a consulting firm, calculated the total taxes paid by a simulated mid-sized service firm in twenty-five different American locales, and estimated that state taxes would be about one-third of pretax income in four cities, and one-fifth or more in six other cities—certainly high enough for even the dullest corporate comptroller to notice—and varied by a factor of three from the highest to the lowest tax locale.[36]

One of the most interesting studies done in recent years involves a comparable simulation of the economic impact of economic development incentives beyond competitive tax reductions. Alan H. Peters and Peter S. Fischer developed economic models of both large and small firms from eight different industries. They then collected data on the "standing offer" of investment incentives available in twenty-four states—usually including more than one locale in each state—and applied the types, terms, and levels of incentives to estimate the economic impact, over the course of twenty years, on each simulated firm.

They estimated that the difference in the rate of return between the locales with the *most* attractive package of state and local incentives, and those with the *least,* was substantial—roughly comparable to a $1 differential in average hourly wages—leading them to conclude that "at least at the extremes, taxes and incentives are potentially large enough to influence location decisions."[37]

NOTES

Chapter One: The Ascendancy of the States

1. Woodrow Wilson, *Constitutional Government in the United States* (New York: Columbia University Press, 1921 edition), p. 175.

2. One reference to Senator Dole's regular display of a card imprinted with the Tenth Amendment is Robert Pear, "Source of State Power Is Pulled from Ashes," *New York Times*, April 1, 1995. At one point Dole declared on the stump (with considerable poetic license) that the "Founding Fathers were concerned about this all-powerful central government in Washington." Katherine Q. Seelye, "Dole Sticks with an Anti-Washington Line," *New York Times*, July 11, 1996. The Clinton quote is from remarks delivered to the Democratic Governors' Association in Washington, D.C., and distributed by the White House Office of the Press Secretary, February 5, 1996; the quote from the platform comes from the on-line version posted on the Democratic National Committee Web site, August 19, 1996.

3. See Vito Tanzi, "Fiscal Federalism and Decentralization: A Review of Some Efficiency and Macroeconomic Aspects," World Bank working paper, May 1995, on the worldwide surge of interest in fiscal federalism and the decentralization of economic authority. For an impressionistic sample of debates over governmental decentralization in other countries, see "Russia's Riddle of the Regions," *Economist*, March 23, 1996; Margaret Atwood, "How Many Canadas?" *New York Times*, November 5, 1995; Matt Moffett, "As Mexico's Leader Cedes Some Authority, Power Scramble Begins," *Wall Street Journal*, March 25, 1996; Celestine Bohlen, "Italy's Northern League Exploits a Growing Army of Malcontents," *New York Times*, June 11, 1996.

4. I am indebted to Robert Z. Lawrence for emphasizing the magnitude of

this trend. See also Daniel J. Elazar, "From Statism to Federalism: A Paradigm Shift," *Publius* (Spring 1995).

5. The Constitution, of course, is not an economics tract; the Framers' chief concern was not prosperity, but liberty. Yet the economic miseries of the brief Federal era—states refused to pay their share of war debts, struck their own separate deals with European trading powers, and passed laws to favor their own producers at the expense out-of-state farmers, merchants, manufacturers, and workers—formed a backdrop to the Constitutional Convention. While the Framers were not economists—especially not in the modern, highly abstract sense of that label—good economics is essentially common sense fortified with mental rigor and catalyzed by imagination. And these qualities the Constitution's authors possessed in abundance.

6. Between 1950 and the mid-1980s, the real cost of international air travel fell by two-thirds and of international air freight by three-fourths; the real cost of international phone calls fell by roughly 95 percent, while average tariff rates dropped by half. "Higher mobility leads to a generalization of arbitrage—a tendency to equalize conditions worldwide." Richard N. Cooper, "The United States as an Open Economy," in *How Open Is the U.S. Economy?* ed. R. W. Hafer (Lexington, Mass.: Lexington Books, 1986), pp. 10, 21.

7. John Kincaid, "The American Governors in International Affairs," *Publius* (Fall 1984): 97; Derek Leebaert, "Innovations and Private Initiatives as Frontiers Fall," *Washington Quarterly* (Spring 1992) p. 114. I am indebted to Robert B. Reich for bringing the Franklin anecdote to my attention.

8. The recent reflections of a freight-flight tourist offer some remarkable vignettes of the degree to which the interweaving of global commerce has become routine. Barry Lopez, "On the Wings of Commerce," *Harper's* (October 1995). Motorola, for example, maintains several Asian design centers intricately integrated into its global operations. An American engineer can work on a project during North America's office hours, send it electronically to engineers in China, India, or Singapore when he leaves the lab, and return the next morning to pick up the relay from his Asian colleagues as their day ends (this extraordinary example comes from Keith Bradsher, "Skilled Workers Watch Their Jobs Migrate Overseas," *New York Times*, August 28, 1995). When sandstone can be quarried in India, air-freighted to Japan for finishing, and then flown to Los Angeles to be installed in a building facade; when American telephone books and insurance claim forms can be processed in Asia; the defense that distance once afforded against the consequences of cold economic calculations has become very minor indeed.

9. Political pressures and the peculiarities of trust-fund accounting have kept appropriations below authorizations, but ISTEA still represents a major block grant initiative. See "Highways, Mass Transit Funded," *Congressional Quarterly Almanac 1991*; Kirk Victor, "Skinner's Last Act," *National Journal*,

December 14, 1991; and General Accounting Office, "Intermodal Freight Transportation: Projects and Planning Issues" (Letter Report, 07/09/96, GAO/NSIAD–96–159).

10. P.L. 104-4 is discussed in "Unfunded Mandate Bill Highlights," *Congressional Quarterly Almanac 1995*, pp. 3–17.

11. Margaret Kriz, "Drinks All Around," *National Journal*, November 18, 1995. The legislation was eventually passed in 1996 as P.L. 104-82. The ill-fated 1993 Clinton health reform plan was inspired in many of its details by state-level innovations, and would have assigned to the states unprecedented responsibilities—to define and police regional health alliances, for example. When the administration effort collapsed, expectations for fixing the health-care system fell largely to the states. See John J. DiIulio, Jr., and Richard P. Nathan, *Making Health Reform Work: The View from the States* (Washington, D.C.: Brookings Institution, 1994).

12. The data on which this figure is based are from Office of Management and Budget, *Budget of the United States Government, Fiscal 1998* (Washington, D.C.: U.S. Government Printing Office, 1997), Historical Tables volume, Table 15.5.

13. Over 1960–64 the division was 65 percent local, 35 percent state. State spending exceeded local spending slightly in 1976 and 1981, and then decidedly in 1992 and 1993. The 1990–93 average is 51 percent state, 49 percent local. Bureau of the Census, Government Division, Government Finance data from *Statistical Abstract of the United States* and Census Bureau Web site, various years.

14. The 1995 federal transfers were 30.8 percent of total public spending, while federal "consumption"—mostly salaries and purchased goods and services—was 19.4 percent. State and local consumption was 29.2 percent of overall government spending, and state and local transfers came to 12.5 percent. NIPA data come from a disk supplied by Virginia Mannering of the National Income and Wealth Division, Bureau of Economic Analysis, U.S. Department of the Census, in November 1996.

15. John J. DiIulio, Jr., and Donald F. Kettl, *Fine Print: The Contract with America, Devolution, and the Administrative Realities of American Government* (Washington, D.C.: Brookings Institution, 1995), p. 18.

16. In 1993—the last year for which complete data on all three levels of government are available—there were 2.7 million full-time federal civilian workers (of whom one-third were civilians working in defense or foreign affairs), compared with 3.9 million state and 9.6 million local workers (overwhelmingly public school employees). Workforce data are from the Census Bureau's annual survey of government employment, as reported on the bureau's Web site as of October 1996. Federal workers are full-time; state and local on a full-time equivalent basis. This comparison misses a small number

of part-time federal workers, but including part-timers would not affect the pattern greatly. (Including contractors probably *would* change the workforce pattern.)

17. Council of Economic Advisors and U.S. Department of Labor Office of the Chief Economist, "Job Creation and Employment Opportunities: The United States Labor Market, 1993–1996," Washington, D.C., April 23, 1996, p. 2.

18. The Gallup and Roper polls from the 1930s are summarized in Robert J. Blendon et al., "Changing Attitudes in America," unpublished paper, September 1996, Table 6.

19. Advisory Commission on Intergovernmental Relations, "Changing Public Attitudes on Governments and Taxes 1994," ACIR Publication S-23, Washington, D.C. All the contemporary polls cited here are telephone surveys with samples ranging from several hundred to over a thousand.

20. Surveys done in 1994 and 1995 by the *Wall Street Journal* and NBC News found majorities favoring state, rather than federal, responsibility for "improving public education" (72 percent versus 22 percent), "reducing crime" (68 percent versus 24 percent) "providing job training," (55 percent versus 31 percent) "reforming welfare" (46 percent versus 42 percent), and "providing assistance to the poor" (44 percent versus 40 percent). Quoted in Blendon et al., "Changing Attitudes in America," Figure 9. A similar Harris-*Business Week* survey in January 1995 found majority support for shifting to the states "control and management" of all six policy areas mentioned—crime prevention, low-income housing, highway construction and maintenance, medical care for the poor, welfare, environmental protection, and farm subsidies. January 1995 Harris–*Business Week* poll (McGraw-Hill News Release, January 23, 1995). The *Wall Street Journal*/NBC News poll did find majorities favoring federal responsibility for improving the health-care system, protecting the environment, protecting civil rights, and strengthening the economy. Sixty percent of those surveyed by Gallup in 1995 felt that the federal government has "too much power," while only 27 percent felt the same about their state government. Asked which level of government was "more likely to administer social programs efficiently," 20 percent of the Gallup sample opted for Washington; 74 percent gave their votes to the states. The Gallup Poll, *Public Opinion* (Washington, D.C.: Gallup, 1995), pp. 143–49, 213. A Hart and Teeter poll conducted in 1995 for the Council for Excellence in Government found 64 percent favoring the concentration of public power at the state level versus 26 percent favoring concentration at the federal level. In no policy area did a majority endorse giving Washington the lead. (The best the federal government did was in "programs to expand opportunities for minorities," where 35 percent called for federal responsibility, 30 percent for state responsibility, and 28 percent for local responsibility.) Welfare, air and water quality, roads and highways, employment and job training, and education were all seen as jobs

for the states; law enforcement and the management of libraries, museums, and the like were seen as local responsibilities. Hart and Teeter poll, conducted March 1995, for the Council for Excellence in Government.

21. Political/Media Research, October 1994 State Races Poll.

22. The gap reflects more a loss of confidence in the federal government than any great enthusiasm for the states; while 75 percent trust the federal government to "do the right thing" only some of the time or never, 64 percent are similarly skeptical of their state governments. November-December 1995 survey, Princeton Survey Research Associates for *Washington Post*, Kaiser Family Foundation, and Harvard University, as summarized by Blendon et al., "Changing Attitudes in America." The last figures, on comparative trust to "do the right thing" are from the version reported on the Kaiser Foundation Web site.

23. *New York Ice Co. v. Liebman*, 285 U.S. 262, 311 (1932). The "laboratories of democracy" metaphor was actually coined by Lord Bryce, as I am grateful to David Osborne for pointing out to me.

CHAPTER TWO: AMERICA'S ENDLESS ARGUMENT

1. Ivo D. Duchacek, *The Territorial Dimension of Politics* (Boulder, Colo.: Westview Press, 1986), p. 92.

2. "Taxation No Tyranny," in *Samuel Johnson: Political Writings*, ed. Donald J. Greene (New Haven, Conn.: Yale University Press, 1977), p. 423.

3. In the Constitutional Convention, Pennsylvania's James Wilson would argue that (plural "States" aside) the joint Declaration of Independence defined the United States as a single entity from the start. Herbert Storing, "The Problem of Big Government," in *Toward a More Perfect Union: The Writings of Herbert J. Storing*, ed. Joseph M. Bessette (Washington, D.C.: American Enterprise Institute Press, 1995), p. 293.

4. Stanley Elkins and Erik McKitrick, *The Age of Federalism* (New York and Oxford: Oxford University Press, 1993), p. 41. One of those young officers, Alexander Hamilton, became the most ardent Nationalist among the Framers, and Elkins and McKitrick suggest that his concern for a strong central government was shaped in part by the searing memory of suffering among the troops as Washington was chronically unable to exact sufficient funding from the separate states (pp. 100–101).

5. Quoted in Merrill D. Peterson, *Adams and Jefferson: A Revolutionary Dialogue* (Oxford: Oxford University Press, 1976), p. 11.

6. Article II, Articles of Confederation, drafted 1777, formally adopted 1781, from Samuel Eliot Morison, ed., *Sources and Documents Illustrating the American Revolution* (London: Oxford University Press, 1923), p. 178.

7. The chaotic currency situation under the Articles is described in

Allan Nevins, *The American States During and After the Revolution* (New York: Macmillan, 1927), pp. 568–70; the quotation is from p. 570.

8. Curtis P. Nettels, *The Emergence of a National Economy 1775–1815*, Vol. II of *The Economic History of the United States* (New York: Holt, Rinehart, and Winston, 1962), pp. 34, 95.

9. See Nevins, *American States During and After the Revolution*, p. 578, for the specific reference to New York and Rhode Island. Elkins and McKitrick, *Age of Federalism*, especially Chapter 3, discuss the fundamental controversy over the assumption of states' war debt.

10. Nettels, *Emergence of a National Economy*, p. 72.

11. Nevins, *American States During and After the Revolution*, pp. 554–58. Oscar Handlin and Mary Flug Handlin, *Commonwealth* (Cambridge, Mass.: Belknap Press, 1969), p. 63.

12. Nevins, *American States During and After the Revolution*, p. 560. See also Albert S. Abel, "The Commerce Clause in the Constitutional Convention and in Contemporary Comment," *Minnesota Law Review* (1941): 448–49, 456–57.

13. Nevins, *American States During and After the Revolution*, p. 562.

14. Quoted in ibid., p. 563.

15. Jefferson is quoted in Nettels, *Emergence of a National Economy*, p. 73.

16. Akhil Reed Amar, "Of Sovereignty and Federalism," *Yale Law Journal* 96, no. 7 (June 1987).

17. See Elkins and McKitrick, *Age of Federalism*, pp. 10–11, 702. This magnificent book is a rich source on the Framers, especially Madison and Hamilton.

18. General sources for this section include Samuel H. Beer, "Federalism, Nationalism and Democracy in America," *American Political Science Review* 72, no. 1 (March 1978); Richard B. Morris, *Witnesses at the Creation: Hamilton, Madison, Jay and the Constitution* (New York: New American Library, 1985); and Elkins and McKitrick, *Age of Federalism*.

19. Federalist 9, *The Federalist Papers* (New York: New American Library, 1961), p. 76. All Federalist references are to this edition. Leading statements in opposition to the Constitution, favoring either separatism or "a more perfect confederation," are collected in *The Anti-Federalist* (Chicago: University of Chicago Press, 1981), with a thoughtful introduction by editor Herbert J. Storing. Martin Diamond, "What the Framers Meant by Federalism," in Laurence J. O'Toole, Jr., *American Intergovernmental Relations* (Washington, D.C.: Congressional Quarterly Press, 1993), gives an interesting account of the subtle shift toward a nationalist perspective in the early days of the convention; see esp. pp. 43–44.

20. Morris is quoted in Abel, "The Commerce Clause in the Constitutional Convention," note 12, p. 436.

21. The references are to Article I, Section 8, and to Article IV, Section 4.

22. Elkins and McKitrick, *Age of Federalism*, p. 62. Madison was a good political stategist; the addition of the Bill of Rights was instrumental in converting North Carolina and Rhode Island.

23. See Hamilton's observations, Federalist 34, *Federalist Papers*, p. 207, which are quoted in the next chapter.

24. U.S. Treasury Department, Office of State and Local Finance, *Federal-State-Local Fiscal Relations: Report to the President and the Congress*, Washington, D.C., September 1985, p. vii.

25. R. Kent Newmyer, "John Marshall, Political Parties, and the Origins of Modern Federalism," in *Federalism: Studies in History, Law, and Public Policy*, ed. Harry N. Scheiber (Berkeley, Calif.: Institute of Intergovernmental Studies, 1988), p. 19.

26. *McCulloch v. Maryland*, 17 U.S. 316 (1819), granted Congress an expansive definition of the "necessary and proper" clause in Article I. *Gibbons v. Ogden*, 22 U.S. 1 (1824), launched the use of commerce clause as the predicate for federal activism.

27. Wilson, *Constitutional Government*, p. 173. See also U.S. Treasury Department, *Federal-State-Local Fiscal Relations*, p. vii; and Richard Cordray, "The Supreme Court's Role in American Federalism," paper presented at the Federalism Summit, Cincinnati, October 23, 1995.

28. Garry Wills claims to have pinpointed the precise time and manner of its occurrence—November 19, 1863, in the passionate evocation of national identity and purpose compressed into Abraham Lincoln's Gettysburg Address. In those 272 words, Wills has written, Lincoln either brought to fulfillment or (depending on one's position) perverted to his own ends the vision of the Founding Fathers. "What had been mere theory—that the nation preceded the states, in time and importance—now became a lived reality of the American tradition." See Garry Wills, "The Words That Remade America: Lincoln at Gettysburg," *Atlantic Monthly* (June 1992), p. 78.

29. Ibid., p. 79.

30. On this debate, see Richard H. Fallon, Jr., "The Ideologies of Federal Courts Law," *Virginia Law Review* 74, no. 7 (October 1988).

31. "We must be careful, when focusing on the events which took place in Philadelphia two centuries ago, that we not overlook the momentous events which followed," Justice Thurgood Marshall went so far as to say in 1987. "While the Union survived the Civil War, the Constitution did not." Remarks to the Annual Seminar of the San Francisco Patent and Trademark Law Association, Magi, Hawaii, May 6, 1987, quoted in David Beam, Cynthia Colella, and Timothy Conlan, "Federal Regulation of State and Local Governments: Regulatory Federalism—a Decade Later," draft report for the U.S. Advisory Commission on Intergovernmental Relations, Washington, D.C., February 1992, p. viii-8.

32. Herbert Croly, *The Promise of American Life* (New York: Macmillan, 1909), p. 18.

33. Ibid., p. 350.

34. Quoted in Michael E. Parish, "Felix Frankfurter and American Federalism," in *Federalism: Studies in History, Law, and Public Policy*, ed. Harry N. Scheiber (Berkeley, Calif.: Institute of Intergovernmental Studies, 1988), p. 28. Frankfurter had been a self-described "hot Hamiltonian" in his younger days; see p. 30.

35. *Hammer v. Dagenhart*, 247 U.S. 251 (1918), quoted in Philip P. Frickey, "The Congressional Process and the Constitutionality of Federal Legislation to End the Economic War Among the States," in *The Economic War Among the States* (Minneapolis: Federal Reserve Bank of Minneapolis, 1996), p. 29.

36. "With the advent of the New Deal," writes political scientist Paul Peterson, "the constitutional power of the national government expanded so dramatically that the doctrine of dual sovereignty virtually lost all meaning." Paul Peterson, *The Price of Federalism* (Washington, D.C.: Brookings Institution, 1995), p. 11.

37. Quoted in Advisory Council on Unemployment Compensation, "National Interests and Federal Responsibilities in the Unemployment Insurance System," April 1995, p. 4.

38. Quoted in Daniel P. Moynihan, "The Politics and Economics of Regional Growth," *Public Interest*, no. 51 (Spring 1978): 4.

39. Harold J. Laski, "The Obsolescence of Federalism," *New Republic*, May 3, 1938, p. 367.

40. U.S. Treasury Department, *Federal-State-Local Fiscal Relations*, esp. p. xx.

41. 336 U.S. 525, 1949, quoted in Julian N. Eule, "Laying the Dormant Commerce Clause to Rest," *Yale Law Journal* 91, no. 3 (January 1982), note 47, p. 434.

42. Peterson, *Price of Federalism*, pp. 59–60.

43. Donald R. Gilmore, *Developing the "Little" Economies* (Washington, D.C.: Committee for Economic Development, 1960), p. 9.

44. See John Shannon, "The Deregulation of the Federal System," in *The Changing Face of Fiscal Federalism*, eds. Thomas R. Swartz and John E. Peck (Armonk, N.Y.: M.E. Sharpe, 1990), esp. Exhibit 2.1, p. 22.

45. Morton Grodzins, "Marble-Cake Federalism," in *The American System: A New View of Government in the United States*, ed. Daniel J. Elazar (Chicago: Rand McNally, 1966).

46. U.S. Treasury Department, *Federal-State-Local Fiscal Relations*, p. xxi.

47. Paul E. Peterson and Kenneth K. Wong, "Toward a Differentiated

Theory of Federalism: Education and Housing Policy in the 1980's," *Research in Urban Policy* 1 (1985): 302–3.

48. Jeffrey L. Pressman and Aaron Wildavsky, *Implementation* (Berkeley: University of California Press, 1973).

49. Jane Perry Clark, *The Rise of a New Federalism* (New York: Columbia University Press, 1938).

50. Samuel H. Beer, "The Idea of the Nation," in *American Intergovernmental Relations*, ed. Laurence J. O'Toole, Jr. (Washington, D.C.: Congressional Quarterly Press, 1993), p. 354.

51. See Thomas R. Swartz and John E. Peck, "The Changing Face of Fiscal Federalism," *Challenge* 33, no. 6 (November-December 1990): 42–43.

52. *Statistical Abstract of the United States 1992*, Table 470, p. 282.

53. There are different ways of counting the number of block grants and consolidated programs. This tally is from the General Accounting Office, in "Block Grants: Lessons Learned" (February 9, 1995, GAO/T-HEHS–95–80).

54. On the rise and fall of intergovernmental grants, see Peterson, *Price of Federalism*, pp. 62–63. See also Richard P. Nathan and Fred C. Doolittle, "The Untold Story of Reagan's 'New Federalism,'" *Public Interest* 77 (Fall 1984).

55. Swartz and Peck, "The Changing Face of Fiscal Federalism," p. 41. The sentiment was not limited to the intergovernmental area, to be sure.

56. John Shannon, "The Return to Fend-for-Yourself Federalism: The Reagan Mark," *Intergovernmental Perspective* 13, no.3/4 (Summer-Fall 1987). Another longtime observer of state government judged in 1992 that the United States was "moving from an era of cooperative federalism to an era of "go-it-alone" federalism." Thad Beyle, "New Governors in Hard Economic and Political Times," in *Governors and Hard Times*, ed. Thad Beyle (Washington, D.C.: Congressional Quarterly Press, 1992) pp. 8–9.

57. See Nathan and Doolittle, "The Untold Story of Reagan's 'New Federalism,'" p. 97.

58. See John D. Donahue, "Business, Government, and Job Training," Chapter 9 in *The Privatization Decision* (New York: Basic Books, 1989).

59. As constitutional scholar Richard Cordray puts it, "the Framers created an awkward balance of power that is, at bottom, a political balance. The precise contours of this arrangement were not clearly fixed and therefore have remained both uncertain and mutable . . ." Cordray, "The Supreme Court's Role in American Federalism," p. 4.

60. 426 U.S. 833 (1976).

61. 469 U.S. 528 (1985), 550, quoted in Cordray, "The Supreme Court's Role in American Federalism," p. 16.

62. In the words of concurring Justice Blackmun: "State sovereign interests . . . are more properly protected by procedural safeguards inherent in the

structure of the federal system than by judicially created limitations on federal power." Quoted in Beam, Colella, and Conlan, "Federal Regulation of State and Local Governments," p. vi-4.

63. Beam, Colella, and Conlan read *Baker* as questioning whether there are any barriers to taxing interest on state debt; ibid., pp. vi-14.

64. Cordray, "The Supreme Court's Role in American Federalism," p. 18.

65. 112 S. Ct. 2408 (1992).

66. 115 S. Ct. 1624 (1995). Linda Greenhouse has suggested that "a re-shaping of the Federal-state balance may prove [Chief Justice William H. Rehnquist's] most enduring legacy." Linda Greenhouse, "Taking States Seriously," *New York Times*, April 14, 1996.

67. Quoted in Nina Bernstein, "An Accountability Issue: As States Gain Political Power, a Ruling Seems to Free Them of Some Legal Reins," *New York Times*, April 1, 1996.

68. Linda Greenhouse, "Justices Take Up Question of Party Donations to Candidates," *New York Times*, April 16, 1996.

69. Quoted in Joan Biskupic, "Justices Shift Federal-State Power Balance," *Washington Post*, March 30, 1996.

70. Alice Rivlin, *Reviving the American Dream: The Economy, the States, and the Federal Government* (Washington, D.C.: The Brookings Institution, 1992).

71. DiIulio and Kettl, *Fine Print*, p. 31.

72. Robin Toner, "Senate Approves Welfare Plan That Would End Aid Guarantee," *New York Times*, September 20, 1995.

73. Pear, "Source of State Power."

74. Michael O. Leavitt, "Rebalancing the American Republic," paper presented at the Federalism Summit, Cincinnati, October 23, 1995.

75. Madison had also opposed "the great compromise" making Senate representation equal by state, rather than proportional to population, and gave in "only with deep disgust." Elkins and McKitrick, *Age of Federalism*, p. 83.

76. Brit Hume reference from *Hotline* (August 1, 1995).

77. Council of Economic Advisors and U.S. Department of Labor Office of the Chief Economist, "Job Creation and Employment Opportunities," p. 2.

78. Organization for Economic Cooperation and Development, *Economic Outlook*, June 1996, p. A31.

79. The data on which Figure 4 is based comes from Office of Management and Budget, *Budget of the United States Government, Fiscal Year, 1998* (Washington, D.C.: U.S. Government Printing Office, 1997), Historical Tables volume, Table 15.5.

80. I am using the term "discretionary" in a somewhat different sense here than its technical meaning in the Budget Enforcement Act. Here, it is simply a

shorthand for federal domestic spending other than debt service, entitlements, and intergovernmental grants.

CHAPTER THREE: UNITY AND AUTONOMY: THE WEIGHTS ON THE SCALE

1. Wilson, *Constitutional Government*, p. 173.

2. Hamilton, Federalist 34, *Federalist Papers*, p. 207.

3. For a fascinating account of Madison's split with Hamilton and his tortured reconsideration of his previous convictions, see Elkins and McKitrick, *Age of Federalism*, pp. 224–34.

4. Madison, Federalist 46, *Federalist Papers*, p. 294.

5. Elkins and McKitrick, *Age of Federalism*, p. 12.

6. Martin Landau, in an interesting perspective, finds advantages in ambiguity and overlap themselves. See Martin Landau, "Redundancy, Rationality, and the Problem of Duplication and Overlap," *Public Administration Review* 29, no. 4 (July/August 1966), esp. pp. 351–53.

7. Nettels, *Emergence of a National Economy*, p. 99, notes that the issuance of paper currency is not an enumerated power. Harvard economist and Reagan economic adviser Martin Feldstein, among others, sees some significant practical defects to a single national currency for a set of economically diverse states. Martin Feldstein, "The Case Against EMU," *Economist*, June 13, 1992, p. 21.

8. The *Harvard Journal of Law and Public Policy* (Winter 1996), Symposium on Originalism, Democracy, and the Constitution, gives a sample of this debate.

9. For an example outside the American context, a World Bank economist argues that "if the European Union forced the Italians and the Germans to pursue a similar stabilization policy objective for inflation and unemployment when in fact Italians might prefer lower unemployment while Germans might prefer lower inflation, some welfare loss would result." Tanzi, "Fiscal Federalism and Decentralization," p. 8.

10. Calhoun is quoted in Beer, "The Idea of the Nation," p. 349.

11. Gerald C. Wright, Jr., Robert S. Erikson, and John P. McIver, "Public Opinion and Policy Liberalism in the American States," *American Journal of Political Science* 31, no. 4 (November 1987), see esp. Table 3, p. 991.

12. The collective choice literature is vast and demanding; some classic readings include Kenneth Arrow, "A Difficulty in the Concept of Social Welfare," *Journal of Political Economy* ([month unknown] 1950), reprinted in *Microeconomics: Selected Readings*, 3rd edition, ed. Edwin Mansfield (New York: Norton, 1979); Knut Wicksell, "A New Principle of Just Taxation" (1886;

translation by James M. Buchanan) in *Classics in the Theory of Public Finance*, eds. Richard A. Musgrave and Alan T. Peacock (New York: St. Martin's Press, 1967); and Erik Lindahl, "Just Taxation: A Positive Solution," German original 1919, translation reprinted in *Classics in the Theory of Public Finance*, eds. Richard A. Musgrave and Alan T. Peacock (New York: St. Martin's Press, 1967); and Anthony Downs, "Why the Government Budget Is Too Small in a Democracy," *World Politics* (1960), reprinted in *Private Wants and Public Needs*, ed. Edmund S. Phelps (New York: Norton, 1965). The Framers' perspective was less formal, perhaps, and less purely economic, but they held what constitutional theorist Albert S. Abel termed a "lively awareness of the need for autonomous solution of special problems not common to all the people." Abel, "The Commerce Clause in the Constitutional Convention," p. 481.

13. Wallace E. Oates, *Fiscal Federalism* (New York: Harcourt, Brace, Jovanovich, 1972), esp. pp. 34–35.

14. Executive Order 12612, 52 F.R. 20, October 30 1987, pp. 41685–88.

15. *Carnival Cruise Lines v. Shutes*, 111 S. Ct. 1522 (1991), referenced in Michael Gottesman, "Draining the Dismal Swamp: The Case for Federal Choice of Law Statues," *Georgetown Law Journal* 80 (1991): 14–15.

16. Wilson, *Constitutional Government*, p. 179. His objections were apparently based as much on pragmatic as on constitutional grounds, as he argued that "[u]niform regulation of the economic conditions of a vast territory and a various people like the United States would be mischievous, if not impossible" (p. 175).

17. For an interesting discussion of the shift toward federal regulation in the 1970s, the resurgence of states amid federal deregulatory efforts in the 1980s, and business's accompanying calls for federal preemption, see Susan Bartlett Foote, "Administrative Preemption: An Experiment in Regulatory Federalism," *Virginia Law Review* 70 (1984). Another good discussion, specific to a single regulatory issue, can be found in Mark King, "Federal Preemption of the State Regulation of Nuclear Power: State Law Strikes Back," *Chicago Kent Law Review* (1984).

18. A. Gerstenfeld, "Government Regulation Effects on the Direction of Innovation: A Focus on Performance Standards," *IEEE Transaction Engineering Management* (August 1977), quoted in Lynn Bollinger, Katherine Hope, and James M. Utterback, "A Review of Literature and Hypotheses on New Technology-Based Firms," *Research Policy* 12 (1983): 12.

19. P.L. 104-290 can be found on THOMAS, the legislative Web site, under its House label H.R. 3005. A good survey article on this general topic is Robert Tannenwald, "State Regulation and Economic Development," paper prepared for "The Effects of State and Local Public Policies on Economic Development," Federal Reserve Bank of Boston, November 1996.

20. Larry E. Ribstein and Bruce H. Kobayashi, "An Economic Analysis

of Uniform State Laws," *Journal of Legal Studies* 25 (January 1996), esp. pp. 138–42. See also Robert P. Inman and Daniel L. Rubinfeld, "A Federalist Fiscal Constitution for an Imperfect World: Lessons from the United States," in *Federalism: Studies in History, Law, and Public Policy*, ed. Harry N. Scheiber (Berkeley, Calif.: Institute of Intergovernmental Studies, 1988), esp. p. 80.

21. Colorado State Representative Ron May termed the end of the national speed limit "the first step in the devolution of power from Washington." James Brooke, "10-State Swath of the West Will Soon Hit 75 MPH," *New York Times*, May 8, 1996. The legislation ending national speed limits and requiring state helmet laws was called the National Highway System Designation Act of 1995.

22. Ironically, many of the policies of the New Deal, an era that marked the federal government's surge to economic preeminence, represent the nationalization of Progressive innovations developed and refined in the states and localities. R. Scott Fosler, "State Economic Policy: An Assessment," *Business in the Contemporary World* (Summer 1989): 87.

23. David Long et al., *LEAP: Three-Year Impacts of Ohio's Welfare Initiative to Improve School Attendance Among Teenage Parents* (Washinton, D.C.: Manpower Demonstration Research Corporation, 1996).

24. Peter Eisinger, *The Rise of the Entrepreneurial State* (Madison: University of Wisconsin Press, 1989), pp. 171–72.

25. Robert Pear, "Laws Won't Let H.M.O.'s Tell Doctors What to Say," *New York Times*, September 17, 1996.

26. These and several other case studies are discussed in David C. Nice, *Policy Innovation in State Government* (Ames: Iowa State University Press, 1994).

27. David Osborne, "A New Federal Compact: Sorting Out Washington's Proper Role," in *Mandate for Change*, eds. Will Marshall and Martin Schram (New York: Berkeley Books, 1993), p. 256, argues that a fraction of intergovernmental grants should be earmarked for diffusion efforts.

28. Sherman is quoted in Diamond, "What the Framers Meant by Federalism," p. 44.

29. William Weld, "The States Won't Be Cruel," *New York Times*, February 9, 1996.

30. I am grateful to William Galston for bringing this example to my attention in a conversation of October 7, 1996, in Washington, D.C.

31. Michael J. Sandel, "America's Search for a New Public Philosophy," *Atlantic Monthly* (March 1996), p. 74.

32. Hamilton's argument, in Federalist 9, is discussed in Storing, "The Problem of Big Government," pp. 288–89.

33. At least one knowledgeable observer finds this highly implausible. See Richard Cohen, "Always the National News," *Washington Post*, May 2, 1995.

34. On this point see Max Weber, "Bureaucracy," in *From Max Weber*, eds. H. H. Gerth and C. Wright Mills (New York: Oxford University Press, 1946), p. 200.

35. The peak of pure administrative efficiency was no doubt reached by Robinson Crusoe (before he met Friday); any *social* arrangement falls short of that admirably uncomplicated standard.

36. Jefferson is quoted in Duchacek, *Territorial Dimension of Politics*, p. 58.

37. Philip M. Burgess, "Federalism: An Overview," paper presented at the Federalism Summit, Cincinnati, October 23, 1995, p. 8.

38. Remarks before the Federalism Summit, Cincinnati, October 23, 1995.

39. George E. Peterson and Demetra Smith Nightingale, "What Do We Know About Block Grants," analysis prepared for the Labor Department by the Urban Institute, July 1995.

40. Peter T. Kilborn, "Michigan's Welfare System: Praise Amid Warning Signs," *New York Times*, October 24, 1995.

41. More realistic than assertions of some uniform efficiency edge for small-scale or large-scale government is a pattern of selective advantages, where some functions are suited to higher levels of government and others to lower. The task, then, is to determine what function fits where, and to boost the odds that duties end up where they belong. There are few simple decision rules concerning governmental scale. It's still hard to beat Madison's formula—small units of government to bind citizens' affinities, united into a larger community whose politics will be too fluid and complex for rigid factions to form. Michael Sandel calls for a slightly different synthesis, arguing that "only a politics that disperses sovereignty both upward and downward can combine the power required to rival global market forces with the differentiation required of a public life that hopes to inspire the allegiance of its citizens." Sandel, "America's Search for a New Public Philosophy," p. 74.

Paul Peterson, a longtime student of American federalism, describes two conflicting bodies of theory on how the capacity and quality of political processes affect the allocation of responsibilities across levels of government. What he terms "legislative theory" is rather pessimistic, predicting that legislators at each level of government will tend to claim and defend authority over policies where they will be least accountable to citizens, and will trade on citizens' gullibility to claim credit for benefits originating elsewhere and "shift governmental burdens to other levels of the federal system." Peterson, *Price of Federalism*, p. 16. In an example consistent with this view, two analysts found that Reagan-era efforts at devolution were more successful where special interests were weak at the federal level, and less successful in policy areas where "well-organized beneficiaries and policy professionals were entrenched"—arguably, just those areas that could benefit most from devolution. Michael A. Pagano and Ann O'M. Bowman, "The State of American Federalism—

1988–1989," *Publius* 19, no. 3 (Summer 1989): 16. The other tradition, which Peterson terms "functional theory," can be viewed as a political analogue of the economist's efficient markets hypothesis. Functional theory "predicts that each level will expand in its arena of competence but will remain limited or will diminish in its less competent arena." Peterson's own position is nuanced, but in general he aligns himself with the more optimistic functional theory, and sees a general trend toward a rational sorting-out of responsibilities. Herbert Croly held a comparable view that levels of government would, over time, come to claim the responsibilities that they are competent to carry out. "The enjoyment by any public authority of a function which it cannot efficiently perform is always a source of weakness rather than of strength." Croly, *Promise of American Life*, p. 43.

42. Political scientist John Chubb has found that voters assign state officials little responsibility for the performance of the state's economy ("Institutions, the Economy, and the Dynamics of State Elections," *American Political Science Review* 82, no. 1 [March 1988], esp. Table 6, p. 148). Robert Stein, analyzing 1982 exit-poll data from twenty-seven states, reached similar conclusions. Robert Stein, "Economic Voting for Governor and U.S. Senator: The Electoral Consequences of Federalism," *Journal of Politics* 52, no. 1 (February 1990). Patrick Kenney, in a regression study of gubernatorial elections in fourteen states from 1946 through 1980, found no discernible relationship between a state's unemployment and inflation rates and the ballot box judgment rendered on incumbent governors. Patrick Kenney, "The Effect of State Economic Conditions on the Vote for Governor," *Social Science Quarterly* 64, no. 1 (March 1983). See esp. Table 1, pp. 158–59.

43. Jonathan Rabinovitz, "State Legislatures Tighten the Rules on Lobbyists' Gifts," *New York Times*, May 3, 1996.

44. Figures on trade associations from Alan Rosenthal, *The Third House: Lobbyists and Lobbying in the States* (Washington, D.C.: Congressional Quarterly Press, 1993), p. 4; see also Lucian Ayre Bebchuk, "Federalism and the Corporation: The Desirable Limits on State Competition in Corporate Law," *Harvard Law Review* 105 (1992): 1503 and note 204.

45. Clifford J. Levy, "Huge Rise in Spending on State Lobbying," *New York Times*, March 14, 1996.

46. Jonathan Elliot, *The Debates in the Several State Conventions on the Adoption of the Federal Constitution*, 1988, quoted in Larry Kramer, "The Power of Congress to Regulate Interstate Economic Competition," in *The Economic War Among the States* (Minneapolis: Federal Reserve Bank of Minneapolis, 1996), p. 35. Woodrow Wilson's observations are again relevant: "It is clear enough that the general commercial interests, the general financial interests, the general economic interests of the country, were meant to be brought under the regulation of the federal government, which should act for all; and it is

equally clear that what are the general commercial interests, what the general financial interests, what the general economic interests of the country, is a question of fact, to be determined by circumstances which change under our very eyes." Wilson, *Constitutional Government*, pp. 173–74.

47. Webster quote from 1930 debates with Calhoun, quoted in Beer, "The Idea of the Nation," pp. 351–52.

48. See Daniel A. Farber, "State Regulation and the Dormant Commerce Clause," *Constitutional Commentary* 3 (1986), esp. pp. 400–401.

49. Fritz W. Scharpf, "Theorie der Politikverflechtung," in Fritz W. Scharpf, Bernd Reissert, and Fritz Schnabel, *Politikverflectung: Theorie und Empirie des kooperativen Foederalismus in der Bundesrepublik* (Kronberg: Scriptor Verlag, 1976), p. 25.

50. Mancur Olson, Jr., "Strategic Theory and Its Applications; The Principle of 'Fiscal Equivalence': The Division of Responsibilities Among Different Levels of Government," *American Economic Review*, 59, no. 2 (May 1969): 483.

51. "8 Die as Blaze Erupts at Fireworks Store," *New York Times*, July 4, 1996.

52. Andrea Adelson, "Pushing Lemons over State Lines," *New York Times*, August 27, 1996.

53. The practice is familiar to any newspaper reader. For a sample of the theory, see Alan Williams, "The Optimal Provision of Public Goods in a System of Local Government," *Journal of Political Economy*, no. 1 (February 1966).

54. The Supreme Court upheld the state's prerogatives in product liability law in 1996, and President Clinton appealed to similar themes in threatening a veto of 1996 legislation that would preempt state liability rules that were more stringent than federal standards. For a sample of the legal debate on the merits of state-based product liability law, see Bruce L. Hay, "Conflicts of Law and State Competition in the Product Liability System," *Georgetown Law Journal* 80, no. 3 (1992). The Supreme Court case rejecting federal preemption was *Medtronic v. Lohr*, No. 95–754. See Clinton's letter to Majority Leader Bob Dole on H.R. 956, the Common Sense Product Liability Legal Reform Act of 1996, in a White House press release dated March 16, 1996.

55. Jesse Burkhead and Jerry Miner, *Public Expenditure* (Chicago and New York: Aldine-Atherton, 1971), pp. 261–62.

56. See Peterson, *Price of Federalism*, pp. 45–46, and Beam, Colella, and Conlan, "Federal Regulation of State and Local Governments," Chapter 1 generally. See also Richard B. Stewart, "Federalism and Rights," *Georgia Law Review* 19 (1985), for a thoughtful discussion of the accountability problems of both unfunded mandates and intergovernmental grants.

57. Intergovernmental grants averaged 21.5 percent of state and local spending over the 1990–95 period, based on data issued as part of the FY 1997 federal budget.

58. The classic example is Pressman and Wildavsky's *Implementation*. For a later, somewhat more nuanced, but essentially parallel critique of the awkwardness of intergovernmental action, see John E. Chubb, "The Political Economy of Federalism," *American Political Science Review* 79, no. 4 (December 1985).

59. Legal scholar Richard Stewart diagnoses an extreme breakdown of political accountability in the power of federal judges to impose detailed conditions on grant recipients invoking the absolute language of rights, with no need to calibrate whether costs and benefits are commensurate. This he terms "Madison's Nightmare"—a perverted version of the multilevel politics Madison sought to set in motion. Stewart, "Federalism and Rights."

60. One promising approach, in principle, is basing grants on performance, as summarized by Osborne, "A New Federal Compact." Many public tasks, however, feature inherently ambiguous measures of performance.

61. In principle, as Fritz Scharpf explains, "for each public task a special decision process must be established, encompassing all people who are affected positively or negatively by the undertaking, and only those people." Scharpf, "Theorie der Politikverflechtung," p. 28; free translation by author. See also Albert Breton and Anthony Scott, *The Economic Constitution of Federal States* (Toronto: University of Toronto Press, 1978), pp. 37–39, on the principle of "perfect correspondence."

62. Gordon Tullock, "Federalism: Problems of Scale," *Public Choice* 6 (Spring 1969): 25.

63. Ibid., p. 2; see also p. 27, esp. Figure 4, for a sense of Tullock's concept.

64. For example, see Eitan Berglas, "On the Theory of Clubs," *American Economic Review* (May 1976), or James Buchanan, "An Economic Theory of Clubs," *Economica* (February 1965). Mancur Olson, in a slightly less cleanslate proposal, would not abolish government, but arrange instead for a system of intergovernmental cash payments to compensate for external costs and benefits. See Olson, "Strategic Theory and Its Applications," esp. p. 486.

65. Oded Hochman, David Pines, and Jacques-Francois Thisse, "On the Optimal Structure of Local Governments," *American Economic Review* 85, no. 5 (December 1995).

66. Bruce Lambert, "City Council Report Lists Abuses in Business Improvement Districts," *New York Times*, November 11, 1995.

Chapter Four: The National Commons

1. Wilson, *Constitutional Government*, p. 192.

2. Fred P. Bosselman, "Replaying the Tragedy of the Commons," *Yale Journal on Regulation* 13, no. 1 (Winter 1996): 391, quoting William H. Rodgers, Jr., *Environmental Law* vol. 39, 1994.

3. Garrett Hardin, "The Tragedy of the Commons," *Science* 162, no. 3859 (December 1968). The specific quotation is from p. 1244.

4. For examples of the voluminous commons literature, see Bruce Benson, "Corruption in Law Enforcement: One Consequence of the 'Tragedy of the Commons' Arising with Public Allocation Processes," *International Review of Law and Economics* 8, no. 1 (June 1988); Hugh Ward, "Game Theory and the Politics of the Global Commons," *Journal of Conflict Resolution* 37, no. 2 (June 1993); William Nordhaus, "How Fast Should We Graze the Global Commons," *American Economic Review* 72, no. 2 (May 1982); and Bosselman, "Replaying the Tragedy of the Commons." I am also indebted to Thomas Sileo, a nature writer and historian, for generous private communications on the management of common lands in colonial and early American New England.

5. Aaron Zitner, "Blood Feud: New Rules in Battle for Donors," *Boston Globe*, March 24, 1996.

6. David C. Morrison, "Litter Aloft," *National Journal* (September 10, 1988), p. 2282.

7. Nettels, *Emergence of a National Economy*, p. 28.

8. Alberta M. Sbragia, *Debt Wish: Entrepreneurial Cities, U.S. Federalism, and Economic Development* (Pittsburgh: University of Pittsburgh Press, 1996), pp. 35–40.

9. The Republicans were much more afflicted by the 1996 process; with an unchallenged incumbent President, the Democratic primaries meant little. The Democratic National Committee also had some rules in place to constrain competitive scheduling.

10. Elizabeth Kolbert, "Primaries Ending Before They Begin," *New York Times*, October 15, 1996, and Chuck Campion, "The Primary Rush Has Hurt the Process," *Boston Globe*, February 29, 1996.

11. Summaries of Republican National Committee plans to fix the primary process can be found in "Presidential Primary Schedule: RNC Meets to Say Once Is Enough," *Hotline*, April 19, 1996, and "Primary Schedule: GOP Admits Mistake," *Hotline*, July 3, 1996.

12. David Broder, an astute observer of the Washington scene, makes some related points in "Small States Lose Their Leverage with Term Limits," *Boston Globe*, December 7, 1995.

13. See Paul M. Barrett, "I Do/No You Don't: How Hawaii Became Ground Zero in Battle over Gay Marriages," *Wall Street Journal*, June 17, 1996.

14. David W. Dunlap, "Congressional Bills Withhold Sanction of Same-Sex Unions," *New York Times*, May 9, 1996; "House to Vote on Same-Sex Marriages," Reuters News Service, July 12, 1996.

15. The source is a Gannet poll summarized in "Dems Up Nine in Generic House Ballot," *Hotline* (July 11, 1996). Twenty-nine percent of voters said a

candidate's position on gay marriage was "very important," and 27 percent said it was "somewhat important."

16. Todd S. Purdum, "Gay Rights Groups Attack Clinton on Midnight Signing," *New York Times*, September 22, 1996.

17. For an interesting discussion of divorce as an economic development tactic, see Barbara Dafoe Whitehead, "The Moral State of Marriage," *Atlantic Monthly*, September 1995, esp. p. 116.

18. The House sponsor of the Defense of Marriage Act was on his third marriage at the time.

19. "Republicans Slam Marijuana Ballot Measures," Reuters News Service, December 3, 1996.

20. Jerry Gray, "House Endorses Bill to Require Notification on Sex Offenders," *New York Times*, May 8, 1996.

21. Quoted in Timothy J. Bartik, "The Effects of Environmental Regulation on Business Location in the United States," *Growth and Change* 19, no. 3 (Summer 1988): 24.

22. H.R. Rep. No. 294, 95th Cong., 1st Sess. 34 (1977) quoted in Richard L. Revesz, "Rehabilitating Interstate Competition: Rethinking the 'Race-to-the-Bottom' Rationale for Federal Environmental Regulation," *New York University Law Review* 67 (December 1992): 1226–27.

23. For an excellent summary of the commons problem in this context, see Richard B. Stewart, "Pyramids of Sacrifice? Problems of Federalism in Mandating State Implementation of National Environmental Policy," *Yale Law Journal* 86 (1977): 1211–12. Stewart also discusses an important point that goes beyond this brief summary—the relatively greater political power of environmental advocates at the national level.

24. Stewart argues that "the indispensable contribution of the states to achieving federal objectives has been (with a few notable exceptions) seriously inadequate . . . [as] weak state agencies are exposed to intensive pressure from politicians, industry, unions, and citizens reacting to the costs (economic and otherwise) of controlling pollution and the possibility of unemployment and curtailment of economic development." Ibid., p. 1201.

25. There was some devolution of responsibilities, but the basic model of national, not state, environmental regulation endured. James P. Lester, "New Federalism and Environmental Policy," *Publius* 16, no. 1 (Winter 1986), esp. Table 4, pp. 99, 162–63.

26. Recent experience with the 1980 Low Level Radioactive Waste Policy Act is discussed in Ronald Smothers, "Waste Site Becomes a Toxic Battlefield," *New York Times*, October 9, 1995.

27. James P. Young, "Expanding State Initiation and Enforcement Under Superfund," *University of Chicago Law Review* 57 (1990). Some states maintain environmental rules that exceed federal standards. In 1992 several states

agreed to exceed the 1990 CAA rules on nitrogen oxides, and in 1991 nine New England states agreed to adopt California's pollution control requirements for automobiles. Revesz, "Rehabilitating Interstate Competition," p. 1228. And several states have dabbled with action to halt global warming, which is utterly at odds with what the commons model would predict.

28. Bartik, "The Effects of Environmental Regulation on Business Location," p. 37.

29. Adam B. Jaffee et al., "Environmental Regulation and the Competitiveness of U.S. Manufacturing: What Does the Evidence Tell Us?" *Journal of Economic Literature* 33 (March 1995), Table 9, p. 149. One exception was Japanese automobile plants.

30. James A. Tobey, "The Effects of Domestic Environmental Policies on Patterns of World Trade: An Empirical Test," *Kyklos* 43 (Fall 1990).

31. Curtis Alva, "Delaware and the Market for Corporate Charters: History and Agency," *Delaware Journal of Corporate Law* 15, no. 3 (1990).

32. Croly, *Promise of American Life*, p. 348.

33. Ibid., p. 356.

34. *Liggett Co. v. Lee*, 288 U.S. 517, 558–59 (1933), quoted in Ralph K. Winter, Jr., "State Law, Shareholder Protection, and the Theory of the Corporation," *Journal of Legal Studies* (1977): note 10, p. 254.

35. William L. Cary, "Federalism and Corporate Law: Reflections upon Delaware," *Yale Law Journal* 83 (1974).

36. From 1960 to 1980, Delaware got fully 16 percent of its total revenue from corporate franchise taxes. Roberta Romano, "The State Competition Debate in Corporate Law," *Cardozo Law Review* 8, (1987): 710.

37. The Senate hearings are described in Winter, "State Law, Shareholder Protection, and the Theory of the Corporation," note 10.

38. Alva, "Delaware and the Market for Corporate Charters." Alva, an attorney for the Skadden, Arps—an important fixture in the Delaware corporate bar—cites as an advantage the fact that "political parties and candidates do not get involved in Delaware corporate law, and very few of the corporations domiciled in Delaware have any employees or major physical assets there" that would impose goals other than efficient chartering (pp. 918–19).

39. See Roberta Romano, "Law as a Product: Some Pieces of the Incorporation Puzzle," *Journal of Law, Economics, and Organization* 1 (1985). On four state-law provisions popular with corporations— explicit standards for indemnifying directors and officers, antitakeover statues, merger vote exemptions, and appraisal rights exemptions—other states followed the innovators (in an S-shaped, classic "innovation adoption" curve) (pp. 233–35).

40. Winter, "State Law, Shareholder Protection, and the Theory of the Corporation," p. 289.

41. Ibid.

42. Daniel R. Fischel, "The 'Race to the Bottom' Revisited: Reflections on Recent Developments in Delaware's Law," *Northwestern University Law Review* 76 (1982): 920–21. Fischel is similarly explicit in condemning federal chartering. "Since founders of corporations have the option of incorporating in any of the fifty states, each state has strong incentives to enact a statute that will attract new incorporators. . . . Federal regulation of corporations would destroy the salutary effect of the market for corporate charters" (pp. 921–22).

43. Frank H. Easterbrook, "Antitrust and the Economics of Federalism," *Journal of Law and Economics* 26, no. 1 (April 1983): 28. Easterbrook's empirical results are summarized on p. 35. See also Romano, "The State Competition Debate," p. 752.

44. Romano, "The State Competition Debate." See also Jonathan R. Macey and Geoffrey P. Miller, "Toward an Interest-Group Theory of Delaware Corporate Law," *Texas Law Review* 65 (1987).

45. Bebchuk, "Federalism and the Corporation."

46. Ibid., p. 1490.

47. Winter curtly declines to discuss "the firms' relationship to the larger society." Winter, "State Law, Shareholder Protection, and the Theory of the Corporation," p. 252.

48. Robert Goodman, *The Luck Business* (New York: Martin Kessler Books, 1995), pp. 7–8.

49. Dirk Johnson, "More Casinos, More Players Who Bet Until They Lose All," *New York Times*, September 25, 1995.

50. Gerald F. Seib, "GOP Faces Tensions as Gambling Interests Meet Family Values," *Wall Street Journal*, October 5, 1995; "Law Sets Up Study of Gambling," *New York Times*, August 4, 1996.

51. Goodman, *Luck Business*, p. 3.

52. This figure is from U.S. Department of Commerce, Bureau of the Census, Survey of Government Finances, Income and Apportionment of State-Administered Lottery Funds: 1994, on-line version as of November 1996.

53. Johnson, "More Casinos, More Players Who Bet Until They Lose All."

54. Kevin Sack, "Gaming Lobby Gives Lavishly to Politicians," *New York Times*, December 18, 1995; Sally Denton and Roger Morris, "Easy Money in Las Vegas," *New York Times*, July 9, 1996; Seib, "GOP Faces Tensions as Gambling Interests Meet Family Values."

55. *Hotline* (November 8, 1995).

56. Johnson, "More Casinos, More Players Who Bet Until They Lose All."

57. Ibid.

58. Goodman, *Luck Business*, pp. 5–6.

59. They lost the 1994 referendum anyway, as it turned out, in an early sign of stiffening resistance to gambling's expansion, despite spending nearly as much as both of that year's gubernatorial candidates combined. Seib, "GOP

Faces Tensions as Gambling Interests Meet Family Values." Another firm used a similar strategy in Illinois, pointing to the prospect of regional gambling centers opening in Wisconsin to overcome resistance to loosening the laws in Illinois. These examples are from Goodman, *Luck Business*, p. 5 (Montana), pp. 71–72 (Florida) and p. 72 (Wisconsin).

60. Raymond Hernandez, "Pataki Panel Says Casinos Could Bring in $2.6 Billion," *New York Times*, August 31, 1996.

61. "Governor Glendening's Stand on Slots," *Washington Post* editorial, August 16, 1996.

62. Barbara Vucanovich (R-Nevada), quoted in William Safire, "New Evil Empire," *New York Times*, September 28, 1995.

CHAPTER FIVE: THE INDUSTRIAL POLICY PARADOX

1. These references are from the Indiana Commerce Department Web site as of November 1, 1996.

2. For the definitive history of Carter-era industrial policy debates, see Otis L. Graham, Jr., *Losing Time: The Industrial Policy Debate* (Cambridge, Mass.: Harvard University Press, 1992). The Economic Report quotation is from p. 52.

3. White House Report on the Program for Economic Recovery, February 18, 1981, from *Administration of Ronald Reagan, 1981* (Washington, D.C.: U.S. Government Printing Office, 1981), p. 117.

4. See, for example, Lester Thurow, *The Zero-Sum Society* (New York: Basic Books, 1980); Ira Magaziner and Robert B. Reich, *Minding America's Business* (New York and London: Harcourt Brace Jovanovich, 1982); Barry Bluestone and Bennett Harrison, *The Deindustrialization of America* (New York: Basic Books, 1982).

5. A committee led by Senator Timothy Wirth produced *Rebuilding the Road to Opportunity* (Washington, D.C.: Democratic Committee on Party Effectiveness, 1982), which outlined an agenda for better education and training, investment in infrastructure, and a sharp increase in governmental support for commercial research and development.

6. See Jeremy Bernstein, "Allocating Sacrifice," *New Yorker*, January 23, 1983.

7. *Business Week*, July 4, 1983, pp. 54, 92.

8. Robert B. Reich, *The Next American Frontier* (New York: Times Books, 1983).

9. Quoted in Graham, *Losing Time*, p. 116.

10. The Greenspan quotation is from *Business Week*, July 4, 1983, p. 57.

11. The Fall 1984 issue of the *Cato Journal*, for example (vol. 4, no. 2), was devoted almost entirely to attacks on industrial policy. Many of the authors

simplified their work by defining "industrial policy" as essentially identical to Soviet central planning. See the introduction by James A. Dorn, "Planning America: Government or the Market," and the article by James C. Miller III, "The Case Against Industrial Policy."

12. *Economic Report of the President 1992*, Table B-2, p. 301; Table B-37, p. 340.

13. A 1986 article in the scholarly paper of record pronounced that "the Reagan revolution sealed the issue, ruling out a U.S. industrial policy for years to come." R.D. Norton, "Industrial Policy and American Renewal," *Journal of Economic Literature* 24, no. 1 (March 1986): 1.

14. See Martha Derthick, "The Enduring Features of American Federalism," *Brookings Review* 7, no. 3 (Summer 1989), esp. p. 35; John Herbers, "The Growing Role of the States Is Greater Than We Knew," *Governing* 3, no. 6 (March 1990); Susan S. Fainstein and Norman Fainstein, "The Ambivalent State: Economic Development Policy in the U.S. Federal System Under the Reagan Administration," *Urban Affairs Quarterly* 25, no. 1 (September 1989), esp. p. 42; Harvey A. Goldstein and Edward M. Bergman, "Institutional Arrangements for State and Local Industrial Policy," *Journal of the American Planning Association* 52, no. 3 (Summer 1986); and Enid F. Beaumont and Harold A. Hovey, "State, Local, and Federal Economic Development Policies: New Federal Patterns, Chaos, or What?" *Public Administration Review* 45, no. 2 (March/April 1985).

15. For a related discussion see Paul Brace and Gary Mucciaroni, "The American States and the Shifting Locus of Positive Economic Intervention," *Policy Studies Review* (Fall 1990). See also Aaron Wildavsky, "Industrial Policies in American Political Cultures," in *The Politics of Industrial Policy*, eds. Claude E. Barfield and William A. Schambra (Washington, D.C.: American Enterprise Institute, 1986), esp. p. 22.

16. Kathryn A. Pischak, "State Economic Development Incentives: What's Available? What Works?" *Municipal Finance Journal* 10, no. 4. (1989): 309. One of the society's promoters was Alexander Hamilton.

17. Handlin and Handlin, *Commonwealth*, pp. 78–79, 125.

18. The emergence of the states as financial intermediaries—and the abortive effort by Albert Gallatin, Jefferson's Treasury Secretary, to launch a national infrastructure investment campaign, are discussed in Sbragia, *Debt Wish*, Chapter 1. In the 1820s Henry Clay developed a grand proposal for using tariff revenues to finance a national campaign of infrastructure spending. But this scheme, labeled the "American System," came undone when Andrew Jackson—deeply antagonistic to centralized authority—won the presidency. See Thomas K. McCraw, "Mercantalism and the Market: Antecedents of American Industrial Policy," in *The Politics of Industrial Policy*, eds. Claude E. Barfield and William A. Schambra (Washington, D.C.: American Enterprise

Institute, 1986), pp. 39–41; and Wildavsky, "Industrial Policies in American Political Cultures," esp. p. 22.

19. Harry N. Scheiber, Harold G. Vatter, and Harold Underwood Faulkner, *American Economic History* (New York: Harper and Row, 1976), pp. 102–3. For many states one consequence of the infrastructure campaign was a mid-century financial debacle. Bond defaults and abandoned projects bequeathed a heritage of political sensitivities about state investments in private projects, and explicit restrictions that endure today in many state constitutions. For a more recent, and generally more optimistic, assessment of subnational economic development policy in American history, see Sbragia, *Debt Wish*.

20. These bonds essentially confer "public" status onto securities that finance private industrial projects, allowing bondholders to exempt the interest they receive from federal taxation.

21. For early histories of Southern-state development efforts, see Gilmore, *Developing the "Little" Economies*, p. 29. The Southern innovations in IRBs and tax concessions are discussed in Benjamin Bridges, Jr., "State and Local Inducements for Industry," *National Tax Journal* 18, no. 1 (March 1965), esp. pp. 6–8.

22. See Roger Vaughan, Robert Pollard, and Barbara Dyer, *The Wealth of States: Policies for a Dynamic Economy* (Washington, D.C.: CSPA, 1985). The success of BAWI and related programs, of course, was in some ways a hollow one, since many of the footloose, low-wage enterprises enticed to move to the South were just as easily enticed to move overseas, for similar reasons, a few decades later.

23. Robert J. Reinshuttle, "Economic Development: A Survey of State Activities" (Lexington, Ky.: Council of State Governments, 1983), p. 2; Sandra Kanter, "A History of State Business Subsidies," in *Proceedings of the Seventieth Annual Conference* (Washington, D.C.: National Tax Association–Tax Institute of America, 1977), p. 151; Edward F. Morrison, "State and Local Efforts to Encourage Economic Growth Through Innovation: An Historical Perspective," in *Technological Innovation-Strategies for a New Partnership* (North-Holland: Elsevier Science Publishers B.V., 1986), p. 60; National Association of State Development Agencies, 1992 Expenditure Survey. But as late as 1970, the states offering the richest packages of industrial incentives were still clustered in the Southeast. See Steven R. Kale, "U.S. Industrial Development Incentives and Manufacturing Growth During the 1970s," *Growth and Change* 15, no. 1 (January 1984), Figures 1 and 2, p. 28.

24. Meanwhile, a raft of studies showed that plant relocations were rare events; for example, see James P. Miller, "Manufacturing Relocations in the United States 1969–1975," in *Plant Closings: Public or Private Choices*, ed. Richard B. McKenzie (Washington, D.C.: Cato Institute, 1984). Miller shows

that, on average, fewer than three hundred plants per year moved from one state to another over the six-year period studied. More recent estimates by Dun and Bradstreet, however, are much higher.

25. The "second wave" was informed in part by an influential but controversial study suggesting the overwhelming importance of indigenous growth and the relative insignificance of industrial relocations. Peter M. Allaman and David L. Birch, "Components of Employment Change for Metropolitan and Rural Areas in the United States, 1970–1982" (Cambridge, Mass.: Joint Center for Urban Studies of Massachusetts Institute of Technology and Harvard University, 1976).

26. See, for example, John Herbers, "A Third Wave of Economic Development" and Doug Ross, "The Principles of the Third Wave," *Governing* 3, no. 9 (June 1990); and Dan Pilcher, "The Third Wave of Economic Development," *State Legislatures* 17, no. 11 (November 1991). Pilcher attributes the "third wave" term to Bob Friedman of the Corporation for Enterprise Development. Two academics summarized the new policies as "based on an export-based model of growth" and involving "less competition with other states than the 'beggar-thy-neighbor' supply-side policies" of previous decades. Virginia Gray and David Lowery, "The Corporatist Foundations of State Industrial Policy," *Social Science Quarterly* 71, no. 1 (March 1990): 5.

27. Robert Howard argues that American small-business policy is overwhelmingly state-based, and finds that forty-three states provided $700 million in startup financing in 1988. Robert Howard, "Can Small Business Help Countries Compete?" *Harvard Business Review* (November-December 1990).

28. State-level financial programs are no recent invention, with many examples—some cited here—dating from the colonial era. The first modern state loan guarantee program, though, was established in New Hampshire in 1955. New Hampshire was also a pioneer in programs that lent state money directly to businesses. But in the early postwar era the heaviest user of direct state lending programs was Pennsylvania. The Keystone State alone issued 77 percent of the $56 million total of state-level business lending between 1955 and 1963. Bridges, "State and Local Inducements for Industry," p. 3.

29. U.S. Department of Commerce, Economic Development Administration, "Strategies for Developing Effective State International Business Development Programs," prepared by Price Waterhouse, distributed by National Technical Information Service, June 1986, p. III-2; National Association of State Development Agencies Expenditure Survey, 1992.

30. National Governors' Association, *States in the International Economy* (Washington, D.C.: National Governors' Association, 1985). National Governors' Association, *International Trade* (NGA State Service Reports Program Brief, August 1989), p. 21. For a relevant, if somewhat unconvincing, article, see Elaine Webster, Edward J. Mathis, and Charles E. Zech, "The Case for

State-Level Export Promotion Assistance: A Comparison of Foreign and Domestic Export Employment Multipliers," _Economic Development Quarterly_ 4, no. 3 (August 1990). Robert Thomas Kurdle and Cynthia Marie Kite, "The Evaluation of State Programs for International Business Development," _Economic Development Quarterly_ 3, no. 4 (November 1989), find that "a generally satisfactory evaluation effort for any activity is rare" (p. 294).

31. Handlin and Handlin, _Commonwealth_, esp. pp. 75–77; Jurgen Schmandt and Robert Wilson, eds., _Promoting High-Technology Industry: Initiatives and Policies for State Governments_ (Boulder, Colo.: Westview Press, 1987), esp. pp. 3–6, 120–40; Robert D. Atkinson, "State Programs for Technology Development," National Association of State Development Agencies, Washington, D.C., April 1988, esp. p. 2.

32. Interview with Marianne Clarke, Program Director, Economic Development, Science, and Technology, Center for Policy Research, National Governors' Association, Washington, D.C., June 14, 1991.

33. Atkinson, "State Programs for Technology Development," p. 3. For a sense of the variety of technology-promotion programs, see F. Gregory Hayden with Douglas C. Kruse and Steve C. Williams, "Industrial Policy at the State Level in the United States," _Journal of Economic Issues_ 19, no. 2 (June 1985); Michael Peltz and Marc A. Weiss, "State and Local Government Roles in Industrial Innovation," _Journal of the American Planning Association_ 50, no. 3 (Summer 1984); Paul B. Phelps and Paul R. Brockman, _Science and Technology Programs in the States, 1992_ (Alexandria, Va.: Advanced Development Distribution, 1992); and (for a discussion that is somewhat more relevant to national than to state-level policy) Richard R. Nelson and Richard N. Langlois, "Industrial Innovation Policy: Lessons from American History," _Science_ 219, no. 4586 (February 18, 1983).

34. One category of programs involves _research funding_; while the federal government remains the major source of support for research and development, most states provide some support for applied technology research and development—usually through the state university system. (The vagaries of state budgeting practices make national spending totals close to meaningless for all state development programs. The problem is especially acute for research funding, since much of the relevant spending is commingled with university budgets.) Aside from the many state-level efforts meant to spur the development of business in general, some states have _high-technology investment-finance programs_ targeted specifically to technology-intensive companies, products, or processes. For example, the Massachusetts Technology Development Corporation was launched in the mid-1970s to make investments in technology-based firms that failed to attract support from conventional sources of venture capital. The MTDC was closed down in the 1990s, though Massachusetts retains a number of technology-promotion initiatives. See

Ronald F. Ferguson and Helen F. Ladd, "Economic Performance and Economic Development Policy in Massachusetts," Kennedy School of Government Discussion Paper, May 1986, p. 160; Schmandt and Wilson, eds., *Promoting High-Technology Industry*, pp. 84–87; Peter S. Fisher, "State Venture Capital Funds as an Economic Development Strategy," *Journal of the American Planning Association* 54 (Spring 1988): 167. Other states, instead of attempting to supplement incomplete capital markets, sought to accelerate the evolution of private financing mechanisms. Utah's Technology Finance Corporation and Pennsylvania's Seed Venture Capital Fund were both launched in the early 1980s to force-feed the venture capital industry in their respective states. Utah, one of the smallest and most fiscally cautious states, budgeted over $2 million for such loans in 1992.

35. Williamson is quoted in Elkins and McKitrick, *Age of Federalism*, p. 276.

36. Susan B. Hansen, for example, argues both (in principle) that "the states . . . are less likely to make the costly mistakes industrial policy critics have feared for federal efforts" and (empirically) that while critics of national industrial policy "predict that the winners will be chosen on the basis of political clout rather than economic logic, to a commendable degree, state industrial policy efforts have not borne out these predictions." Susan B. Hansen, "Targeting in Economic Development: Comparative State Perspectives," *Publius* 19, no. 2 (Spring 1989): 60, 51.

37. Peter Eisinger, *The Rise of the Entrepreneurial State*, p. 288.

38. Leonard Smith's shopping cart brake is described in "Start-Up Companies Find States Becoming Their Biggest Boosters," *Wall Street Journal*, January 13, 1989. I interviewed the pet-food condiment entrepreneur as one of several beneficiaries of a state technology extension program that (the reader will appreciate) must remain nameless. One somewhat subtle instance of a Type I error concerned the Massachusetts Technology Development Corporation (MTDC). The MTDC, founded in 1978 and in operation until the mid-1990s, was one of several state programs meant to promote the growth of technology-intensive businesses by making equity investments in specific research and development schemes undertaken by private firms. Most observers credited the MTDC as one of the more successful such programs. One appraisal, undertaken nearly a decade after the MTDC began making investments out of its state-appropriated initial capital, concluded approvingly that "operating income . . . has been sufficient to preserve the public's capital and to begin to augment it" (Fisher, "State Venture Capital Funds as an Economic Development Strategy," p. 170). Otherwise put, the corporation's net worth stayed essentially constant, in nominal dollars, over an eight-year interval. This represents an inflation-adjusted loss, on average, for a type of enterprise whose risk level implied a requirement for quite high average returns. MTDC funded

relatively few clear failures, but its portfolio was laden with the "living dead"—ventures making money, but too little money to graduate from venture capital sponsorship. In the absence of large and convincing social benefits to offset the financial costs, many of MTDC's investments must be counted as Type I mistakes, where government alters market judgments that turn out to be correct—in this case, judgments that the potential payoff of many high-technology startups is too low to justify the risk.

39. This is an advantage in principle, not necessarily in practice. See Frank J. Mauro and Glenn Yago, "State Government Targeting in Economic Development: The New York Experience," *Publius* 19, no. 2 (Spring 1989). For an interesting discussion of a related issue, see Hugh Heclo, "Industrial Policy and the Executive Capacities of Government," in *The Politics of Industrial Policy,* eds. Claude E. Barfield and William A. Schambra (Washington, D.C.: American Enterprise Institute, 1986).

40. See Harvey A. Goldstein, "The State and Local Industrial Policy Question," *Journal of the American Planning Association* 52, no. 3 (Summer 1986): 262–63. On the claim that regional diversity is a distinctive American advantage in economic adjustment, and a major argument against national industrial policy, see Norton, "Industrial Policy and American Renewal," pp. 25–27.

41. See L. Harmon Ziegler, "Interest Groups in the States," in *Politics in the American States,* eds. Virginia Gray, Herbert Jacob, and Kenneth N. Vines (Boston: Little, Brown, 1983).

42. For a provocative and ambitious (if not entirely convincing) empirical study concluding that organized occupational and business interests are able to arrange for profitable policies that fail to deliver promised broader benefits, see Margery Marzahn Ambrosius, "The Role of Occupational Interests in State Economic Development Policy-Making," *Western Political Quarterly* 42, no. 1 (March 1989).

43. See Ziegler, "Interest Groups in the States," p. 113. For some suggestive evidence on related issues see Virginia Gray and David Lowery, "Interest Group Politics and Economic Growth in the U.S. States," *American Political Science Review* 82, no. 1 (March 1988): 128; and Sally McCally Morehouse, *State Politics, Parties, and Policy* (New York: Holt, Rinehart and Winston, 1981), esp. Table 3-1, pp. 108–12.

44. Mack C. Shelley et al., "State Legislators and Economic Development: University-Industry Relationships and the Role of Government in Biotechnology," *Policy Studies Review* 9, no. 3 (Spring 1990): 457–58.

45. See David Osborne, "Refining State Technology Programs," *Issues in Science and Technology* 6, no. 4 (Summer 1990), esp. p. 56.

46. Bill Clinton's Arkansas and Al Gore's Tennessee were two of the seven states with the most powerful economic development agencies, accord-

ing to Dennis O. Grady, "Economic Development and Administrative Power Theory: A Comparative Analysis of State Development Agencies," *Policy Studies Review* 8, no. 2 (Winter 1989), Table 5, p. 334.

47. National Association of State Development Agencies, 1992 Expenditure Survey. Average state appropriations fell from $32.5 million to $25.2 million, though much of the decline was concentrated in a few large states and (because of federal transfers) spending fell far less than did appropriations. See also Eileen Shanahan, "The Other Side of Recession," *Governing* (March 1991).

CHAPTER SIX: THE COURTSHIP OF CAPITAL

1. While the intensity of competition has risen and fallen over time; while the federal government's stance has ranged from disengagement to intervention in disadvantaged (mostly Southern) states' favor; and while a few states have on occasion sought to limit business growth, throughout American history the courtship of industry has been standard state practice. Dividing lines are inevitably artificial, but the modern era of business-attraction policy may be marked by the "Balance Agriculture with Industry" campaign launched in Mississippi in 1936. For one reference, see Vaughan, Pollard, and Dyer, *Wealth of States.* A general increase in industrial mobility in the early postwar era helped set the stage for interstate competition. Chinitz and Vernon trace the mid-century dispersal of industry from the Northeast, and attribute it to several factors, including the generally declining importance of proximity to raw materials; the shift to highway-based transportation; and, in some industries, greater sensitivity to labor and other input costs. Benjamin Chinitz and Raymond Vernon, "Changing Forces in Industrial Location," *Harvard Business Review* 38 (1960).

2. Hard data are scarce, but what evidence there is suggests that states devote three to twelve times as much to targeted tax reductions as they spend on direct economic development programs. Timothy J. Bartik, "Jobs, Productivity, and Local Economic Development: What Implications Does Economic Research Have for the Role of Government?" *National Tax Journal* (December 1994): 848.

3. Quoted in Michael R. Gordon, "With Foreign Investment at Stake, It's One State Against the Others," *National Journal* 18, (October 1980): 1746–47. See also Norman J. Glickman and Douglas P. Woodward, *The New Competitors: How Foreign Investors Are Changing the U.S. Economy* (New York: Basic Books, 1989), p. 232. Kentucky's state government, at around the same time, sold $78 million in state bonds in Japan to create a public fund for luring Japanese corporations, using subsidized loans conveniently denominated in yen instead of dollars. Penelope Lemov, "Sunset for IDBs," *Governing* 2, no. 10 (July 1989): 49.

4. "Hubsidies," *Economist*, January 4, 1992, p. 27; other information from May 1996 presentation by Arthur J. Rolnick, Conference on Economic War Among the States, Washington, D.C.

5. Brett Pulley, "New York Makes Staying Put Irresistible to Coffee Exchange," *New York Times*, October 13, 1995.

6. Jerry Ackerman, "Lower Taxes, Murky Results," *Boston Globe*, September 17, 1995, and "Fidelity Links Building Plan to Tax Cuts," *Boston Globe*, May 10, 1996. All told, mid-1990s legislation delivered lower tax breaks for defense contractors, manufacturers in general, banks, and mutual fund companies, as well as lowering both the capital gains and estate taxes. Charles Stein, "State Losing Taxachusetts Tag Among Executives," *Boston Globe*, August 9, 1996.

7. The National Association of State Development Agencies publishes a biennial *Survey of State Economic Development Expenditures*, but categories of spending are highly aggregated, and reporting states use their own judgment about what kinds of spending to count as development-related. While the NASDA tallies are informative to practitioners, they shouldn't really be used for research, though they frequently are.

8. Director of KPMG-Peat Marwick's Business Incentives Group, quoted in David Cay Johnston, "Boom Seen in State and Local Tax Aid to Business," *New York Times*, September 21, 1995.

9. "New York and California Losing Jobs, South Atlantic and Mountain States Gaining," Dun and Bradstreet, Murray Hill, New Jersey, January 1997. Ten states, mostly in the Southeast, gained over 10,000 jobs each. California and New York both *lost* around 80,000 jobs.

10. Sophia Koropeckyj, "Do Economic Development Incentives Matter?" *Regional Financial Review* (February 1996): 16.

11. Two such books published in 1995 alone are Kenneth C. Wagner, *How to Create Jobs in the 90s* (Albany: Wagner Group, 1995), and Eric P. Canada, *Economic Development: Marketing for Results* (Wheaton, Ill.: Blane, Canada, 1995).

12. KPMG-Peat Marwick LLP, Business Incentives Group, "Business Incentives and Tax Credits: A Boon for Business or Corporate Welfare?" New York, September 1995, p. 5.

13. A special issue of *Business Week* may mark the popular debut of the term. *Business Week*, "Multinational Companies: A Special Report," April 20, 1963.

14. The same pace of growth is unlikely to continue—indeed, an equal acceleration for another decade is probably impossible to achieve—but foreign direct investment has recovered from its 1992 collapse. Data on foreign direct investment are published annually, usually in March, in the *Survey of Current Business*, U.S. Department of Commerce, Bureau of Economic Analysis.

15. For one illuminating historical perspective, see Ann M. Carlos and Stephen Nicholas, "Giants of an Earlier Capitalism: The Chartered Trading Companies as Modern Multinationals," *Business History Review* 62, no. 3 (Autumn 1988).

16. Cleona Lewis, *America's Stake in International Investments* (Washington, D.C.: Brookings Institution, 1938); reference to oil investments, pp. 94–98; motives for early investments, pp. 310–13. See also Peter J. Buckley and Brian R. Roberts, *European Direct Investment in the USA Before World War I* (New York: St. Martin's Press, 1982), and Robert F. Lipsey, *Changing Patterns of International Investment in and by the United States* (Cambridge, Mass.: National Bureau of Economic Research, 1987).

17. See Edward M. Graham and Paul R. Krugman, *Foreign Direct Investment in the United States* (Washington, D.C.: Institute for International Economics, 1989), p. 44.

18. "The mere spot they stand on," Jefferson continued, "does not constitute so strong an attachment as that from which they draw their gains." Letter to Horatio Spafford, March 17, 1814, quoted in Bernard Snoy, *Taxes on Direct Investment Income in the EEC: A Legal and Economic Analysis* (New York: Praeger Publishers, 1975), p. x.

19. Thorstein Veblen, *The Vested Interests and the Common Man* (New York: B. W. Huebsche, 1920), p. 132.

20. C. P. Kindleberger, *American Business Abroad: Six Lectures on Direct Investment* (New Haven, Conn.: Yale University Press, 1969), p. 207. At around the same time, George Ball, then Undersecretary of State, argued that "to achieve its full potential, the multinational corporation must be able to decide and to act with little regard for national boundaries—or in other words, for restrictions imposed by individual national governments—and this implies, of course, a considerable erosion of the rigid concepts of national sovereignty. Such an erosion is not new; it is an inescapable feature of the modern age; and it is taking place every day as national economies grow increasingly interdependent. It is a process that should, I think, be consciously encouraged." Quotation from a 1967 official speech in Japan, quoted in Jack N. Behrman, *National Interests and Multinational Enterprise: Tensions Among the North Atlantic Countries* (Englewood Cliffs, N.J.: Prentice-Hall, 1970), p. 182. For especially good samples of the rich literature on multinational firms, see Raymond Vernon, *Sovereignty at Bay* (New York: Basic Books, 1971), Gregory Adam, "New Trends in International Business: Worldwide Sourcing and Dedomiciling," *Acta Oeconomica* 7, no. 3–4 (1971), and John H. Dunning, "Explaining Changing Patterns of International Production: In Defense of the Eclectic Theory," *Oxford Bulletin of Economics and Statistics* 41, no. 4 (November 1979); Stephen H. Hymer, *The International Operations of National Firms: A Study of Direct Foreign Investment* (Cambridge, Mass.: MIT Press, 1976 (written 1960),

in shorter form as "The Internationalization of Capital," *Journal of Economic Issues* 6, no. 1 (March 1972). A little-noticed but poignant illustration of the American economy's integration into world markets occurred in the late 1980s when a historically evocative piece of American real estate—the Watergate—was sold by one European owner to another European owner. Peter Rashish, "Still Discovering America," *Europe*, no. 296 (May 1990): 17.

21. Neela Banerjee, "Russia's Many Regions Work to Attract Funds from Foreign Investors," *Wall Street Journal*, June 30, 1996.

22. See Snoy, *Taxes on Direct Investment Income in the EEC*, esp. Table 27.5, p. 289. For similar research focused on Scotland, see Keith P.D. Ingham, "Foreign Ownership and the Regional Problem: Company Performance in the Mechanical Engineering Industry," *Oxford Economic Papers* 28, no. 1 (March 1976).

23. For example, economists Graham and Krugman write, "The real problem with state-level investment incentives is not the absence of offsetting performance requirements, but rather the inherent tendency of interstate competition to transfer rents from the United States to foreign firms." Graham and Krugman, *Foreign Direct Investment*, p. 119.

24. In a non–U.S. setting, Dermot McAleese and Michael Counahan found "no evidence that MNC's [multinational corporations] behave in a systematically different fashion from their Irish-owned counterparts. Apparent differences in employment stability turned out to be entirely attributable to industry mix." Dermot McAleese and Michael Counahan, "Stickers or Snatchers? Employment in Multinational Corporations During the Recession," *Oxford Bulletin of Economics and Statistics* 41, no. 4 (November 1979): 346–48. For some observations in the American setting, see Norman J. Glickman, Amy Glasmeier, Geoffrey Bannister, and William Luker, Jr., "Foreign Investment, Industrial Linkages & Regional Development" (Austin: Lyndon B. Johnson School of Public Affairs, University of Texas at Austin, 1989), esp. pp. 46–53, 221–22.

25. Robert Perrucci, *Japanese Auto Transplants in the Heartland* (New York: Aldine de Gruyter, 1994). The cost per job for the Honda package is even less if subsequent rounds of investment are taken into account. A team of scholars that studied the deal have suggested that in this deal at least, the incentives were not of great *financial* importance to Honda—but were significant nonetheless. American attitudes toward Japanese automakers were by no means uniformly warm in early 1980, and Honda officials were eager to avoid anchoring a major plant in a hostile or culturally unwelcoming locale. The incentives symbolized public officials' willingness to accommodate Honda, and in that sense may have mattered greatly. John P. Blair, Carole Endres, and Rudy Fichtenbaum, "Japanese Automobile Investment in West Central Ohio: Economic Development and Labor-Management Issues," in *The Politics of In-*

dustrial Recruitment: Japanese Automobile Investment and Economic Development in the American States, eds. Ernest J. Yanarella and William C. Green (Westport, Conn.: Greenwood Press, 1991), p. 127.

26. Blair, Endres, and Fichtenbaum, "Japanese Automobile Investment in West Central Ohio," p. 133.

27. Gordon, "With Foreign Investment at Stake," pp. 1744–45, and Eisinger, *Entrepreneurial State*, p. 294.

28. Except where noted otherwise, estimated cost-per-job figures for the auto assembly plant investments come from H. Brinton Milward and Heidi Newman, "State Incentive Packages and the Industrial Location Decision," *Economic Development Quarterly* 3, no. 3 (August 1989), Table 4, p. 212.

29. Lynn W. Bachelor, "Flat Rock, Michigan, Trades a Ford for a Mazda: State Policy and the Evaluation of Plant Location Incentives," in *The Politics of Industrial Recruitment: Japanese Automobile Investment and Economic Development in the American States*, eds. Ernest J. Yanarella and William C. Green (Westport, Conn.: Greenwood Press, 1991), p. 98.

30. William Fulton, "The Rabbit That Got Away," *Governing*, June 1982, p. 47.

31. There was in fact some resistance on the part of Bloomington-Normal to a new auto assembly plant. As state officials launched into negotiations— and as a gubernatorial election stepped up the sense of urgency—they had to reassure not just Diamond-Star, but local officials as well. Nancy S. Lind and Ann H. Elder, "Who Pays? Who Benefits? The Case of the Incentive Package Offered to the Diamond-Star Automotive Plant," *Government Finance Review* 2, no. 6 (December 1986): 19–21.

32. Other incentives came from Bloomington and Normal city governments; from the county and township governments; and from the school and sewer districts and the airport authority. Lind and Elder, "Who Pays? Who Benefits?" Table 1, p. 22. See also Margaret L. Chapman et al., *Mitsubishi Motors in Illinois* (Westport, Conn.: Quorum Books, 1995), pp. 25–30. Nancy Lind raises the point that firms have an interest in getting as many types and levels of government as possible to cooperate in assembling an incentive package for a site. Economists would say this is analogous to summing individual demand curves for a public good. See Nancy S. Lind, "Economic Development and Diamond-Star Motors: Intergovernmental Competition and Cooperation," in *The Politics of Industrial Recruitment: Japanese Automobile Investment and Economic Development in the American States*, eds. Ernest J. Yanarella and William C. Green (Westport, Conn.: Greenwood Press, 1991), pp. 110–12.

33. The joint venture dissolved in the early 1990s, and the plant became an exclusive Mitsubishi operation.

34. Ernest J. Yanarella and Herbert G. Reid, "Problems of Coalition Building in Japanese Auto Alley: Public Opposition to the Georgetown Toyota

Plant," in *The Politics of Industrial Recruitment: Japanese Automobile Investment and Economic Development in the American States*, eds. Ernest J. Yanarella and William C. Green (Westport, Conn.: Greenwood Press, 1991), pp. 154–55.

35. *Automotive News*, December 11, 1995.

36. In part they were merely leapfrogging the quantitative restrictions on imports of Japanese autos under the Voluntary Restraint Agreement negotiated by the Reagan Administration. Longer term, they were attempting to enlist U.S. workers and officials as allies, and Americanize the public face of their companies, to insulate themselves against protectionist sentiments in the future.

37. *Automotive News* gave the cost per job as $65,000; a National Public Radio program gave a figure of $75,000. As always, these figures cannot be taken entirely seriously, but it is probably true that the BMW deal was a bit richer than previous packages.

38. Mark Tran, "$300 m Tax Break Clinches Mercedes Plant for Alabama," *Manchester Guardian* (Manchester, England), October 1, 1993.

39. Allen R. Myerson, "Oh Governor, Won't You Buy Me a Mercedes Plant?" *New York Times*, September 1, 1996.

40. "When each of the states are offering essentially similar incentive packages in terms of the types of benefits being provided," David Lowery concluded in a study focused on the recruitment of the Japanese automakers, "their next recourse is to offer more of each." David Lowery, "The National Level Roots of the Failure of State Industrial Policy," in *The Politics of Industrial Recruitment: Japanese Automobile Investment and Economic Development in the American States*, eds. Ernest J. Yanarella and William C. Green (Westport, Conn.: Greenwood Press, 1991), p. 200. See also Milward and Newman, "State Incentive Packages and the Industrial Location Decision," p. 219.

41. This is not a phenomenon limited to the United States. In mid-1996 General Motors announced plans to build its first assembly plant in Asia. The Philippines offered a site developed to GM's specifications rent-free for five years, an eight-year tax holiday, duty-free equipment imports, and taxpayer-financed worker training—in other words, the kind of package that came to be seen as an American standard. Seth Mydans, "GM to Tap Asian Markets, and Two Nations Bid for Plant," *New York Times*, May 28, 1996.

42. Calculated from Table 5 and Table 6, Milward and Newman, "State Incentive Packages and the Industrial Location Decision," pp. 214–15.

43. See Robert B. Reich and John D. Donahue, *New Deals: The Chrysler Revival and the American System* (New York: Times Books, 1985), esp. Chapter 7.

44. Long ago Raymond Vernon termed the link between policy and business location "a subject steeped in pure emotion and impure data," and the characterization still holds good. Edgar M. Hoover and Raymond Vernon, *Anatomy of a Metropolis* (New York: Doubleday Anchor Books, 1962), p. 55.

45. I am indebted to Ann Hoeffer Pax for helping me track down this half-remembered exchange.

46. For examples of the "Pascal's wager" perspective, see Harold Wolman, "Local Economic Development Policy: What Explains the Divergence Between Policy Analysis and Political Behavior?" *Journal of Urban Affairs* 10, no. 1 (1984); and Paul Peretz, "The Market for Industry: Where Angels Fear to Tread?" *Policy Studies Review* 5, no. 3 (February 1986).

47. Two well-known researchers have argued just the opposite—that state taxes and spending *did* affect employment growth (especially in manufacturing) from the mid-1960s to the mid-1980s, but have more recently lost their punch. Robert Carroll and Michael Wasylenko, "Do State Business Climates Still Matter? Evidence of a Structural Change," *National Tax Journal* 47, no. 1 (March 1994), esp. Tables 3 and 4, pp. 28–29, and the concluding sections on pp. 30–31. Carroll and Wasylenko suggest that competitive pressures from overseas may now swamp the effects of interstate competition. Another team of empirical researchers also dissent from the "revisionist" view of increasingly potent state policies, finding that "the evidence that tax policies have become more important determinants of economic growth in recent years is weak"— though even they find somewhat stronger evidence for the post-1975 period than earlier that state tax policy affects economic growth. Wei Yu, Myles S. Wallace, and Clark Nardinelli, "State Growth Rates: Taxes, Spending, and Catching Up," *Public Finance Quarterly* 19, no. 1 (January 1991): 91.

48. Allen R. Myerson, "Follow the Leader," *New York Times*, October 13, 1995.

49. Most surveyed executives perceived no competitive advantage in location incentives, since they assumed all their rivals had them as well. KPMG-Peat Marwick LLP, Business Incentives Group, "Business Incentives and Tax Credits," p. 9.

50. Handlin and Handlin, *Commonwealth*, p. 79.

51. Alan A. Altshuler and Jose A. Gomez-Ibanez, *Regulating for Revenue: The Political Economy of Land Use Exactions* (Washington, D.C.: Brookings Institution, 1993), Chapter 6.

52. Press release from State Senator Charles Horn, Columbus, Ohio, September 20, 1995.

53. Johnston, "Boom Seen in State and Local Tax Aid to Business."

54. Robert G. Lynch, "Do State and Local Tax Incentives Work?" (Washington, D.C.: Economic Policy Institute, 1996).

55. Ken Gepfert, "North Carolina Recruiters Set New Bait for Firms," *Wall Street Journal*, Southeastern edition, August 14, 1996.

56. Kale, "U.S. Industrial Development Incentives," esp. p. 29.

57. Myerson, "Oh Governor, Won't You Buy Me a Mercedes Plant?" A private communication with a senior Mercedes official who prefers not to be

identified confirms that Alabama would not have been chosen without the incentive package.

58. Few workers hired by Mercedes jump up from Alabama's average wage to the higher Mercedes wage; most move to Mercedes from better-than-average previous jobs. In that sense, the back-of-the-envelope calculation is probably biased high. On the other hand, the number of jobs attributable to Mercedes will likely be higher than two thousand—the plant itself is scheduled to employ as many as ten thousand, and predictions of job "multipliers," while characteristically overblown, are not *entirely* spurious. Moreover, the figures cited for the cost of the Mercedes deal—ranging from $160 million to $300 million—are biased upward by the failure to discount costs that occur in future years, among other factors. Calibrating the *net* effect on a state's economy of business-attraction policies is a complex and much-studied issue. For early examples of the literature, see James R. Rinehart, "Rates of Return on Municipal Subsidies to Industry," *Southern Economic Journal* (April 1963); and William Morgan and Merlin Hackbart, "An Analysis of State and Local Industrial Tax Exemption Programs," *Southern Economic Journal* (October 1974). For a recent example of the theoretical literature, see James R. Rogers, "The Futility of State Tax Competition for Business Site Selections," paper prepared for delivery at the Midwest Political Science Association meeting, Chicago, April 18–20, 1996.

59. Bartik, "Jobs, Productivity, and Local Economic Development," p. 852. Bartik's own estimate is that, long term, about 20 percent of the new jobs in a metropolitan area go to original local residents (p. 854); the figure for a *state* is probably somewhat higher.

60. Competitiveness Policy Council, "Saving More and Investing Better: A Strategy for Securing Prosperity," Fourth Report to the President and Congress, September 1995, p. 47.

61. Many analysts, notably Timothy Bartik, have emphasized that the net benefits of location incentives depend crucially on whether they shift jobs not just across state borders, but into areas of high joblessness or underemployment. This line of reasoning has long been invoked to justify the distinctive business-attraction aggressiveness of Southern states from the Depression years until the 1980s. For a related observation, see Peterson, *Price of Federalism*, p. 29.

62. Graham S. Toft, "Doing Battle over the Incentives War: Improve Accountability but Avoid Federal Noncompete Mandates," in *The Economic War Among the States* (Minneapolis: Federal Reserve Bank of Minneapolis, 1996), pp. 8, 10.

63. One of the more prominent themes in most proposals for smarter interstate competition is the use of "clawback" provisions that require subsidized firms to reimburse states and localities if they fall short of promises about the

quantity, quality, or duration of employment that motivated location incentives. (These provisions are essentially variants of the "performance requirements" long common in Western European and some less developed nations.)
For a good discussion of this theme, see Blaine Liner and Larry Ledebur, "Foreign Direct Investment in the United States: A Governor's Guide" (Washington, D.C.: Urban Institute, 1987), pp. 7, 10.

64. Competitiveness Policy Council, "Saving More and Investing Better."

65. Brian Dabson, Carl Rist, and William Schweke, "Business Climate
and the Role of Development Incentives," in *The Economic War Among the
States* (Minneapolis: Federal Reserve Bank of Minneapolis, 1996), p. 19.

66. Jack Behrman, "Impact of Inward Direct Investment on North Car-
olina Development" in *The Costs and Benefits of Foreign Investment from a State
Perspective*, U.S. Department of Commerce, International Trade Administra-
tion, prepared by the Southern Center for International Studies, distributed by
U.S. Department of Commerce, Office of Trade and Investment Analysis,
Washington, D.C., August 1982, pp. 137–38.

67. For a fairly representative example, see Joe Mattey and Mark Spiegel,
"On the Efficiency Effects of Tax Competition for Firms," in *The Economic
War Among the States* (Minneapolis: Federal Reserve Bank of Minneapolis,
1996). Mattey and Spiegel are worried about distortions resulting from efforts
to curb competition—certainly a valid concern—and are spectacularly un-
troubled by the prospect of states losing resources, suggesting that costs can be
cut or transfers from the federal government arranged if problems arise.

68. U.S. Bureau of the Census, State Government Tax Collections, series
GF, no. 1, summarized in *Statistical Abstract of the United States 1994*, Table
479; 1994 data from Commerce Department on-line data.

69. Tax data from U.S. Bureau of the Census, *Government Finance*, various
issues; corporate income data from U.S. Department of the Treasury, Internal
Revenue Service, *Statement of Income Bulletin*, Spring 1996. The figures given
are for corporate income on a NIPA basis; stated on a statement-of-income basis the increase between 1970–73 and 1990–93 is smaller.

70. National Conference of State Legislatures, *State Tax Actions 1995*
(Washington, D.C.: National Conference of State Legislatures, 1995), Table
1, p. 8.

71. Information on these more aggressive forms of tax incentives came
from conversations with development officials and from a review of New Jersey, Michigan, and Kentucky state government Web sites in July, August, and
September 1996. Similar innovations are in place or under development in
other states.

72. Lawrence J. White, "Should Competition to Attract New Investment
Be Restricted?" *New York Affairs* 9, no. 3 (1986): 13.

73. Eisinger, *Entrepreneurial State*, pp. 146, 150–51.

74. Trico and Gulf States anecdotes from Myerson, "Oh Governor, Won't You Buy Me a Mercedes Plant?" For commentary on this general issue I recommend an essay of shining common sense (though its conclusions differ somewhat from mine) by Dick Netzer. He calls on states to concentrate on training and technology, remedy irrational distortions in their tax codes, and avoid the kinds of capital and credit subsidies that are more likely to be wasteful. But development incentives, on balance, are "neither very good nor very bad from the standpoint of efficient resource allocation in the economy. . . . Given the low cost-effectiveness of most instruments, there is little national impact, only a waste of local resources in most cases." Five years ago when Netzer wrote, the consequences of draining discretionary resources from states may have seemed smaller than they do today. Dick Netzer, "An Evaluation of Interjurisdictional Competition Through Economic Development Incentives," in *Competition Among States and Local Governments*, eds. Daphne Kenyon and John Kincaid (Washington, D.C.: Urban Institute Press, 1991), p. 127.

75. For an experienced perspective on calls for adopting positive-sum business-attraction policies, see Morrison, "State and Local Efforts to Encourage Economic Growth."

76. Detailed field research done in the early 1980s suggested that Japanese firms, in particular, focus almost entirely on firm-specific skills. State assistance to cover the cost of such training would have few meaningful differences from a simple grant. Duane Kujawa, "Production Practices and Strategies of Foreign Multinationals in the United States—Case Studies with a Special Focus on the Japanese," paper prepared for Bureau of International Labor Affairs, U.S. Department of Labor, December 1984, Appendix, Table 16.

77. Richard Lester et al., "Tough Questions for Manufacturing in Massachusetts," report commissioned by Raytheon Company, September 1995, pp. ii, 8–9.

78. Alan H. Peters and Peter S. Fisher, "Do High Unemployment States Offer the Biggest Business Incentives? Results for Eight States Using the 'Hypothetical Firm' Method," *Economic Development Quarterly*, forthcoming. Peters and Fisher found "no evidence to suggest that states and cities with less competitive tax structures tend to offer more incentives." While high-unemployment areas showed *some* tendency to offer higher incentives, these areas also had higher average tax rates to begin with, so there was "no discernible tendency for [posttax and subsidy] returns to be more attractive in high-unemployment or in low-unemployment places."

79. KPMG-Peat Marwick LLP, Business Incentives Group, "Business Incentives and Tax Credits," pp. 6–8.

80. Mary B. W. Tabor, "In Bookstore Chains, Display Space Is for Sale," *New York Times*, January 15, 1996.

81. The classic article on this point is R.H. Coase, "The Nature of the Firm," *Economica* (November 1937).

82. Efforts by developing nations to form a common front against global capital have a three-decade history of failure. The August 1993 NGA initiative is discussed in Competitiveness Policy Council, "Saving More and Investing Better," p. 48. See also Wolman, "Local Economic Development Policy," esp. p. 27.

83. On LDC efforts to forge investment alliances, see Kindleberger, *American Business Abroad*, p. 204.

84. Treaty of Rome's Article 92 (1), 14-003 to 14-103.

85. Robert Knox, *Towards 1992: State Aids to Industry* (Brussels, European Commission), p. 39. "The Commission forbids all forms of aid that cause too marked a distortion of competition, but in the past it has been obliged to let many trespassers go unpunished." William Molle, *The Economics of European Integration* (Brookfield, Vt.: Dartmouth University Press, 1990), p. 370. For general discussions of EU restrictions on member-state industrial subsidies, see Conor Quigly, "The Notion of a State Aid in the EEC," *European Law Review* (August 1988); Piet Jan Slot, "Procedural Aspects of State Aids: The Guardian of Competition Versus the Subsidy Villains?" *Common Market Law Review* 27 ([month unknown] 1990); Despina Schina, *State Aids Under the EEC Treaty Articles 92 to 94* (Oxford: ESC Publishing, 1987); Commission of the European Communities, "Second Survey on State Aids in the European Community in the Manufacturing and Certain Other Sectors," 1990; and Manfred Caspari, "The Aid Rules of the EEC Treaty and Their Application," in *Discretionary Powers of the Member States in the Field of Economic Policies and Their Limits Under the EEC Treaty*, ed. Jurgen Schwarze (Baden-Baden, Germany: Nomos Verlagsgesellschaft, 1988).

86. For example, C. Fred Bergsten and Edward M. Graham have advocated multinational investment rules featuring curbs on subnational investment incentives; Robert B. Reich once proposed the creation of a "U.S. Investment Representative" analogous to the U.S. Trade Representative, to act as the single agent of the American workforce in negotiations with multinational capital. See C. Fred Bergsten and Edward M. Graham, "Global Corporations and National Governments: Are Changes Needed in the International Economic and Political Order in Light of the Globalization of Business," mimeo; Institute for International Economics, 1990; Robert B. Reich, "Who Is Them?" *Harvard Business Review* (March-April 1991), esp. pp. 87–88. Multinational negotiations on an investment accord were under way at the time of this writing, and some delegations (notably New Zealand's) were calling for limits on subnational investment incentives.

87. Melvin L. Burstein and Arthur J. Rolnick, "Congress Should End the

Economic War Among the States," Federal Reserve Bank of Minneapolis, 1994 Annual Report, March 1995, p. 10.

88. Ibid., p. 7.

89. *Metropolitan Life Insurance Co. v. Ward*, 470 U.S. 869, 879 (1985), and *West Lynn Creamery v. Healy*, 114 S. Ct. 2205, 2214 (1994).

90. Walter Hellerstein, "Commerce Clause Restraints on State Tax Incentives," in *The Economic War Among the States* (Minneapolis: Federal Reserve Bank of Minneapolis, 1996), p. 33. Peter D. Enrich, "Saving the States from Themselves: Commerce Clause Constraints on State Tax Incentives for Business," *Harvard Law Review*, vol. 110, no. 2 (December 1996).

91. Graham and Krugman, *Foreign Direct Investment*, p. 119.

92. Executive Director of Louisiana Office of Commerce and Industry, quoted in S. Young and B. L. Kedia, "Costs and Benefits of Foreign Investment from a State Perspective: The Case of Louisiana," U.S. Department of Commerce, International Trade Administration, "The Costs and Benefits of Foreign Investment from a State Perspective," prepared by the Southern Center for International Studies, distributed by ITA's Office of Trade and Investment Analysis, Washington, D.C., August 1982, p. 120.

93. U.S. General Accounting Office, "Foreign Direct Investment in the United States—The Federal Role," June 3, 1980, p. 34. For a discussion of similar attitudes on the part of subnational officials in Germany, Canada, Britain, Italy, and France, see Behrman, *National Interests and Multinational Enterprise*, p. 146.

Chapter Seven: Commonwealth and Competition

1. Elkins and McKitrick, *Age of Federalism*, Chapter 4.

2. Hartz is quoted in Sbragia, *Debt Wish*, p. 29.

3. Charles M. Tiebout, "A Pure Theory of Local Expenditures," *Journal of Political Economy* 64, no. 5 (October 1956). It does not diminish Tiebout's accomplishment to point out that the idea is hardly novel; the basic theme of competition as a check on governmental power is central to the Constitution, and figures explicitly in Federalist 10, for example.

4. Tiebout, "A Pure Theory of Local Expenditures," pp. 422, 418.

5. The Tiebout model enchants theorists by seeming to subordinate political logic to economic logic once and for all. The particulars of running a community become as irrelevant to the scholar as the particulars of running an assembly line—amid the competitive struggle, *somebody* will get things right, and resources and consumers will sort themselves out accordingly.

6. Perhaps the most full-blown recent example of this theme is Thomas R. Dye, *American Federalism: Competition Among Governments* (Lexington, Mass.: Lexington Books, 1990). "Competitive federalism envisions a marketplace for governments where consumer-taxpayers can voluntarily choose the

public goods and services they prefer, at the cost they wish to pay, by locating in the governmental jurisdiction that best fits their policy preferences. In this model of federalism, state and local governments compete for consumer-tax-payers by offering the best array of public goods and services at the lowest possible costs. The preferences of all individuals in society are better met in a system of multiple governments offering different packages of services and costs than of a single monopoly government, even a democratic one, offering a single package reflecting the preferences of the majority. The greater number of governments to select from, and the greater the variance in public policies among them, the closer each consumer-taxpayer can come to realizing his or her own preferences" (p. 14).

7. Advisory Commission on Intergovernmental Relations, *Interjurisdictional Tax and Policy Competition: Good or Bad for the Federal System?* ACIR (April 1991), p. 4.

8. Edgar K. Browning and Jacqueline M. Browning, *Public Finance and the Price System* (New York: Macmillan, 1983), p. 469.

9. Peterson, *Price of Federalism*, p. 27.

10. Gary S. Becker, "The Commonwealth's Best Chance Is Competition," *Business Week*, February 3, 1992.

11. Croly, *Promise of American Life*, p. 347.

12. F. M. Scherer and David Ross, *Industrial Market Structure and Economic Performance*, 3rd edition (Boston: Houghton Mifflin, 1990), p. 18.

13. Ibid., p. 31. An interesting argument that increasing competition in technology-based industries is depressing the level of basic research can be found in Andrew M. Odlyzko, "The Decline of Unfettered Research," paper prepared for Bell Labs, Murray Hill, N.J., October 1995.

14. Kevin C. Blackman and Dan R. Miller, "Public Investment in Professional Sports: An Analysis of the Economic and Credit Implications," Policy Analysis Exercise, John F. Kennedy School of Government, April 1996.

15. This illustrates the broader point that market power is defined by context. The integration of once-segmented national economies changes conventional metrics of market power. A cozy monopoly becomes vulnerable if falling transaction costs or lowered trade barriers give customers the option of imports. The Federal Trade Commission—a major enforcer of the antitrust laws that are meant to protect consumers by forbidding business collusion—is beginning to redefine market power, and recalibrate the degree of domestic combination it will permit, by taking into account non-American players in an industry. See *Anticipating the 21st Century: Competition Policy in the New High-Tech, Global Marketplace*, Federal Trade Commission Staff Report, Washington, D.C., May 1996.

16. Milt Freudenheim, "$2.3 Billion Deal Creates Giant in Managing of Doctors' Offices," *New York Times*, May 15, 1996.

17. Steven Greenhouse, "Podiatrists to Form Nationwide Union; A Reply to H.M.O.'s," *New York Times*, October 25, 1996.

18. Dr. Apolinair A. Henriquez, quoted in Peter T. Kilborne, "Feeling Devalued by Change, Doctors Seek Union Banner," *New York Times*, May 30, 1996. In a more garden-variety example of the economic power of organization, several large corporations, including Chrysler and Procter & Gamble, formed a consortium in 1996 to negotiate fares with airlines. Adam Bryant, "Southwest in Accord on Corporate Fares," *New York Times*, April 1, 1996.

19. See James Sterngold, "Boeing's Deal Quickens Pace for Arms Industry Takeovers," *The New York Times*, December 17, 1996.

20. Federalist 11, *Federalist Papers*, pp. 85–86, p. 91. See also Abel, "The Commerce Clause in the Constitutional Convention."

21. Alan Dembner, "Schools Vying for Students Add Merit Aid," *Boston Globe*, September 12, 1995 (in which Thomas Gerety, the president of Amherst, laments that this "path leads to less opportunity for the poor and more for the wealthy. It's a bidding war for the well-to-do student"). See also Davidson Goldin, "Ivy League Plans an Audit to Enforce Its Policy Against Athletic Scholarships," *New York Times*, April 5, 1996.

22. The sickest 10 percent cost an average of $28,120 per year; the rest, an average of $1,340. The figures come from Health Care Finance Administration, *Medicare: A Profile*, February 1995, cited in Scott MacStravic, "The Disease Management Dilemma," *Health Care Strategic Management* (June 1996).

23. *Washington Post*/Kaiser Family Foundation/Harvard University 1995 poll data, as tabulated in Blendon et al., "Changing Attitudes in America," Figure 8.

24. Peterson and Nightingale, "What Do We Know About Block Grants."

25. The 1.5 percent savings is based on Michigan officials' prediction of administrative costs discussed in Kilborne, "Michigan's Welfare System."

26. John J. DiIulio, Jr., *No Escape: The Future of American Corrections* (New York: Basic Books, 1991), esp. pp. 19–26, 204–8.

27. David Osborne, "A Federal Challenge for Local Ingenuity," *Washington Post*, June 1, 1995.

28. One clear imperative for the next several years is to ensure that these innovations are evaluated and, where successful, replicated; this holds good even for those skeptical about the broader benefits of wholesale devolution.

29. A 1991 New York program *did* avoid most of the major problems, but its expertise came from its own experience with a 1983 early retirement program, not from data gleaned from other states. See Michael deCourcy Hinds, "Early Retirements to Reduce Budgets Cost States Money: Poor Planning Is Blamed," *New York Times*, November 16, 1992.

30. Melody Peterson, "A Group of Accountants Controls Audits of Localities," *New York Times*, September 10, 1996.

31. Albert O. Hirschman, *Exit, Voice, and Loyalty* (Cambridge, Mass.: Harvard University Press, 1970).

32. It is interesting to observe how casual some advocates are about the point that intergovernmental competition, to be efficient, must meet the same conditions as market competition, and then some. An official report highly supportive of tax competition raises, then drops, the following observation: "One major theme of this [theoretical] literature is that the conditions under which a competitive governmental structure will lead to a Pareto optimum are considerably more stringent than the conditions necessary for achieving a Pareto optimum in the private market." Advisory Commission on Intergovernmental Relations, *Interjurisdictional Tax and Policy Competition*, p. 63. Yet analysts who wouldn't dream of endorsing unregulated competition by, say, pharmaceutical companies seem to accept with little comment calls for competition among governments. Easterbrook is more realistic in conceding that intergovernmental competition won't lead to a perfect arrangement of laws. "But allowing for all of the difficulties with interjurisdictional competition, one still can show that exit causes a power *tendency* toward optimal legislation to the extent four conditions are satisfied: (1) people and resources are more mobile; (2) the number of jurisdictions increases; (3) jurisdictions can select any set of laws they desire; and (4) all the consequences of one jurisdiction's laws are felt within that jurisdiction" (Easterbrook, "Antitrust and the Economics of Federalism," p. 35). At several points in this book, I argue that these conditions are seldom met. In particular, condition (1) is unevenly met—some institutions, resources, and individuals are highly mobile; others, not—and condition (4) applies with low and falling frequency.

33. "Federalism as an Ideal Political Order and an Objective for Constitutional Reform," *Publius* (Spring 1995): 21. A somewhat more formal version of this same logic is laid out in James M. Buchanan and Roger Faith, "Secession and the Limits of Taxation: Towards a Theory of Internal Exit," *American Economic Review* (December 1987).

34. Easterbrook, "Antitrust and the Economics of Federalism," pp. 28, 35.

35. The common defect of Paul Peterson's and Alice Rivlin's otherwise acute assessments of American federalism is that both hinge on an implausibly clean dichotomy between "developmental" and "distributive" policies. See Alice Rivlin, *Reviving the American Dream: The Economy, the States, and the Federal Government* (Washington, D.C.: Brookings Institution, 1992), and Peterson, *Price of Federalism*, esp. pp. 64–65.

36. Wallace E. Oates and Robert M. Schwab, "Allocative and Distributive Implications of Local Fiscal Competition," in *Competition Among States and Local Governments*, eds. Daphne Kenyon and John Kincaid (Washington, D.C.: Urban Institute Press, 1991), pp. 140–41.

37. Paul E. Peterson and Mark Rom, "American Federalism, Welfare

Policy, and Residential Choices," *American Political Science Review* 83, no. 3 (September 1989): 724.

38. The 1940–85 reference is from ibid., p. 715; the Clinton quote is from "Clinton Okays Changes to Welfare," Reuters on-line wire, July 16, 1996.

39. Philip B. Levine and David Zimmerman use longitudinal data to test whether welfare-eligible families are more likely than others to move to high-benefit states, and conclude that welfare is a minor factor in migration patterns. Philip B. Levine and David Zimmerman, "An Empirical Analysis of the Welfare Magnet Debate Using the NLSY," Cambridge, Mass., NBER Working Paper No. 5264, September 1995. Edward M. Gramlich and Deborah S. Laren, using somewhat different methods and data series, find a small but measurable "welfare magnet" effect. While the poor (like most people) move out of state only rarely, when they *do* move it is more likely to a high-benefits state. From the 1960s through the mid–1980s Gramlich and Laren see a "very sluggish migration process toward high-benefit states, which is gradually reducing the real level of AFDC benefits as it becomes perceived." Edward M. Gramlich and Deborah S. Laren, "Migration and Income Redistribution Responsibilities," *Journal of Human Resources* 19, no. 4 (1984): 509. For the entire 1900–87 period two scholars find "strong statistical evidence that, all else being equal, higher per-capita income leads to a greater rate of net in-migration" for population overall. Robert J. Barro and Xavier Sala-I-Martin, "Convergence Across States and Regions," *Brookings Papers on Economic Activity* no. 1 (1991): 132.

40. For references to California and Wisconsin, see Sam Howe Verhovek, "States Are Already Providing Glimpse at Welfare's Future," *New York Times*, September 21, 1995; for references to New York, see Kenneth B. Noble, "Welfare Revamp, Halted in Capital, Proceeds Anyway," *New York Times*, March 10, 1996; and Raymond Hernandez, "Pataki's Plans for Welfare: Strict Rules and Job Incentives," *New York Times*, February 6, 1996. Shortly before the welfare reform bill became effective a New York state senator sought to assemble a coalition for reforming the state's constitution to limit antipoverty efforts, warning that "delay may well be cataclysmic. Thousands of poor Americans from other states could trek to New York." John J. Marchi, "New York's Welfare Meltdown," op-ed, *New York Times*, August 12, 1996. According to Paul Peterson, "Massachusetts has reported that welfare recipients are already leaving the state in response to cuts enacted in the spring of 1995." Peterson, *Price of Federalism*, p. 187.

41. The federal entitlement ended as of October 1, 1996 (though states had nine months to submit their plans for meeting the terms of the legislation and collecting their block grants). But Wisconsin, Michigan, Ohio, Florida, Vermont, Massachusetts, Maryland, Oregon, Oklahoma, Tennessee, and Maine submitted their plans earlier, and Wisconsin and Michigan had been approved—that is, certified as consistent with the reform legislation, the only

criterion for approval—the evening before the law became effective. Robert Pear, "Actions by States Hold Keys to Welfare Law's Future," *New York Times,* October 1, 1996.

42. Kevin Sack, "In Mississippi, Will Poor Grow Poorer with State Welfare Plans?" *New York Times,* October 23, 1995.

43. Mickey Kaus, "The Revival of Liberalism," *New York Times,* August 9, 1996.

44. Robyn Meredith, "Michigan Welfare Plan Draws Unlikely Support," *New York Times,* January 22, 1996; Jason Deparle, "Aid from an Enemy of the Welfare State," *New York Times,* January 28, 1996; see also Jennifer Preston, "Whitman Proposes Welfare Plan Intended to Ease a Shift to Work," *New York Times,* January 30, 1996; and the *New York Times* editorial, May 3, 1996, hailing Wisconsin's plan.

45. The late Stephen Gold, then director for the Center for the Study of the States and later director of a major research effort on the impact of devolution, assessed Michigan's plan bluntly in 1995. "You can see they're not going to have enough money. They will say, 'Well, we can't raise taxes, so we will have to cut spending more.' They are sowing the seeds of further cuts in social spending." Kilborne, "Michigan's Welfare System." Robert Reischauer, former director of the Congressional Budget Office and later a Brookings Institution researcher, predicts that the shift to block grants will cause state spending on vulnerable populations to "drop like a rock." Robert Reischauer, "The Blockbuster Inside the Republicans' Budget: In the Rush to Fiscal Devolution, Has Anyone Figured Out How to Divvy Up the Cash?" in *Dollars and Sense: Diverse Perspectives on Block Grants and the Fiscal Responsibility Act,* Institute for Educational Leadership, Washington, D.C., September 1995, p. 60.

46. James Sterngold, "Agency Missteps Put Illegal Aliens at Mercy of Sweatshops," *New York Times,* September 21, 1995. For an interesting (but extreme) thought experiment, see Steven Kelman, "The Ethics of Regulatory Competition," *Regulation* (May-June 1982): 42–43.

47. Ela Trivedi, "Unionism and Public Policy: An Investigation of the Effects of Welfare Expenditures, Protective Labor Legislation, and Right-to-Work Laws," doctoral dissertation, Northern Illinois University, 1994, Table 2.1, p. 26. There has been no recent increase in the number of right-to-work states; the framework I outline here would predict otherwise. It may be that the decline of the labor movement nationwide has made state right-to-work laws less significant. If this is the case, any national resurgence of organized labor should generate greater state interest in passing new right-to-work legislation.

48. In the realm of social policy, competitive logic may help to explain the difficulty of ensuring that absent fathers support their children. About one-quarter of the absent fathers required by courts to pay child support live in a

separate state from their children. A General Accounting Office study found that 45 percent of these men are usually or always delinquent in child-support payments, versus 28 percent of absent fathers living in the same state. (U.S. General Accounting Office, "Interstate Child Support" [January, 1992], Figure 1, p. 3, and Figure 2, p. 4.) Much of this differential is doubtless due to the simple effect of distance on absent fathers' consciences and to the administrative complexity of one state's government enforcing another state's court decrees. But there may be other factors at work. Divorced men (especially those who haven't remarried) tend to have relatively high incomes and to place relatively low demands on schools and other government services, making them desirable citizens—at least by states' narrow budgetary calculus. Previously married adults—covering those widowed, divorced, or separated—are almost 10 percent more likely than married adults to move from one state to another, based on mobility data from 1981 to 1994. There is certainly no evidence that states craft explicit strategies to become havens for deadbeat dads. But competitive pressures could subtly soften in practice officials' hard line of rhetoric if special stringency on child-support enforcement would make a state marginally *less* attractive to unencumbered men and *more* attractive to divorced or abandoned women with children.

49. I am grateful to Claudia Goldin for emphasizing this point.

50. Some states that exempt from taxes contributions to retirement funds (in parallel with federal law) do tax payouts in retirement. A few of these states have attempted to collect these taxes from retirees who have moved to other states with no personal income tax. California had collected $25 million per year from out-of-state retirees, for example. Senator Harry Reid (D-Nevada) sponsored a law barring the practice, which Congress passed and Clinton signed in 1996. This *could* strengthen incentives for retirees to move, though the stronger effect will probably be on state taxation of retirement savings. See David Cay Johnston, "Clinton Signs Law Barring Some State Tax on Retirees," *New York Times,* January 11, 1996.

51. Richard J. Cebula, "A Brief Empirical Note on the Tiebout Hypothesis and State Income Tax Policies," *Public Choice* 67, no. 1 (1990): 89.

52. Philip J. Grossman, "Fiscal Competition Among States in Australia: The Demise of Death Duties," *Publius* 20, no. 4 (Fall 1990): 150–51. In the United States, the federal government offers credits against estate tax liability for state death duties "to assure that the states do not destroy this source of state revenue by engaging in competition through tax concessions to the wealthy aged." Burkhead and Miner, *Public Expenditure,* p. 278.

53. If all tax costs were passed down the line to less mobile suppliers or customers, ultimately all taxes must fall on landowners. "Although it is hard to name other things as mobile as corporate charters and investment capital, it is also hard to find resources—save for land—that are immobile in the long run."

Easterbrook, "Antitrust and the Economics of Federalism," p. 28. Many con-
tributors to the Tiebout literature assume that the effects of all government
taxing and spending decisions are incorporated into the value of land, and
concentrate their analysis on the interactions between landowners and public
officials. For example, see Dennis Epple and Allan Zelenitz, "The Implications
of Competition Among Jurisdictions: Does Tiebout Need Politics?" *Journal of
Political Economy* 89, no. 6 (December 1981), whose modeling confirms the intuition that local governments "can exploit the immobility of land and share
in the rents accruing to that land" (p. 1216).

54. See Stewart, "Federalism and Rights," pp. 932–33.

55. Glenn Blackmon and Richard J. Zeckhauser, "Fragile Commitments and
the Regulatory Process," *Yale Journal on Regulation* 9, no. 1 (Winter 1992): 77.

56. Deregulation and new technologies increasing large customers' options
are major parts of this trend, but interstate competition plays a role. Doug
Rothwell, director of the Michigan Jobs Commission, pointed to other states'
efforts to lower energy costs for industrial customers as a competitive threat to
Michigan. "Just cutting taxes is not enough. You have to deal with the total
cost of doing business in the state, and electricity costs play a role." Agis
Salpukas, "Utilities Rewrite the Rate Card," *New York Times*, April 5, 1996.

57. The Committee on Economic Security report is quoted in Advisory
Council on Unemployment Compensation, "National Interests and Federal
Responsibilities in the Unemployment Insurance System," April 1995, p. 7.

58. Laurie J. Bassi et al., "The Evolution of Unemployment Insurance,"
Advisory Council on Unemployment Compensation staff paper, August 1995,
p. 24. Howard P. Foley, an official of a group called the Massachusetts Taxpayers' Foundation, cast his argument for tightening eligibility criteria and shrinking the unemployment insurance trust fund entirely in terms of the need to
"make our unemployment insurance system more competitive with other
states." "Make the system friendlier to firms," Boston *Globe*, June 18, 1996.
Proposals for reducing unemployment insurance costs are detailed in "Reducing the High Cost of Doing Business in Massachusetts," Massachusetts Taxpayers Foundation, Boston, 1995. It is also poignant to note that on the day he
left the Senate to set out on his campaign full-time, Bob Dole joked to re-
porters traveling with him, "I'm going around the country to see where they
have the best unemployment benefits." Adam Nagourney, "'Out-of-Work'
Dole Starts What He Calls 'the Real Campaign,'" the *New York Times*, June
13, 1996.

59. Katherine Baicker, Claudia Goldin, and Lawrence F. Katz, "A Distinctive System: Origins and Impact of U.S. Unemployment Compensation," January 1997 working paper, Harvard University, pp. 8–9. I am grateful to Larry
Katz for his generous advice on the U.I. issue.

60. George F. Break, *Intergovernmental Fiscal Relations in the United States*

(Washington, D.C.: Brookings Institution, 1967), pp. 23–24. A more recent literature review also finds a "tendency for interjurisdictional competition to reduce reliance on ability-to-pay taxes." Advisory Commission on Intergovernmental Relations, *Interjurisdictional Tax and Policy Competition*, p. 63.

61. One analyst found that by most measures, all state tax codes are regressive, and only Delaware is progressive by *any* measure. Donald W. Keifer, "A Comparative Analysis of Tax Progressivity in the United States: A Reexamination," *Public Finance Quarterly* 19, no. 1 (January 1991).

62. Advisory Commission on Intergovernmental Relations, *Significant Features of Fiscal Federalism 1995*, Washington, D.C., September 1995.

63. Ronald Snell, ed., *Financing State Government in the 1990s* (Washington, D.C.: National Council of State Legislatures and National Governors' Association, 1993), p. 66. A review of 1990–93 personal income tax reforms— the most common of which was simply lifting top rates—can be found in Steven D. Gold, "State Fiscal Problems and Policies," in *The Fiscal Crisis of the States*, ed. Steven D. Gold (Washington, D.C.: Georgetown University Press, 1995), pp. 19–21.

64. Anne C. Case, James R. Hines, Jr., and Harvey S. Rosen find robust statistical evidence that "a state's level of per capital expenditure is positively and significantly affected by the expenditure levels of its neighbors," even when other factors are taken into account. Anne C. Case, James R. Hines, Jr., and Harvey S. Rosen, "Budget Spillovers and Fiscal Policy Interdependence: Evidence from the States," *Journal of Public Economics* 53 (1994): 287. They also observe that states mold their tax policies in response to policies of neighboring states (note 4, p. 286) but don't attempt to prove this.

65. 1994 data are from Bureau of the Census, *State Government Finances Series*; 1995 and 1996 tax changes from *State Tax Actions*, National Conference of State Legislatures, 1995 and 1996 issues, employing the "baseline" method for measuring tax changes.

66. "Average Sales Tax Rates Reach Record High," press release from Vertex, Inc., Berwyn, PA, January 1997.

67. This generalization is complicated where a single metropolitan region includes two or more states. But the patterns one sees in the Boston area, for example, are best considered special cases of competition among local governments, rather than a general example of interstate rivalry.

68. Averaging over the 1988–94 period, Americans age twenty-five and over with family income between $25,000 and $50,000 had about a 2.4 percent probability of moving interstate in a given year, while those with incomes over $50,000 had about a 3.0 percent probability. Calculated from U.S. Bureau of the Census, Current Population Reports, P-20 series, various years. While mobility rates vary from year to year, at no time over the period were higher-income people less likely to move interstate than middle-income peo-

ple. Empirical research by Marian Vallaint Wrobel confirms that individuals do migrate in response to interstate tax differentials, constraining the progressivity of state taxation, though data limitations make it difficult to verify that better-off individuals are more mobile than the broad middle class. Marian Vallaint Wrobel, "The Quantity Effects of the Variation in State Personal Income Taxes," thesis chapter, Harvard Economics Department, October 1995; telephone conversation, December 6, 1996.

69. Calculated from Kristen A. Hansen, "Geographical Mobility: March 1993 to March 1994," Current Population Reports, U.S. Department of Commerce, August 1995, Table 1.

Chapter Eight: The Stewardship of Skills

1. Claudia Goldin, "How America Graduated from High School: 1910 to 1960," NBER Working Paper No. 4762, June 1994, p. 2.

2. For example, see Richard B. Freeman and Lawrence F. Katz, editors, *Differences and Changes in Wage Structures* (Chicago: University of Chicago Press, 1995).

3. Data on changes in real weekly earnings are from the U.S. Bureau of Labor Statistics' Current Population Survey.

4. Lynn A. Karoly, "Anatomy of the US Income Distribution: Two Decades of Change," *Oxford Review of Economic Policy* 12, no. 1 (1996), Table 2, p. 84. Shifts in family structure—such as the tendency of single parents to be less educated, or of college-educated men to marry college-educated working women—intensify the trend, but rising returns to education are a major part of the story.

5. See Donall O'Neil, "Education and Income Growth: Implications for Cross-Country Inequality," *Journal of Political Economy* 103, no. 6 (December 1995), esp. p. 1299.

6. *Statistical Abstract of the United States 1994*, Table 227. This is biased somewhat high, since the statistics miss on-the-job training and the value of students' time. Yet government's role in education, however reckoned, is a weighty one, especially for lower-income groups.

7. Statement by Federal Reserve Chairman Alan Greenspan before the House Budget Committee, March 27, 1996, reprinted in *Daily Labor Report*, March 28, 1996.

8. Paul Peterson refers to CETA as "a block grant that gave local governments considerable flexibility in designing training." Peterson, *Price of Federalism*, pp. 61–62.

9. The origins and structure of JTPA, and the logic for assessing training policy, are discussed in Donahue, *Privatization Decision*, Chapter 9.

10. Abt Associates, *The National JTPA Study*, Overview of the Final

Report, October 22, 1993. The researchers examined about sixteen thousand applicants to JTPA programs in sixteen different locales, who were randomly divided between a "treatment" group assigned to JTPA training services, and a "control" group that was not. Two and a half years later their earnings and employment were measured, both through direct surveys and (as a check) through consulting official earnings data from the unemployment insurance system. The methodology was not perfect—local programs volunteered for inclusion in the study, inviting a positive bias; participants assigned to the treatment group didn't necessarily complete the training prescribed for them, and control group members often had access to alternative sources of training. But overall the study was impressively sound.

   11. Exhibit 4, p. 9. For young men with an arrest record, the study showed JTPA participation produced a large, statistically significant *decline* in earnings—though this was probably a fluke of the data or design. Overall the net benefits of JTPA—taking into account earnings gains, savings on public-assistance benefits, and the cost of providing training—were tiny but positive for adults (about $500 to $600, spread out over thirty months) but negative for young people (-$1,170 for young women, -$2,900 for young men). Exhibit 16, p. 37.

   12. See *What Works (and What Doesn't)*, U.S. Department of Labor, Office of the Chief Economist, 1995.

   13. Kassebaum's "Work Force Development Act of 1995" was published in the *Daily Labor Report* of June 15, 1995.

   14. While some programs would have been consolidated, many were left free-standing, with the decision over whether to preserve a separate program or fold it into the broader system more dependent on a constituency's political clout, in most cases, than on the distinctiveness of the program's mission. A governance system made up of public, private, and labor officials at federal, state, and local levels was to be the main instrument for enforcing efficiency on providers, with individual choice playing a strictly limited role. The use of voucher-style arrangements was narrowly circumscribed, and the word itself was banished.

   15. Tuition deductibility, like any tax incentive, would confer much of its benefits on families who would have invested in education in any event. The extra postsecondary education would be small, most likely in the range of 3 percent. But the proposal targets tax cuts to families facing special pressures on their budgets, and by phasing out deductibility as income rises the benefits are targeted on the middle class. Unlike cash subsidies or 100 percent credits, deductibility preserves families' resistance to tuition increases, and won't simply fuel cost inflation.

   16. U.S. Department of Labor, "A G.I. Bill for America's Workers," February 3, 1995.

17. Kassebaum had disputed charges by Reich that her bill would invite governors to deploy federal funds as weapons in economic devilment competition, pointing to provisions in the legislation that barred using training subsidies to lure firms from out of state. But the administration worried that some governors would find the short-term payoff of business-location incentives irresistibly more attractive than long-term investments in workers' skills, especially the skills of older, poorer, and less able workers. And much stronger safeguards in the Job Training Partnership Act, while preventing explicit federal subsidies for identifiable smokestack-chasing forays, had still allowed states to burnish their business-climate claims by channeling federal training money to private firms. On this debate see *Daily Labor Report*, August 9, 1996, p. AA-2, and August 10, 1996, p. A-10, as well as Michael Booth and Mark Eddy, "State Hands Welfare to Rich," *Denver Post*, February 18, 1996, on JTPA funding for tailored training programs for Anheuser-Busch, Lockheed Martin, Merrill Lynch, Bechtel, and others. Provisions added to JTPA in 1992 that forbid the use of funds "to encourage or induce the relocation of an establishment," and that impose a penalty of double the funds thus deployed, have never been invoked, in part because actual relocations are rare and in part because disentangling the impact of training funds proved extraordinarily difficult.

18. Two bills were passed by their respective chambers and came to a conference in the summer of 1996. But the administration was dismayed that the conference was heading toward what Reich called a "very watered-down version of the voucher idea," with the dominant themes emerging as simple funding cuts, shifting authority from federal and local officials and toward the states, and only feeble steps toward a market-driven system. See Deborah Billings, "Reich Concerned Training Reform Bill Will Not Embrace Mandatory Skill Grants," *Daily Labor Report*, May 10, 1996.

19. These figures are from the National Center for Education Statistics' on-line service as of September 1996. The state share had been slightly higher than the local share through the mid-1980s.

20. *Statistical Abstract of the United States 1994*, Table 227.

21. U.S. Bureau of the Census, *State Government Finance*, 1995. Except for a slight shift toward postsecondary programs, the allocation of state education budgets has changed little since 1980.

22. U.S. Department of Education, *Mini-Digest of Educational Statistics* 1995, Table 30.

23. President's Remarks to the National Governors' Association Education Summit, March 27, 1996, Palisades, New Jersey.

24. *Projections of Education Statistics to 2005*, U.S. Department of Education, National Center for Education Statistics, 1995.

25. The GAO figure is cited in Peter Applebome, "Enrollment Soars,

Leaving Dilapidated School Buildings Bursting at the Frayed Seams," *New York Times*, August 25, 1996.

26. *Statistical Abstract of the United States 1994*, Table 477.

27. Charles Babington, "Cautious Glendening Proposes a Bare-Bones Budget," *Washington Post*, January 18, 1996.

28. See Jennifer Preston, "Whitman's Budget Calls for a Drop in State Spending," *New York Times*, January 28, 1996, and Neil McFarquar, "Whitman Offers Fiscal Plan for Parity in Schools," *New York Times*, May 18, 1996.

29. Frank Phillips, "Weld Gives State a Populist Agenda," *Boston Globe*, January 10, 1996. "The key question is whether the state can afford both the investment in education reform and the tax cut," according to the president of the Massachusetts Taxpayers' Foundation, Michael Widmer. "I think it will be difficult to achieve both in the immediate future."

30. Fosler, "State Economic Policy," p. 88. For anecdotes about the economic development payoff of a top-flight community-college system, see Fred R. Bleakley, "To Bolster Economies, Some States Rely More on Two-Year Colleges," *Wall Street Journal*, November 26, 1996.

31. Jay Mathews, "Corporations Vow to Favor States That Boost Academic Standards," *Washington Post*, March 28, 1996.

32. Antonio Ciccone and Robert E. Hall, "Productivity and the Density of Economic Activity," *American Economic Review* 86, no. 1 (March 1996), esp. p. 54 and Figure 2, p. 64. This is the most recent and prestigious study of the issue. Most, but not all, empiricists agree on the importance of education for productivity. One provocative but ultimately not very plausible regression study found that a state's level of education spending was *inversely* related to short-term economic growth rates in the mid-1970s. Thomas R. Dye, "Taxing, Spending and Economic Growth in American States," *Journal of Politics* 42 (1980), Table, p. 1100.

33. Goldin, "How America Graduated from High School."

34. Brad Hayward, "Wilson Takes Aim at Taxes, Welfare," *Sacramento Bee*, January 11, 1996. An earlier proposal, abandoned under pressure, would have sharply cut funding for California's superb community colleges.

35. After the longest budget fight in New York history, the legislature blocked most of the proposed education cuts. Clifford J. Levy, "Pataki's Budget to Sharply Cut Spending for Poor and Colleges," *New York Times*, December 16, 1995; James Dao, "Pataki's Budget Plan in Brief: Amid Austerity, a Tax Break," *New York Times*, January 2, 1996; Raymond Hernandez, "After Standoff, Both Sides Can Claim Credit for Victories," *New York Times*, July 12, 1996.

36. The state and local share of postsecondary education finance peaked at 62 percent in 1979, and had fallen to 53 percent by 1992. Michael S. McPherson and Morton Owen Schapiro, "Are We Keeping College Afford-

able? Student Aid, Access, and Choice in American Higher Education," paper presented at the Princeton Conference on Higher Education, March 1996, Table 1. McPherson, the president of Macalester College, declared that "we're going to have to face up to the fact that states are no longer willing or able to continue to provide the across-the-board access that they provided 20 years ago." Quoted in Karen W. Arenson, "College Tuition Rates Show Steady Growth, Report Says," *New York Times*, September 26, 1996.

37. Melvin L. Burstein and Arthur J. Rolnick, "Congress Should End the Economic War for Sports and Other Businesses," *Region*, Federal Reserve Bank of Minneapolis, June 1996, p. 5.

38. Robert Tomsho, "Rio Rancho Wooed Industry and Got It, Plus Financial Woes," *Wall Street Journal*, April 11, 1995. Other information on the Rio Rancho plant comes from Albuquerque on-line information.

39. Myerson, "Oh Governor, Won't You Buy Me a Mercedes Plant?"

40. Andale Gross, "Schools Should Have Say on Abatement, Board Says," *Kansas City Star*, November 8, 1995.

41. These averages are based on data from U.S. Bureau of the Census, Current Population Reports, P-20 series, various issues.

42. The most recent data, for 1994, show 1.8 percent of adult high school dropouts and 3.3 percent of college graduates moving out of state. In 1971 the differential was much higher—1.6 percent of dropouts and 5.1 percent of graduates.

43. A study of detail data from the 1980 Census Public Use Microdata Sample suggests that the differential tendency of educated workers to migrate meant that sixteen states *increased* their average level of human capital (based on estimated future earnings potential) over the 1975–80 period, either by losing population but holding on to more-educated people, or by increasing population with the increase biased toward human capital. The other states saw their average level of human capital *lowered* by migration. Randall G. Krieg, "Human-Capital Selectivity in Interstate Migration," *Growth and Change* 22, no. 1 (Winter 1991), esp. Table 1, pp. 72–73. And on conceptual grounds, a similar point is made by Douglas Holtz-Eakin: "For the nation as a whole, the parameters indicate that greater rates of accumulation of either physical or human capital will raise productivity. For states, however, the effects are not symmetric. Policies to foster physical capital accumulation will translate to a higher marginal product of labor, and thus improved real wages for the states' workers. In contrast, the greater mobility of labor, at least in the short term, raises the possibility that each state may not reap the benefits of its policies to enhance human capital investment." Douglas Holtz-Eakin, "Solow and the States: Capital Accumulation, Productivity, and Economic Growth," National Bureau of Economic Research Working Paper No. 4144, 1992, p. 13. The unitary countries within the OECD spend a bit more on education, on average,

than the federal countries—6.1 percent versus 5.6 percent—offering some tentative support for the notion that decentralized funding may tend to lower the rate of education investment. Data on education spending can be found in Organization for Economic Cooperation and Development, *Education at a Glance: OECD Indicators*, 3rd edition (Paris: OECD, 1995). It is worth stressing the fragility of the finding that unitary countries spend more on education. When weighted by 1990 GNP figures (drawn from various sources and compiled in *Statistical Abstract of the United States 1994*, Table 1366), the federal average is 5.3 percent of GDP and the unitary average is 4.8 percent; the huge difference between weighted and unweighted averages reflects Japan's very low rate of measured education spending and its dominance of the unitary-country weight pool. For information on the division of authority over education in European countries—and illustrations of how imprecise the OECD categories are—see EURYDICE (European Information Network), *Structures of the Education and Initial Training Systems in the Members States of the European Community* (Luxembourg: Office for Official Publications of the EC, 1991).

44. Claudia Goldin and Lawrence F. Katz, "The Decline of Non-Competing Groups: Changes in the Premium to Education, 1880 to 1940," NBER Working Paper No. 5202, August 1995, p. 30.

45. Elkins and McKitrick, *Age of Federalism*, p. 198.

46. Lower-level governments' incapacity to sustain policies with a redistributive component is among the fundamentals of federalist theory, and the precept that higher levels of government should handle redistribution can be found in virtually every discussion from the classic Tiebout article onward. For example, see Breton and Scott, *Economic Constitution of Federal States*, pp. 120–25. But as one economics text observes, "distributional concerns are only partially implemented by taxes and transfers. . . . Implementation also comes by way of resource allocation—by decisions to spend more or less on programs that benefit specific income groups." Burkhead and Miner, *Public Expenditure*, p. 26.

Chapter Nine: The Endless Argument's Next Stage

1. "Why Don't Americans Trust the Government?" November-December 1995 survey by Princeton Survey Research Associates for *Washington Post*, Kaiser Family Foundation, and Harvard University; these figures are from the version reported on the Kaiser Foundation Web site, Questions 4 and 5.

2. Office of Management and Budget, *Budget of the United States Government, Fiscal Year 1998*, Historical tables 6.1, 12.1, and 15.4. The figures don't sum to 100 percent because of rounding and because of minor inconsistencies among data series.

3. For more on this and related points see Dwight R. Lee and Richard B. McKenzie, "The International Political Economy of Declining Tax Rates,"

National Tax Journal 42, no. 1 (1989); Michael L. Marlow, "Fiscal Decentralization and Government Size," *Public Choice* 56 (1988), esp. p. 267; John D. Wilson, "A Theory of Interregional Tax Competition," *Journal of Urban Economics* 19 (1986); John D. Wilson, "Trade, Capital Mobility, and Tax Competition," *Journal of Political Economy* 95, no. 4 (August 1987); David E. Wildasin, "Interjurisdictional Capital Mobility: Fiscal Externality and a Corrective Subsidy," *Journal of Urban Economics* 25 (1989); Dieter Helm and Stephen Smith, "The Assessment: Decentralization and the Economics of Local Government," *Oxford Review of Economic Policy* 3, no. 2 (Summer 1987); Philip J. Grossman, "Fiscal Decentralization and Government Size: An Extension," *Public Choice* 62 (1989); George R. Zodrow and Peter Mieszkowski, "Pigou, Tiebout, Property Taxation and the Under-Provision of Local Public Goods," *Journal of Urban Economics* 19 (1986), esp. p. 356; J. Fred Giertz, "Centralization and Government Budget Size," *Publius* (Winter 1981); and (most remarkably) Michael J. Boskin, "Local Government Tax and Product Competition and the Optimal Provision of Public Goods," *Journal of Political Economy* 81, no. 1 (January/February 1973).

4. Storing, "The Problem of Big Government," p. 305.

5. Most aspects of law enforcement are suited to state or local control—local preferences matter, scale economies are modest, and consequences are largely contained—calling into question a two-decade expansion of the federal role that continues into our present devolutionary times. Relatedly, it is intriguing to speculate on the potential for enlarging the role of the state National Guards—the heirs of what the Framers meant by a "well-regulated militia." If America's defense challenges come to consist of the kinds of limited interventions (as in Bosnia and Haiti) that a smaller national force can handle, and if threats requiring national mobilization will emerge gradually (allowing time for the protracted debate that would be required to support the coordinated deployment of state forces), then a defense posture based on a compact national force and a larger, looser collection of state forces could make sense. It also has at least as much philosophical justification as the devolution of economic functions; nothing in today's America would be harder to explain to the Framers than the maintenance of a large federal army. Robust national guards under the governors' control could also serve as an insurance policy against the unlikely but not impossible prospect of antidemocratic intrigue at the federal level. Daniel Elazar tells how the state police, controlled by governors, were an important counter to the federal armed forces in Brazil during the 1970s. Elazar, "From Statism to Federalism," p. 16.

6. The nineteenth-century English poor laws restricted paupers' mobility to make decentralized poor relief sustainable, which is not an option for modern America. On the poor laws see Karl Polanyi, *The Great Transformation* (Boston: Beacon Press, 1944). Relevant U.S. court cases include *Shapiro v.*

Thompson, 394 U.S. 618 (1969), and *Memorial Hospital v. Maricopa County*, 415 U.S. 250 (1974). See also Stewart, "Federalism and Rights." It is interesting to note, in this regard, that the Articles of Confederation specifically exclude "paupers" from the provision that "the people of each state shall have free ingress and regress to and from any other state." Article IV, Articles of Confederation, from Morison, ed., *Sources and Documents*, p. 178.

7. Corporate income taxes are only around 7 percent of total state tax revenue, and it is neither possible nor desirable to shore up state finances by concentrating only on the corporate side. The revenues that states and cities raise themselves accounted for around 90 percent of total revenues in the early postwar years, fell towards 70 percent in the 1970s, and rose back to around 80 percent from the mid-1980s onward. Data are calculated from Historical Table 15.3 in the FY 1997 federal budget.

8. A similar proposal figures in Rivlin, *Reviving the American Dream*, esp. Chapter 8.

9. The quotation from Washington's farewell address—which was published, though never delivered—is taken from Elkins and McKitrick, *Age of Federalism*, p. 491.

APPENDIX: RESEARCH ON THE IMPACT OF BUSINESS-ATTRACTION POLICIES

1. Eisinger, *Entrepreneurial State*, p. 201.

2. Abelardo Limon, Jr., "The Use and Effectiveness of Local Government Incentives Designed to Attract Foreign Direct Investment," master's thesis, University of Texas at Austin, 1987, pp. 39–42, 44.

3. Eva Mueller and James N. Morgan, "Location Decisions of Manufacturers," *American Economic Review* 52, no. 2 (May 1962), esp. Table 1 and Table 2, pp. 208–9.

4. Ibid., pp. 211–12.

5. Bridges, "State and Local Inducements for Industry," p. 177.

6. Rodney A. Erickson, "Business Climate Studies: A Critical Evaluation," *Economic Development Quarterly* 1, no. 1 (1987), esp. p. 69; and Roger Wilson, *State Business Incentives and Economic Growth: Are They Effective? A Review of the Literature* (Lexington, Ky.: Council of State Governments, 1989), pp. 13–14.

7. Michel Falise and Armand Lepas, "Les Motivations de Localisation des Investissements Internationaux dans L'Europe du Nord-Ouest," *Revue Economique* 21, no. 1 (January 1970), esp. Table 1, p. 107. Bernard Snoy, *Taxes on Direct Investment Income in the EEC*.

8. H.I. Chernotsky, "Selecting U.S. Sites: A Case Study of German and Japanese Firms," *Management International Review* 23 (1983).

9. Takeshi Nakabayashi, "A Study of Locational Choices of Japanese Manufacturing Companies in the U.S.: Guidelines for State and Local Governments to Attract Japanese Firms' Investments" (Cambridge, Mass.: John F. Kennedy School of Government, Harvard University, Policy Analysis Exercise, April 13, 1987), p. 23. Appendix 4 summarizes responses on taxes, incentives, and other location factors.

10. Ibid., pp. 25–30.

11. Bennett Harrison and Sandra Kanter, "The Political Economy of State Job-Creation Business Incentives," in *Revitalizing the Northeast,* eds. Richard Sternlieb and Roger Hughes (New Brunswick, N.J.: Rutgers University Center for Urban Policy, 1978), pp. 265–66, 254–60.

12. Reported in Eisinger, *Entrepreneurial State,* p. 146.

13. Arthur Andersen and Co., "Trends in State and Local Taxation" March 1989, p. 5.

14. John P. Blair and Robert Premus, "Major Factors in Industrial Location: A Review," *Economic Development Quarterly* 1, no. 1 (1987), esp. pp. 78–79.

15. Ibid., pp. 84–85.

16. Robert T. Walker and David Greenstreet, "The Effect of Government Incentives and Assistance on Location and Job Growth in Manufacturing," *Regional Studies* 25, no. 1 (February 1991): 13.

17. KPMG-Peat Marwick LLP, Business Incentives Group, "Business Incentives and Tax Credits," p. 8

18. Ferguson and Ladd, "Economic Performance and Economic Development Policy in Massachusetts," p. 127.

19. On this point, see Dick Netzer, "What Should Governors Do When Economists Tell Them That Nothing Works?" *New York Affairs* 9, no. 3 (1986): 21.

20. One distinction sometimes treated as central that I see as less important is the difference between "general" and targeted business-location policies. In principle, the distinction is fairly clear, and sometimes it is in practice: A cash grant to one specific firm is certainly different from a quarter-point decline in the top rate of taxation on corporate profits. But more commonly the distinction is blurred by tax abatements, exemptions, and holidays granted in a manner that affects firms differentially. Seldom is there a precise dividing line between general and targeted policies.

21. Wilbur R. Thompson and John M. Mattila, *An Econometric Model of Postwar State Economic Development* (Detroit: Wayne State University Press, 1959), p. 7.

22. Ibid. Thompson and Mattila's results are summarized in Table 3, p. 19.

23. Jane S. Little, "Locational Decision of Foreign Direct Investment in the U.S.," *New England Economic Review* (July/August 1978).

24. Dennis W. Carlton, "The Location and Employment Choices of New Firms: An Econometric Model with Discrete and Continuous Endogenous Variables," *Review of Economics and Statistics* 65, no. 3 (August 1983), esp. p. 447.

25. L. Jay Helms, "The Effect of State and Local Taxes on Economic Growth: A Time Series-Cross Section Approach," *Review of Economics and Statistics* 67, no. 4 (November 1985), esp. pp. 578–79.

26. Thomas R. Plaut and Joseph E. Pluta, "Business Climate, Taxes and Expenditures, and State Industrial Growth in the United States," *Southern Economic Journal* 50 (1983), esp. pp. 112–14. While Plaut and Pluta seek to explain why these peculiar results may be misleading, the pattern of significant and expected results, inconclusive coefficients, and statistically significant anomalies urge caution in using their results.

27. Robert J. Newman, "Industry Migration and Growth in the South," *Review of Economics and Statistics* 65, no. 1 (February 1983). The quotation is from p. 77, results from Table 2, p. 81. Results are given at the 10 percent significance level, and the r-squared of the model specifications were mostly in the 30 percent range.

28. Robert J. Newman and Dennis H. Sullivan, "Econometric Analysis of Business Tax Impacts on Industrial Location: What Do We Know, and How Do We Know It?" *Journal of Urban Economics* 23, no. 2 (1988).

29. Therese J. McGuire, "Interstate Tax Differentials, Tax Competition, and Tax Policy," *National Tax Journal* 39, no. 3 (September 1986): 371–73. See also Eisinger, *Entrepreneurial State*, Chart 8.2, p. 211, for a sense of the conventional wisdom in the late 1980s.

30. William Wheaton, "Interstate Differences in the Level of Business Taxation," *National Tax Journal* 36, no. 1 (March 1983): 93.

31. Leslie E. Papke, "Interstate Business Tax Differentials and New Firm Location: Evidence from Panel Data," *Journal of Public Economics* 45 (1991): 66.

32. James R. Hines, Jr., "Altered States: Taxes and the Location of Foreign Direct Investment in America," NBER Working Paper No. 4397, July 1993, esp. pp. 28–29.

33. Timothy J. Bartik, "Business Location Decisions in the United States: Estimate of the Effects of Unionization, Taxes, and Other Characteristics of States," *Journal of Business and Economic Statistics* 3, no. 1 (January 1985).

34. Timothy J. Bartik, *Who Benefits from State and Local Economic Development Policies* (Kalamazoo, Mich.: Upjohn Institute for Employment Research, 1991); and Bartik, "Jobs, Productivity, and Local Economic Development." Bartik is careful to specify that this assumes the tax reduction has no effect on the level of public services. He also amends the 3 percent figure I cite with a more cautious estimate that the actual impact is very likely in the range of 1 to 6 percent.

35. James A. Papke and Leslie E. Papke, "Measuring Differential State-Local Tax Liabilities and Their Implications for Business Investment Location," *National Tax Journal* 39, no. 3 (1986): 357.

36. Vertex, Inc., Berwyn, Pa. *City Business Tax Study,* 1993, Table IV-A. See also Thomas Vasquez and Charles W. deSeve, "State/Local Taxes and Jurisdictional Shifts in Corporate Business Activity: The Complications of Measurement," *National Tax Journal* 30 (September 1977). This early simulation study illustrates the complexity of assessing the burden of state and local taxes, but does show that under some entirely realistic circumstances they can matter a great deal. See Tables 7–10, pp. 294–96.

37. Peter S. Fisher and Alan H. Peters, "Taxes, Incentives and Competition for Investment," in *The Economic War Among the States* (Minneapolis: Federal Reserve Bank of Minneapolis, 1996), p. 25. For a variant of the same research, see Peters and Fisher, "Do High Unemployment States Offer the Biggest Business Incentives?"

INDEX